Also by Paul Jacobs

Is Curly Jewish?
The State of the Unions
The New Radicals (with Saul Landau)
Labor in a Free Society (with Michael Harrington)
Old Age and Political Behavior (with Frank Pinner and Philip Selznick)

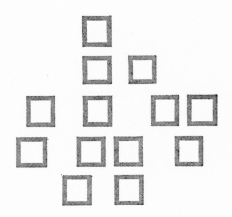

Prelude to Riot

A View of Urban America from the Bottom

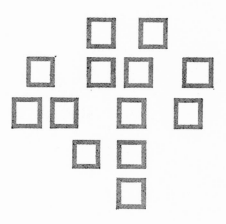

Paul Jacobs

Prelude to Riot

A View of Urban America from the Bottom

Sponsored by the Center for the Study of Democratic Institutions

Random House • New York

SECOND PRINTING

© Copyright, 1966, 1967, by Paul Jacobs
All rights reserved under International and Pan-American Copyright Conventions. Published in New York by Random House, Inc., and simultaneously in Toronto, Canada, by Random House of Canada Limited.

Library of Congress Catalog Card Number: 66-21487

Manufactured in the United States of America
by The Haddon Craftsmen, Inc., Scranton, Pennsylvania
Typography and binding design by Victoria Dudley

To Phil

Acknowledgments

Books like this customarily open with the author's acknowledgment of debt to a variety of people, ending with the spouse, "without whose constant encouragement, etc., etc., etc., this book would not have been, etc., etc., etc." In the past my wife has expressed the hope that one day I would acknowledge her role with a phrase something like, "and to Ruth, without whose constant nagging and complaining this book would have been finished much sooner and would probably read a lot better." But I cannot do this; considering the amount of time I spent away from home gathering material for this book, she was remarkably patient, and remarkably tolerant, too, of the moods of depression through which every writer passes in the frustrating attempt to make clear on paper what seems so clear in the mind.

A fantastic number of people helped make this book possible. Hundreds, literally hundreds of Los Angelenos assisted me in a variety of ways—taking me into their homes, submitting to my lengthy interviews, questioning my questions, and passing me on to others in their communities. They are the men, women, and children without whom this book could not have been written. And even though I must thank them in this impersonal and collective way, I am truly grateful for their individual help.

The entire staff of the State Service Center in Watts was a bulwark of assistance. The aides of the Neighborhood Adult Participation Project educated me about their own barrios and areas. The people of Operation Bootstrap, a remarkable non-governmental training project, gave me a sense of perspective and helped me keep my sense of humor. Irving Warner allowed me to make a message center of his office in L.A.; I am grateful for his tolerance and the help of his staff, especially Sheila Silverman.

Every chapter in this book was read and criticized by experts in and out of government; I am in debt to all of them for their aid in finding errors and for their discussions with me about perspective. Some of them disagreed with my interpretations, but none withheld their generous help. I am especially grateful to Paul Bullock, Fred Case, Grant Cattaneo, Walter Ehrhardt, Harold Horowitz, Truman Jacques, Wade McClain, Mildred Messinger, Eugene Mornell, William Rivera, Jerome N. Sampson, Arthur Stein, Brooks Truitt, Mary Whittaker, and Al German, all of whom took time to read and criticize sections of the book. I thank them all.

My colleagues at the Center for the Study of Democratic Institutions were, as always, a patient and critical audience during the progress of this book. Joan Bowman was much more than a research assistant, for she contributed ideas and viewpoints which were consistently helpful.

The title of this book was suggested by Frances Bardacke, to whom I express my thanks.

Frances Strauss and Barbara la Morticella never balked at typing what must have seemed like endless rewrites of these chapters; both of them acted as critics, too, and aided me a great deal.

Saul Landau argued with me, patiently pointing out the errors of my ways. John J. Simon, my editor at Random House, encouraged me warmly all during the gestation and birth of this book. Rachel Whitebook of Random House helped considerably in bringing the manuscript into focus. I am a debtor to all of them.

Contents

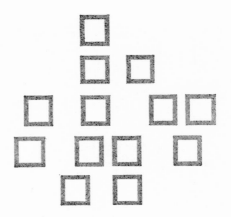

Prelude to Riot

A View of Urban America from the Bottom

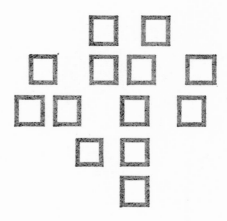

Introduction

The spittle sprayed against my face. I spun around, astounded, and saw no one except a tall young Negro, walking rapidly alongside me. It was he who had spat at me, I realized, and instantly I was flooded with anger, fright, an insane worry that his spittle was diseased, and then shame at the thought of such a disgusting fear.

"Why did you do that?" I shouted at him.

"You spit on me, you white motherfucker!"

"I did not, I've just been walking along. I never saw you until you spat on me," I answered, looking up and down the street to see if there was anyone else near enough to have done it. But no one was close.

"You did spit on me, you white motherfucker, and you tried to push me off the street, too!" he almost screamed, his face contorted with hate, his eyes crazed and rolling. He was in his late twenties, his features more Caucasian than Negroid, his clothes shabby, his shoes worn down. But he shouted clearly, enunciating as if he had been well-educated. We stared at each other—he working himself into a frenzy, I scared and wondering how I could reason with him and thinking, too, that if he'd been a white man, wouldn't I have hit him instinctively, even though he was so much bigger? When I was a soldier, I had been walking on a street when suddenly, without any warning, a mentally disturbed teen-ager had knocked me against the side of a car. Big as he had been, I had fought him bitterly, and ended up in a hospital with a concussion. But now, because this was a Negro, I didn't want to get into a fight; instead, I wanted him to know who I was and that I was writing a book about ghettos. I wanted to tell him about my Negro friends and about my history in the civil rights movement. Because he was a Negro, I wanted him to see me as his friend, and so I was willing to submit to behavior from him that I wouldn't have accepted from a white man.

Then I realized that nothing, absolutely nothing I could say to him would make any impression: he was beyond conversation, beyond rational explanations, beyond anything but hate for me solely because I was Whitey, and I couldn't get through to him.

"I wish I was man enough to hit you, you white motherfucker. I just wish I was man enough to hit you!" he kept repeating as I walked rapidly, frantically down the street. At the corner, I turned while, to my great relief, he continued walking straight across the intersection, still muttering angrily to himself. I felt a sense of deliverance that the episode had ended without a bad fight, but then a terrible depression pulled me down, compounded partly from the shame I felt because I had been afraid of him, partly from my having not hit him just because he was a Negro, but mostly from my failure to connect with him in any way.

Driving out of a ghetto housing project, I sometimes felt the same hostility from the strangers in the parking lot. In my car, waiting for a traffic light to change, a car filled with Negro teen-agers on one side or perhaps even on both sides, I would imagine them looking at me and thinking, "Should we take this white motherfucker and teach him a lesson?" Sometimes, too, a group of kids or young adults would be lounging on the street in front of a liquor store or hamburger joint, and in my mind I could see and hear them judging me while I stared straight ahead, impatiently waiting for the signal to go to green. I always drove cautiously in the ghettos, fearful of any accident that would get me involved in an argument. And

I had to make a conscious effort to overcome these feelings, for most of the time I knew my fears were imaginary and my anxiety induced partially by what my father had taught me when, driving through Harlem, he lectured me on how dangerous it would be if we had an accident among the *"schwartzes."*

So often in my car in the ghetto I had a sense of trying to get from sanctuary to sanctuary, from one place I was known to an office, someone's house, a housing project, a school, or any place where I had friends, confident that if I could just get there, I would be all right.

But this insane encounter had taken place on a street in the predominantly white downtown part of the city, not in a black ghetto or a brown barrio. And it seemed ominous, for until recently, downtown has been where white Americans feel safe.

No more, though. Now the people downtown are frightened, too. The boundaries of the war in the cities have expanded and the battles are no longer confined to the ghettos: downtown Detroit was under siege, downtown Newark was a ghost city, downtown San Francisco has had its dose of looting, and shop windows have been broken on Fifth Avenue, the haughty queen of all New York streets.

And although there *are* differences in the ways the cities fight the war, depending on the political style of the cities' rulers, the basic causes of the war are the same, no matter who the mayor is or which man governs the state. Sam Yorty, the vulgar, reactionary Democratic Mayor of Los Angeles, views government quite differently from Jerome Cavanagh, the sophisticated liberal Democrat, but it doesn't matter: the havoc wreaked on Detroit in 1967 was even worse than what happened in Los Angeles in 1965. Mayor Hugh Addonizio of Newark has very little in common with Mayor John Lindsay across the river in New York, but both cities have suffered from racial disturbances. Governor Ronald Reagan of California pleases every hater of minorities in the country when he threatens, in advance, to use the National Guard to crush the "mad dogs" who participate in riots, while Governor Richard Hughes of New Jersey, Nelson Rockefeller of New York, and George Romney of Michigan speak more carefully, but it doesn't matter: they also have to call out the National Guard, for the substantive issues that brought the internal war are the same for every city.

Those who govern American cities today face such terrible problems that no solutions seem achievable. The cities' administrative structures are anachronistic carryovers from earlier periods of development; the financial basis for conducting the business of government is completely inadequate and unjust. Clearly, the cities cannot continue to be governed as they have been. One model for the terrible anarchy of city life is Los Angeles. There, responsibility for the lives and problems of the citizens living in the same physical locations is divided among a county form of government, with a board of supervisors, a city government, with a council and a mayor, state agencies responsible to an absentee legislature, and the federal government with its own bureaucracy. "Local government," which seems so attractive to the great number of Americans resentful of the federal "encroachment" on their lives, is being lived out in its most developed form in Los Angeles. The county is responsible for welfare programs, the city for the school system; the county for health programs and air-pollution control, the city for the police and for garbage collections. Some county services duplicate the city's, others overlap, a few conflict. Primary taxing authority is vested in the county, but the city government controls the spending of some of the tax funds. And the chaos of governance in Los Angeles demonstrates how useless a notion "local government" is for the city of this century and the ones to follow.

Yet neither the federal nor the state governments have demonstrated that they are any more capable of helping the people in the cities deal with what they face. In the most crucial and agonizing crises of urban life it doesn't matter much whether you live in New York, Detroit, Rochester, Des Moines, Newark, Cambridge, Chicago, Sacramento, Los Angeles, or any other city—or Los Angeles, just as, for Negroes and Spanish-speaking people, all the cities are almost identical.

For example, the powerful groups in all cities, those loosely linked groups which still exercise effective political power, resist any real attempt at racial desegregation in the school system and in housing. And the white people of all cities are so interchangeable in their *real* attitudes on racial questions that once outside the ghettos and barrios, very few black or brown faces can be seen in the same apartment houses with whites or in the same schools with white children.

Thus, when the young Negro spat in my face in downtown Los Angeles, he was spitting on all of white America. I was Whitey, and he hates Whitey because he believes Whitey despises and hates him.

And he is right. The pattern of life of poor whites in America is determined by the contempt in which they are held for having failed to achieve the individual affluence which is the society's basic value. The life of poor Puerto Ricans, Mexicans, and Indians is marked by the same contempt, mixed with some fear about their odd behavior, the kind of fear that resulted in the infamous "zoot-suit" riots in Los Angeles during the war, when gangs of servicemen roamed the streets, savagely beating every teen-ager who looked like a Mexican. But the lives of the poor Negroes in American cities are marked not only by contempt and fear but by active hate. And it is hate which makes ghettoization continue and intensify.

Another characteristic of life common to all the poor but qualitatively different for minorities is their continual contact with government agencies. Most middle-class people in cities have minimal contact with government: occasionally they get a traffic ticket; once a year they write checks to the collector of internal revenue and the state treasurer; every few years an assessor from the county tax office makes an appraisal of their possessions; they vote every two years if they are public-spirited citizens; they go to PTA meetings if they are concerned about their children's education.

But the poor—white, Mexican, Puerto Rican, Indian, and Negro alike—are in continual contact with government agencies. They spend a large proportion of their time waiting for interviews in welfare offices or answering caseworkers' questions in their homes; when they are sick, they wait in the county clinic to see a doctor; they go to a state employment agency for jobs. Because their children frequently get into trouble at school, they are visited by truant officers. Their children get into more trouble outside of school, too, and they have more contact with the police, then the courts, then the jails, then the probation and parole officers, and then the police again, as the whole cycle repeats itself. They see the marshals, too, very often when they stop making payments on the TV and the credit store tries to repossess the set. Their cars are old, they have more accidents in them, and they get more traffic tickets which they cannot pay; so they end up being arrested rather than just cited. If they need psychiatric help, they must be committed to state hospitals, unlike those with higher incomes who can remain at home while undergoing treatment.

For most of the poor, then, government is seen as a network of agencies that affect their lives directly and often. These frequent and affective contacts tend to be either abrasive, rubbing raw their physical and psychic skins, or non-supportive, because their real problems are ignored or not understood. The abrasive quality of the relationships between the poor and such institutions as welfare bureaus or the police departments, which inevitably come into some degree of conflict with citizens, is carried over into poor people's relationships with schools and hospitals, which for the rest of the population are either supportive or at least neutral.

The poor, and especially the minority poor, generally tend, in their contacts with city, county, state, and federal government agencies, to be treated either punitively or in ways which reinforce their feelings of dependency, and frequently both. The help extended to the poor is grudging, tight-lipped, and censorious, for it is generally assumed that they are responsible for their own bad condition and that if they wanted to get out of it badly enough, they could do so.

It is also assumed that they are incapable of running their own lives and that therefore they need not be given the same rights as the rest of society. They are thought of as being somehow subhuman, not truly men and women. That is why the looting and the burning and the sniping take place: a man squinting down the sights of a rifle, hidden from view behind a curtained window, feels powerful, for now he can decide on life or death. A man hurling a Molotov cocktail into a supermarket and watching it burst into flames can say, as one said to me, "That was the first time in my life I ever felt like a man." Another man, who proudly showed me a closetful of suits, said, "Those are loot suits."

And it doesn't matter if the suits don't fit, for they are important as symbols. Looting in the cities can be just as much an act of politics as it is a desire for goods. It is a way in which the poor can make a representation to the society, for they have no other kind of representation; it is a way in which the black poor can express their hate of the white world for not giving them their chance to share in the goodies. And it doesn't matter whether the store being looted is owned by a black man or a white man; *owning* a store is what white people do, not black ones.

The ideas of law and order held by the minority poor can be different from those held by the rest of society. The poor guard their possessions as best they can, but they view the theft of them as being an inevitable part of the world in which they live, rather than as an abnormal circumstance, which is how stealing is perceived outside the ghettos.

So, too, whether or not it is only Jewish men who come to the doors of the poor Negroes selling cheap, shoddy merchandise at high prices, all of them are thought of as Jews, as "Goldbergs in Their Jew Canoes," the Cadillacs in which it is believed they drive into the ghetto to collect the money of the poor. The ghetto dwellers believe it is in the natural order of things for them to be cheated by the Jewish merchants, since they believe cheating to be part of the Jewish psyche. And so, when a "selective demolition program," as the burnings are described, breaks out, the Jewish-owned stores become immediate targets.

But Negro businessmen exploit Negroes viciously, too, and there are Mexican-Americans fattening on the troubles of their community. The ghettos have their own ministers, too, who thrive while their flocks starve (a Cadillac is also called a "Baptist preacher" in the ghetto), their cynical politicians who exploit their ethnic or racial background but do nothing for their constituents, and their "community leaders" seeking only to advance themselves rather than the people they claim to serve. As many organizational jealousies can be found in the ghettos as outside them, and as many groups fighting desperately for the right to speak in the name of the whole community.

So we must learn, painfully, not to romanticize any group and not to expect that a group that is discriminated against is therefore less capable of prejudice against other groups. We must learn how complex are the problems of the urban poor, who have fewer resources to deal with their difficulties than any other group in society. Take health, for example. A family with a pregnant wife, an unemployed sick husband, and two children, one of whom is ill, must get to four different physical locations at four different times in order to even try to solve their health problems: the pregnant mother goes to a prenatal clinic, which meets only twice a week; she takes one child to a Well Baby clinic, which is held on a different day, and the sick child to another clinic, which also meets on a different day; the unemployed father must visit the county hospital for treatment of his illness. In each of these places the waiting time will be interminable; and the family may have to pay for the treatment and care they get.

Or consider what is required to help one unemployed, unskilled Negro teen-ager get a job and keep it: he will probably need a basic education that includes learning how to read, write, and speak intelligibly; his past arrest record will need to be expunged or ignored; he will need many hours of vocational counseling; his poor health will need repairing, some of his bad and rotting teeth replacement; he should spend hours with a psychiatric social worker, and another worker may need to spend hours or days with his family. When all this and a good deal more has been done to help him in his personal life, he will probably still be living in a ghetto from which he cannot escape and be part of a social condition which itself requires fundamental and radical transformation.

The brutal fact about American society today is that a whole constellation of forces, agencies, and circumstances, whose origins are different, whose operations are fragmented, and whose jurisdictions are separate, have converged in the cities. The effect of this constellation bearing down upon us has been disastrous.

This is not to suggest that the ghettos are always frightening, for they are not. Fun and games can be found in them, and there are great sources of humor and deep springs of strength among the ghetto people. In the housing projects the women come and go, laughing with each other about the latest tricks of their little James; on a crowded street a young Negro teen-ager says hello to me and asks as I walk by, "Who you bullshittin' today, white boy? You scarin' the white folks again today?" And when I laugh in answer, he continues with a grin, "You know, white boy, you really should be payin' me so I don't have to go and hustle me some bread. Where you be without me, stirrin' it up around here? You white mother, you should be hiring me and then I won't have to advertise for no job like I'm doin' now. See, I cut this article out of the paper, where it says I'm a black nationalist, a extremist, and I'm going to stick it up on the wall right here on the street. That way, I figure, some white mother might walk down the street, looking to hire a extremist and, like, I'm available. How about it, white boy, you know anybody wants to hire him a black extremist? Like man, I need bread."

In some important ways the ghettos even give strength and security to the people who live in them, and they are a source of great inner vitality. But this strength, security, and vitality can also be a source of weakness, for it makes the ghetto dwellers want to remain inside the ghetto rather than venture beyond its borders.

Until recently another consequence of remaining inside the ghetto has been that some of its inhabitants, especially the kids and teen-agers, always live part of their lives in a fantasy world. School dropouts, unable to face the reality of working in a car wash, talk about becoming jet pilots. They dream about the hi-fi they will buy when they become wealthy entertainers, for their psyches cannot stand the knowledge that they will be poor all their lives. In their minds the boys see themselves as sexual giants, the girls as sought-after beauty queens. Their transistor radios are turned on all the time to the Negro or Spanish stations; the radio is their fix, the music the drug that takes them out of the ugly reality into a private fantasy world. And if the talk and the radio fail them, they can always light up a joint—for to "blow grass," smoke marijuana, helps greatly to soften the sharp outlines of their lives.

It is hard for such ghetto children to grow up, for they think they have nothing to grow up to, and few of the usual ways in which children become adults are open to them. They do not graduate from high school and then take their first steps toward adulthood and maturity in college or in a job. They have no adult occupations with which to identify, and so they remain caught in the matrix of childhood. Even when the fourteen- or fifteen-year-old becomes pregnant and gives birth, she is not really a mother; her baby is no more to her than some kind of doll, and she plays with it happily, her own mother's eyes on her, until baby begins to cry. Then the child-mother grows impatient and slaps the doll, until the thirty-three-year-old grandmother takes the infant away from her.

These people, adults by chronology but not personality, never have an opportunity to break with the patterns they have learned: to lie to and run from the agencies of government, which they see only in negative and oppressive roles. Their lives run by a clock that keeps C.P.T., Colored People's Time, which assumes that appointments made won't be kept, work promised won't be delivered, jobs found won't be gone to, since those are all part of the outside world. Like Mexican Time and the onetime J.P.T., Jewish People's Time, C.P.T. is a phrase that draws the lines of the ghetto.

This book is about one city, Los Angeles, which erupted into violence, but it could be about Detroit, Newark, New York, Rochester, Chicago, Sacramento, or any other city. This book is about the relationships between government and the minority poor in Los Angeles, but it could be any city—for in analyzing those relationships, I have discovered that Los Angeles *is* America and it's terrible.

The Police

"*Mr. Jacobs is a bleeding heart,*" *the police captain said contemptuously to his secretary as he asked her to get me some data, "but I guess we have to give him what he wants."*

The secretary glowered at me and flounced into her office, her back stiff with disapproval. While she was gone I asked the captain and his aide, a lieutenant, another question and got another grudging reply. Neither of them made any attempt to disguise their dislike for me and their disgust at being in a position where they had to answer me.

Not every police official I talked with responded to my interviewing in such a surly way. Some were as cooperative as their positions allowed them to be, and a few were even helpful. All of them attempted, understandably, to defend the institution which they were serving and present it to me as favorably as they could. But always, no matter how pleasant the conversation, a sense of tension hovered over us, for no matter how I tried, it was impossible to shake off the feeling that they thought of me as their enemy.

While I was in Los Angeles, just beginning work on this book, I was invited to participate in an annual training seminar for police officials from all over the country conducted by the University of

Southern California. The men attending the classes were all of high rank in their own departments and seemed a fairly typical cross-section of police officers, much like the men I was meeting in the Los Angeles Police Department. In class the men looked at me either impassively or with open hostility as I spoke to them. I looked back at them, wondering why they wore guns and carried handcuffs to the sessions they were attending.

During these sessions it was very difficult for me to overcome my own angry reactions to their angered response to what I told them about relations between the ghetto communities and the police. They all seemed to have crew cuts, thick necks, and cold eyes. The white officers among them all seemed to be vulgar, crude, and loud, while the few Negroes and Mexican-Americans seemed so concerned with keeping the good will of their peers that they were even more vicious than the white officers in their attacks on their own.

And it was always clear to me that to them I was the embodiment of evil. I began the lectures by explaining that I had a radical past of which I was not ashamed, that I identified myself today with groups that they undoubtedly thought of as radical, that I had been arrested, and that in their view I was undoubtedly some kind of criminal. And even though I tried to joke about this, trying to ease some of the tension in the room, it never worked. They sat grimly, the very positions of their bodies and heads showing that they did believe I was what I joked about being—a criminal.

Twice groups of them walked out on the lectures. The first time was when I was proposing that perhaps a new kind of policeman might be recruited for work in the minority groups: community police officers—men, women, youths from the neighborhoods who might not fit the standards demanded for the regular police officers. I suggested, too, that perhaps even a police record might not be a bar to hiring such people.

There was a shocked silence, followed almost instantly by an angry outburst from a number of the officers. One of them, from another city, shouted at me, "I suppose the next thing you'll be saying is that we should be hiring queers for policemen!"

Flippantly, I answered, "What makes you think police depart-

ments don't hire some queers now without knowing it?"

That did it. The sergeant, his face flushed with fury, got up from his chair and stomped out of the room, followed by a number of other officers. I continued with the discussion but they did not return until after the session had ended. I saw the sergeant come back into the room where I was still sitting, having a cup of coffee and talking with a few of the policemen. He sat down, glowering at me. I said, "Sergeant, I'm sorry you got so mad at what I said. I'll be in your city in a couple of weeks. How about having a cup of coffee together?"

"Jacobs," he said to me, "I wouldn't have a cup of coffee with you if you were the last person on earth. I'll tell you something else, too: you just watch your goddamned step when you get in my area. You just step out of line once and I'll bust your ass so fast you won't know what trouble is."

I was stunned by his vehemence, and some of the other police officials were obviously uncomfortable at his behavior, but no one said anything.

A few minutes later I left. In the hall outside one of the other officials stopped me. "Don't pay too much attention to him," he said. "He's badge-heavy. Some of us don't agree with his ideas about police work."

"How come none of you spoke up, then, if you don't agree with him?"

He shrugged. "Look, I'm a lieutenant, I'm the acting chief in my department. It's a small one and I want to get ahead—I'd like to be chief in a big department some day—so I'm not going to get the reputation of being a troublemaker. I just sit tight and don't argue."

A few months later I was back at the university with a different group—juvenile officers from all over the country attending a delinquency control institute. They were even more openly hostile than the others, for some of them had read the abridgment of this chapter about the police that had by then been published in a national magazine. Even worse, only a week earlier the newspapers had carried a story about my wife and me having been arrested in San Francisco for questioning the behavior of the police *in arresting a group of "hippies" in the Haight-Ashbury district, the city's newest "scene."*

The matter of my arrest came up almost immediately as I gave my version of what had happened. It was apparent that they were convinced of my guilt even though I had not yet been tried. (A week later I was tried and acquitted of the three charges lodged against me.) As one of them, a huge man, almost a caricature of the "cop" type, said, "Wise guys like you always get in trouble. You were interfering with an officer performing his duty. Who gave you the right to question a police officer? I'd arrest you, too, if you ever did that to me." All over the room, I saw the heads nod in agreement. Faithful to my own stereotypes, I looked at a young Mexican-American officer from a city in Arizona, hoping he would give me some support. Instead, he said, "I don't like people like you. You interfere with the enforcement of law. I know you're smarter than I am, but you're a bad influence. You may shake me up but I'll never like you."

Not to be liked by police officers isn't very nice. I need as much love and affection as I can get. But what is far more disturbing is to see how police all over the country, not just in Los Angeles, respond so frantically to what they believe are threats to their authority. There is a sense of crisis in the police world, a feeling that while they are surrounded by enemies at a time when they are the last bulwark of civilization, they are under attack from outsiders who misunderstand them and they are not supported vigorously enough by the public at large.

So even those police officials who are willing to take a more open view of their possible role remain silent lest they be accused of betrayal by their peers. And Mayor Yorty was so angry about my article on the LAPD that he wrote a vitriolic letter to the magazine, denouncing me and stating that I ought to be investigated for having written the article. Indeed, he even suggested that my political views were well known to the authorities, for they had been "aware" of my activities for a long time. And I'm sure that's true, for I know that a dossier on me is in the LAPD's files.

"Drive very carefully in Los Angeles," a police officer who is a friend of mine told me after the abbreviated magazine version of this chapter was published. "If they ever catch you out of line, you'll have a bad time." I believe him, and these days I do drive very carefully in Los Angeles.

Few other police departments in the country are as well known as the LAPD. Jack Webb made it famous for radio listeners and TV viewers in *Dragnet,* and the popular image of the LA policeman as Webb portrayed him was continued by all *Dragnet* imitators. Indeed, no greater contrast in TV images of police departments can be found than in the short-lived comedy about police work *Car 54, Where Are You?,* which portrayed the New York City police officers as bumbling, good-natured fools who survived only through luck, while the slender, athletic, clean-cut, and intelligent men of the efficient LAPD (in *Dragnet*) fight crime with all the tools of modern science.

The air always seems charged with a sense of urgency at the Los Angeles Police Department headquarters in the downtown section of the city. No one just ambles through the corridors of the modern eight-story building known as "The Glass House"; the atmosphere is of a GHQ, the directing center of a war: police officers and civilians all move rapidly, as if they were on missions of the utmost importance. A constant stream of traffic flows from the building to the streets; motorcycle officers in white crash helmets, goggles, black boots, and black jackets roar down the ramps; black-and-white patrol cars stream from the garage; and in the parking area police buses, loaded with equipment and ready for any emergency, wait only to be filled with officers.

The military tone at headquarters is not accidental. The LAPD, like all police departments, believes it is engaged in a never-ending war against crime, a war in which it can function best as a para-military force. Its famous head, now deceased, Chief William H. Parker, who stamped his own imprint indelibly on the department, wore four stars on the shoulders of his dress uniform; his deputy chiefs, with two stars, were called "the general staff"; he issued "general orders"; his subordinates called the internal phones connecting them directly to him "the panic phones," and when they rang, the men at the other end jumped, answering Parker with a continuous stream of "Yes, sir," "Yes, sir," "Immediately, sir."

The LAPD's sense of itself as at least a semi-military organization is pervasive: applicants for the department must be five feet, eight inches tall because "they may face hand-to-hand combat, and they must be able to cow any suspect"; police officers are judged by their superiors on a form modeled after that used in the U.S. Marine Corps, and the qualities for which they are assessed have soldierly connotations—"force," which the department defines as "the faculty of carrying out with energy and resolution that which is believed to be reasonable, right, or duty," and "loyalty," explained as "the quality of rendering faithful and willing service and unswerving allegiance."

The military feeling extends deeply into the police officers' lives, too. When a man applies for admission to the department, he is judged by a board of police officials and civilians; but once accepted and inside the department, he is under the total control of his own police superiors. His promotions to higher rank depend not only upon his passing written exams but, far more importantly, upon the oral interviews he is given by the department's high-ranking officers. And since every police officer knows the views of his superiors, he knows that just as in the military forces, acceptance and conformity to the system's values, as expressed by its high-ranking officials, is one necessary condition for advancement. A police department, like an army, has little use for those who question the value of discipline and obedience to commands: very often lives are at stake when orders are given, and a police officer who cannot shoot accurately may be a menace to himself, his fellow officers, and the public.

In the LAPD another instrument exists for maintaining internal cohesion and "unswerving allegiance": the pension system. Both the police officer and Los Angeles contribute to the pension fund, but unlike most others, the pension plan provides that if a police officer quits the department before he has served the minimum of twenty years required to draw pension, he loses not only the city's contribution but his own as well. And, of course, the longer he stays in the department, the greater his financial stake in remaining; for after he has been contributing his own money to the pension fund for a few years, he cannot afford to leave without suffering a large financial loss.

Two distinct views are current in American society about the role of police. The most widely held is based on the belief that maximum efficiency in enforcing the law is impossible without the sacrifice of some constitutional guarantees; that law enforcement is impossible without a certain amount of secrecy on the part of the police; that all laws must be enforced exactly as enacted; that law violators, in effect, give up their civil rights; and that it may sometimes be necessary for the police to violate laws in the interests of effectively protecting the broader interests of society.

Basically, this has been the dominant view. Most policemen reject or only reluctantly accept the concept that constitutional guarantees against coerced or otherwise illegally obtained confessions or admissions, against unwarranted search and seizure, against illegal arrests and confinements are among the most important elements of a free society, even though these guarantees may be barriers to an "efficient" police service. And in opposing such guarantees, the LAPD is typical of most police departments in the country. It is considered a model department—one of the best if not the best in the country, one whose operations other cities seek to copy. Its practices are typical of what American police activity is evolving toward; its modes of thought are truly representative of what most American policemen believe.

But the philosophy of the police is not a special one; it accurately reflects the views and prejudices held by a majority of people in the community. They, too, see the primary function of the police as the protection of life and property and the preservation of order through the active repression of crime, the apprehension, arrest, and speedy conviction of suspects. A great many people in the country have only a little regard for concepts of crime prevention through positive social action or for the preservation of individual rights which may interfere, substantively, with the efficient apprehension of criminals. This is reflected in the LAPD just as the feelings of the police toward Negroes and Mexicans derive from the community's view of these groups. The department stresses automatic efficiency and absence of compassion; its greatest concern is with "fundamental" police work—crime detection and the capture of law-breakers.

The LAPD reflects the views of the community just as Chief Parker accurately reflected and voiced the views held both in his department and by the majority of police officers in the country. He was probably the second-best-known law officer in the United States, nearly as famous as J. Edgar Hoover, who was not only his enemy but his sole rival for national attention. In the fifteen years after publicity-conscious Parker took over the scandal-ridden and corrupt LAPD and converted it into an efficient, technologically advanced, and incorruptible operation, he became nationally and internationally prominent, a model emulated by other police chiefs.

Before Chief Parker the Los Angeles Police Department could be corrupted; today it is incorruptible. This is not to say that every officer in the department is unbribable; obviously some of them are, for some of them have been bribed. But its atmosphere is not conducive to venal corruption; indeed, the department metes out the severest possible penalties against those of its members found guilty of such acts as taking bribes or stealing, which were mortal sins to Chief Parker, offenses against the moral order, not to be condoned under any circumstances.

The once familiar, and sometimes in other cities still familiar, figure of the policeman selling tickets to the Policeman's Ball is unknown in Los Angeles, where the police are prohibited from soliciting financial assistance for any cause and where the department's monthly magazine accepts no ads. The LAPD's present

structure, with its great emphasis on impersonality and efficiency, grew partially from a reaction against the kind of department which existed in the pre-Parker period, when the way in
which the police exercised their discretionary power was either
haphazard or susceptible to a variety of influences, and when a
citizen didn't know why he was being arrested, or whether or not
his arrest could be prevented by a bribe or the exercise of influence. The relationships between some of the police and some of the
criminals in Los Angeles was so close that it was difficult to distin-
guish one from the other. One of Chief Parker's qualities that
held great appeal for the city's influential business and political
community was that he seemed a man who would bring order, reason, and impersonal bureaucratic efficiency to the police operations. Today most Los Angelenos know that they cannot bribe one
of the "vigilantes," as the motorcycle policemen are known, out of
giving them a citation for speeding on the freeway; and they know,
too, that graft in its more usual form is virtually non-existent inside the LAPD.

Despite the LAPD's incorruptibility, despite its efficiency, despite all the latest technological advances which it uses, despite its
own powerful internal loyalty, despite its officers' bravery, despite
its tradition of service, it is incapable of dealing with the major
problems growing from racial and economic tensions. Indeed, the
case might be made that a primary source of the department's
inadequacy is precisely the set of qualities of which it is so proud.

In recent years, for example, the LAPD insisted repeatedly that
racial conflict would not occur in Los Angeles, where the minority
groups were, according to the department, part of the "compatible
community." "Compatibility between the community and the
police was well-established," said the department in January 1964,
and as late as January 1965 its Annual Report for 1964 asserted
that those "detractors of law-enforcement" predicting an outbreak
of violence in the city were "false prophets" who failed to "consider that many conditions which contributed to chaos in other
parts of the country did not exist in Los Angeles." And in July
1965, only a month before the outbreak which shook up the whole

country, recruits received only a few perfunctory hours of training in race relations in a total of 529 hours spent at the Police Academy!

Still, despite the department's rhetoric stressing the harmonious relationships between the police and minority groups, Chief Parker knew or suspected otherwise: more than a year before the events of August 1965 he had discussed with Governor Brown the possibilities of race riots in Los Angeles. In June 1964 he had even expanded the department's community-relations program, although at the time it was unclear to anyone in the department what function the expanded department was to perform. At the same time Parker responded more characteristically to the problem when he "acquired helmets for all the men in the field that were mobile," although, as he later said, "I did not permit them to wear them, and the helmets were carried in the back of the vehicle, concealed. Those things were done in anticipation that we might have a problem."

The fact is, however, that the country's police departments are caught up in a hopeless position for solving the problems of the era, a position in which their helmets are of no use, a position in which they have been placed both by the conflicting and ambiguous demands society makes upon the police and by their own internal failures.

Generally, the citizens of America make ambivalent and conflicting demands upon their police department: when they are speeding along the freeways which crisscross their spreading city, they resent the sight of a police car; but when an accident occurs during the rush hours and brings any creeping traffic to a halt, they look for a police officer to get the cars moving again, and they are angry if one doesn't appear quickly enough.

A variety of often conflicting public pressures are transmitted to the police officer. If a bar in a "nice" neighborhood becomes a well-known hangout for homosexuals, the community exerts pressure to get it closed, caring little if the methods used are illegal, immoral, or insensitive. The Fire Department, the Health Department, and the Alcoholic Beverage Control Board check the bar for any violations; if those checks fail to yield any evidence which can serve as a basis for action and if the community pressure then continues, a police officer may be stationed in a police car directly in front of the bar. Every twenty minutes he goes inside and checks the bar, looking hard at each patron's face, questioning anyone he recognizes or thinks susceptible to overt pressure. Occasionally he will be able to make an arrest if for nothing else than that one of the homosexuals refused to "cooperate" in being questioned; the "roust" arrest may not hold up, but its effect is just as good. Outside the bar, the police may enforce the traffic laws with great rigidity, giving citations for even the most minor violations. The homosexuals quickly learn that going to drink at that bar is fraught with anxiety and the danger of arrest, and so they move on to another one. The neighborhood is satisfied, and the police return to other duties.

Yet the police know that if they treated middle- or upper-class people in the neighborhood as they do the homosexuals, the entire police force would be denounced. As a result of the public's ambivalent attitude toward the police and their work, most police officers suffer from a great sense of frustration and soon develop a cynical view of the society.

Despite the police department's rhetoric about Los Angeles' being a "compatible community," great variations exist in the attitude taken by the police toward the various sectors of the community. The rich who live in Beverly Hills, hidden from public view by tall hedges, generally have contact with the police only in their role as traffic regulators. The rich get drunk in their own houses, not in public bars; when they quarrel, they shout at each other as loudly as do the poor, but their voices can't be heard by their neighbors as can the voices of those who live cramped next to each other in Boyle Heights or Watts.

"My men are not educators," said Chief Parker. "If you just want to believe that the human being will respond to kindness, that he's not an evil thing, you are just living in a fool's paradise." And most police officers share this view as they ride around the cities looking out the windows of their mobile fortresses at a hostile world, a world filled with enemies, with themselves as the only barrier between society and the beasts who would tear it down, that "horde of migratory perpetrators" of crime, as the department describes its enemies.

Police officials like Parker develop a deeply pessimistic view of the world. "It is . . . hard for me to believe that our society can continue to violate all the fundamental rules of human conduct and expect to survive. I think I have to conclude that this civilization will destroy itself, as others have before it. That leaves, then, only one question: When?"

Parker reflected the views of most police officers, who believe they are fighting alone "to protect the moral reputation of the community." They are convinced that they have been "tragically weakened by the courts of the country," which in their view have relegated "the status of the agents of local law enforcement to a position not unlike that of the accused himself." Thus, the department believes, "it is more than significant that the rise in crime has been paralleled by a metamorphosis of judicial thought and action . . ."

The future is grim, too, in the LAPD's view, for "as long as the populace fails to realize the necessity of order through self-discipline and does not condone the imposition of order through government, the police can only function in a stopgap capacity as the depredations of the criminal element act to disintegrate the social order." And, Parker said, "The main source of Los Angeles crime just happens to be in the areas populated heavily by the Negroes, and the Negroes just happen to be figuring in most of the city's crime. I don't say this from opinion. This comes from the record."

Convinced as the police are that Parker's statements accurately describe reality, the patrol officers drive into the Negro or Mexican-American neighborhoods as if into occupied territories in which almost everybody is likely to be either a criminal or willing to protect criminals from apprehension by the police. This strained view of the area is reinforced by the technical conditions under which the patrol force operates in Los Angeles. The city is so huge and sprawling that almost all patrol work is done by officers in cars, rather than by men walking beats on foot. In smaller cities, and even in a large city like New York whose physical community is vertical, the walking patrol officers have some opportunity to learn about the community. They see its decent people as well as its criminal elements, and they develop neighborhood connections which allow them to act as preventers of crime as well as apprehenders of criminals.

Sitting in their cars, surrounded by their shotguns and riot equipment, the Los Angeles police officers learn about the community primarily through the radio calls that come from the dispatcher, and these calls are always related to the occurrence of crime. The dispatcher never tells them to stop by and congratulate Mrs. Johnson because her son has just won a scholarship to college—the police officers don't even know Mrs. Johnson exists, and the only time they see her is when her next-door neighbor gets drunk and beats up his wife, and then Mrs. Johnson is just another black face to them, peering at them from the outskirts of the crowd.

So it is that the very sight of the police car rounding a corner in a Negro or Mexican-American ghetto and cruising slowly down the street is enough to scatter the gang of kids standing in front of a house. Fear sweat-staining their shirts, the nervous police officers drive down the street, already convinced that those "studs" are up to no good; they show their distrust and suspicion by the very way in which they look the teen-agers over: every Negro and Mexican-American kid has learned to see himself as something evil reflected in the cold, distrustful police stare, the blank look behind which lurks the policeman's knowledge that he is Authority, equipped by the state with the legal power to interrogate, arrest, and, if necessary, shoot to kill.

"They can stay away from me forever," says the young Mexican-American neighborhood aide in one of the anti-poverty projects in Los Angeles. "They look at you like you're dirt if you're a Mexican, and if they don't like the way you look back, they can arrest you. I saw it once on my own street, when a kid wearing boots and gloves, a sharp kid, was walking down the street and got stopped by the cops. He started to argue with them that they didn't have a right to stop him, and the one cop just got out of the car and hit the kid right in the gut with his fist."

"I guess maybe I hate the cops for what they did to me,"

says another Mexican-American youth. "When the cops come out of their academy and get assigned to a barrio, everybody tells them, 'Man, it's rough out there. Those Mexicans'll give you a bad time. Don't let them put anything over on you.' So if you're walking down the street the first night the cop is on duty in a barrio, it's just too bad for you, because you can get arrested for nothing. Maybe he's going to make you stand and look right into his badge and if you just lift your eyes, it's into the jail. Once you're inside, they put you right in a cell and they book you. The two police make up their report and they can put down anything. You go before the judge and he reads the report, all the time holding his hand on his chin, and you think to yourself, What did I do?, and then the judge says, 'Oh, you're a cop beater, huh? You resist arrest, huh? Hundred-and-fifty-dollar fine or twenty-five days.' If you haven't got the money, it's boom, into the jail. In the old days, it was even worse. What the police did then was to wear gloves and work you over so they wouldn't leave any marks on you."

"The old days" were those immediately before and during World War II, when the Negro community of Los Angeles was quite small and the predominant minority group was the Mexican-American community, against whom the police leveled the same kind of charges that they make today against the Negroes. (In June 1943 a Citizen's Committee appointed by Governor Earl Warren to investigate the so-called zoot-suit riots in Los Angeles found, among other things, that "most of the persons mistreated during the recent incidents in Los Angeles were either persons of Mexican descent or Negroes," and asserted that "Mass arrests, drag-net raids and other wholesale classifications of groups of people are based on false premises and tend merely to aggravate the situation." And in view of the committee's 1943 recommendation that "Law enforcement agencies should provide special training for officers dealing with minority groups," the still slight instruction in race relations being given twenty-four years later has a special note of bitter irony.)

It is true that there is much less physical brutality now than in the pre-Parker times when, according to one official, the walls of the interrogation room were sometimes spattered with blood; but in its place there have developed patterns of both psychological and non-verbal brutality very often not understood by the police themselves. When these two types of mistreatment are linked with the occasional real case of physical violence, a body of support begins to grow for the charge of "police brutality."

Judging the physical behavior of the police is difficult in any situation, and especially in the highly charged ones in which racial prejudice is involved. What the police officer learns in the academy about the use of force he must quickly unlearn in his work. Initially he may be no more disposed toward violence and brutality than is the community of which he is a part. But the potentially dangerous nature of his mission, *i.e.,* the repression of crime through the apprehension of criminals, the way in which he views this mission as more important than the preservation of individual liberties, and the skewed view he gets of the world from seeing it primarily in terms of relative rates of criminal activity, all combine to justify the police officer's use of violence. And since he is assumed, because of the character of his work, to be defending society against antisocial types, his use of violence has been sanctioned.

In recent years more and more limitations have been placed upon the police by the courts, and the characteristic police response has been to attack the courts. But the change in the nature of the law has also affected the way in which the police now do their work. As one high police official describes the problem, "Until recently if an officer saw a car that seemed suspicious, he could stop it on the pretext of making some kind of a check for a possible traffic violation. Then, if he could detect visually that there were guns or stolen merchandise inside the car, he could make a search and arrest. But the courts started throwing out these arrests because no traffic citations had been issued, which the courts took to mean that the original stopping of the car had no basis in fact. So now, if an officer sees a car that seems suspicious, he stops it and finds some reason to give it a citation. Then he can make his visual check without worrying that if he makes an arrest it won't stand up in court. But of course lots of times there isn't anything wrong and so somebody has gotten an unnecessary citation."

In some situations, a conflict exists between the legal and moral sanctions on the police. Is a police officer who kicks down a door to get at a suspected narcotics peddler carrying out his duty zealously or is he violating the rights of a private citizen? What is the measure of how much physical force a police officer should use in making an arrest? Many police officers bristle even at the question and have their usual simple answer about those who raise it: "An old tactic . . . an old Communist tactic," says a police lieutenant in a division accused of condoning brutality.

A Negro social worker described a typical incident involving the use of force after she called the police to a settlement house when she found a teen-ager sniffing glue: "As soon as the police came into the settlement house and the boy realized he was going to be arrested, he got very frightened. I asked the officers not to be rough with him. They told him they were arresting him and he should come with them. But he just stood there and looked at them. Then one of them jumped over and put a headlock on him so that the boy started choking. He began to kick, so they threw him down on the ground and put handcuffs on him. All the other kids started crying as they saw what was happening, and one little nine-year-old threatened us with 'We're going to start a Watts riot.' I think the police should have handled it better. They could have done something besides choke the boy, who was really badly bruised. Maybe they were new, because they seemed inexperienced. I guess they were frightened, too."

Such stories of physical violence are repeated again and again, so that they have become part of the folklore among most minority groups. "My boy was picked up one day by the police in the schoolyard," says a Negro lady who lives in a housing project. "The police says he looked suspicious. They pushed a shotgun at him and said, 'Nigger, hit the ground. I give you one second to hit the ground and then you're a dead nigger.' My son said to them, 'I hate your guts,' and they hit him in his sex organ."

Is her story true or false? There's no doubt that her son was arrested, and it's entirely possible that the police did push a shot-gun at him, for that's not an uncommon way of handling what the police believe to be dangerous situations. Did the officers call him a nigger and threaten to shoot him? Maybe. Did the boy say "I hate your guts"? Perhaps he did, and perhaps he may have added "you white motherfucker" to it, but not even that is enough to justify the use of physical violence by the police. Yet despite the dangerous potential of the use of violence in racial situations, despite the basic violation of individual dignity inherent in the unnecessary use of violence, and despite the fact that the use of unnecessary violence breaks down the society's commitment to principles of law, the police in America have generally been exempted from either moral sanctions or legal punishment when they do use violence, including unnecessary killing in situations where it is not required.

In Los Angeles the responsibility for making the initial decision about a homicide rests with the coroner's jury. The case of Johnny Grissom, an eighteen-year-old who was killed by white policemen, is reasonably typical. Johnny wasn't shot during the Los Angeles revolt; his death, on April 10, 1965, was one reason the revolt took place. To the Negroes who live in the same housing project as the Grissom family, the way in which Johnny was killed, the be-havior of the police afterwards, the finding of a coroner's jury that the killing was justifiable homicide, and the arrest of his mother later on a perjury charge were typical of what many minority people have come to expect in their daily lives.

According to Mrs. Grissom, Johnny was "a little disturbed," although it was not a very serious problem. On the night of his death he had quarreled with his mother and she had called the police, asking them to come and talk with him; she told them he had a gun in the house. When the two police officers arrived at the apartment, says Mrs. Grissom, Johnny was sitting on a sofa, hold-ing his infant son in his arms. The police claim he had a gun in his hand; Mrs. Grissom and her other sons deny this. The police drew their pistols, chased the other members of the family out of the house, and eight or ten minutes later emerged with Johnny, who still carried the baby, and walked him to the police car. Johnny stood with one police officer as he radioed for assistance. When the other car arrived, the police suddenly started shooting, and Johnny fell to the ground, on top of his baby, dead from four bullet wounds.

The police claim that the eighteen-year-old was threatening them with a gun, even though he carried a baby in his arms; Mrs. Grissom maintains that the gun was in the house during the entire episode and that the police tore the house apart looking for it after the shooting. According to the inquest report there was a period of time in which no gun was at the death scene, but the police claim that an officer had taken it to police headquarters and then returned it for photographing. There is no doubt, however, that first one police officer and then another, both perhaps frightened, shot Johnny dead, even though he still held his son in his arms.

In the two and a half years immediately preceding the Los Angeles revolt 60 people were killed by police and 4 by security guards protecting public institutions, according to Hugh Manes, a Los Angeles attorney who has repeatedly questioned the present relations between the police and the public. The police shot 27 in the back or the side. Of the 64, 25 had been completely unarmed; 23 had been suspected only of burglary or theft; 4 had not committed any crime when they were killed. Nevertheless, in 62 of the 64 cases the coroner's juries returned verdicts of "justifiable homicide."

On the basis of the record it is clear that a conscious or unconscious pressure to protect the police is always present in the coroner's operations. The coroner works in close cooperation with the police and the district attorney; at a coroner's hearing cross-examination of witnesses by an attorney representing the dead person's family is not permitted.

In addition to those shot dead by the police, others were shot and survived, or were shot at and missed. City Councilman Thomas Bradley, a former police lieutenant, reports that between January 1, 1964, and April 20, 1965, the Los Angeles police were involved in 178 shootings, some of which were completely senseless.

Michael Squalls, a twenty-year-old Negro, was a typical victim of one such shooting. He was driving in his car with a Negro friend, Robert Lee Vance, on September 13, 1964, when they saw a car with a Goldwater bumper strip. Vance shouted at the other driver that he ought to take off the strip because he was "voting for the wrong man." At that point the driver, DeWayne Anderson, who was on his way to work, pulled out a gun and fired five shots at Squall's car, wounding him but missing Vance. When the shooting was over, Anderson alleged that Vance had been waving a gun at him; Vance, arrested on charges of brandishing a weapon and disturbing the peace, was acquitted by a jury on both counts. But Anderson, the man who fired the shots, was neither arrested nor prosecuted: he was a Los Angeles policeman. Anderson apparently wasn't even disciplined by the police department for this episode. But a year later he left the department after getting into another altercation, this time with a fellow police officer.

It is a commonplace in the United States that there are separate systems of justice for the rich and the poor. As part of the War on Poverty, government programs have been designed to correct some of the inequities by organizing legal services for the poor. But for the poor the rule of law carries with it what amounts to a third system of justice. This is the system that exempts the police, in a city like Los Angeles, from their responsibility to society. For example, in August 1964 Richard Price, a white police officer, shot a Negro, Carl Adams, in the back while chasing a prostitute suspect. Adams was arrested for assault with intent to commit murder, but was acquitted in minutes by a jury. Officer Price and his police partner, Daniel M. Samaniego, later were charged with planting Samaniego's knife in Adams' hand and then falsely charging Adams with assault with intent to commit murder. What happened to the two white policemen? They were convicted of falsifying a report and given suspended sentences. Price was pressured into resigning from the police force, while Samaniego, whose knife had been used to justify the false arrest, drew a 180-day suspension from the force; but neither was charged with attempted murder or assault.

So, too, nothing happened to the police officers who killed eighteen-year-old Johnny Grissom and then justified the killing on the basis that he was threatening them with a gun. Instead Johnny's mother was arrested for perjury because she had testified at the coroner's inquest that when Johnny was shot, he didn't have a gun on him, although he owned one. The fact that the perjury charge against her was dismissed by the court for lack of evidence would seem to have called for an investigation of the police officers, but no such inquiry took place.

A whole series of questions needs to be asked about the power of the police to shoot and kill without being penalized. Quite apart from the whole problem of prejudiced officers, should the police be allowed, for example, to kill someone who has committed a crime or who is fleeing from a crime which does not itself call for the death penalty? No one found guilty of stealing, for example, can be sentenced to death for it by an American court, but an American police officer can judge a man, find him guilty, and execute him—on suspicion—all in the instant it takes to pull the trigger of his gun. And if he is predisposed to believe that Negroes or Mexicans or Puerto Ricans are suspicious, he is more likely to shoot at them than at whites. Perhaps most stories of police brutality have passed by now from the level of reality to that of apocrypha, but the apocrypha is still based on the minority groups' perception of reality, a perception that *is* accurate at the psychological and non-verbal level.

More frequent than the misuse of a police gun is the wounding use of language. Every member of the LAPD may be instructed to say "sir" to a man being stopped for a traffic violation, but the way in which the "sir" is pronounced can be an insult or a courteous greeting. And since the police represent the community, it is inevitable that they will reflect the hostility many people in Los Angeles feel toward the presence of a large group of uneducated, unemployed Negroes. And the hostility and prejudice *do* spill over: if a police officer stands inspection in a room whose bulletin board has a picture of Eleanor Roosevelt with "nigger lover" scrawled across it, he is unlikely to think it improper to call a little boy over to his car by shouting "Hey, nigger baby, come over here."

The photo of Eleanor Roosevelt with "nigger lover" on it did exist, as did the prejudice of the LAPD against Negroes and Mexicans-Americans. Until 1961 the handful of Negro police officers in the LAPD worked only with other Negroes on patrol duty, and then in just a few divisions. There were only two Negro motorcycle officers then, and the only Negro officers assigned to any duty in the police headquarters were those working in the jail. It was also characteristic that the moment a Negro police officer, including the few who reached the status of lieutenant, reached the twenty-year retirement age, he quit, often becoming the department's sharpest critic. During those years the department had only a few Mexican-Americans, too. Since then more Negroes and Mexican-Americans have joined, but their number is still far below their percentage in the population.

The few Negro and Mexican-American officers who were in the department, on a segregated basis, prior to Chief Parker's integration order of 1961 were in an extremely difficult and anomalous position: as members of the department, they had to defend its practices; as members of the minority groups, they were the subjects of prejudice inside it and the objects of scorn from their own ethnic groups. Sometimes the response of the Negro and Mexican-American police officers to the painful pre-1961 situation in which they were caught was to be even more aggressive and brutal toward Negroes and Mexican-Americans than were their white counterparts. In return they were often more feared, hated, and despised by the minority groups than were the white officers; the Mexican-American policemen have been described as particular offenders against other Mexican-Americans.

Prior to 1961, according to one Negro officer assigned to a division in a predominantly Negro area, brutality "happened every day." It was common practice when booking a prisoner to have the booking officer try to antagonize him. The arresting officer used to join in, too, shouting insults and taunting him. "Sometimes the prisoner would go past the breaking point . . . make some kind of move. Then they'd really beat him. Sometimes they'd push the prisoner up to the booking window so the booking officer could slug him through the slot. Everyone down there knew about it but no one did anything . . . I didn't do anything either. Things were miserable for a Negro officer in those days. You had to go through channels, and things like that wouldn't go through channels."

A Mexican-American sergeant says, "In those days, all someone had to do was fail to pass the 'attitudes test' and they'd get worked over. Then they'd get booked on resisting arrest or something like that. There wasn't anything we could do about it if we wanted to stay in the department."

Since the 1961 order integrating the department, the internal practices have improved. But a large proportion of the officers in the department prior to 1961 are now moving upward into positions of authority, carrying with them their past attitudes even though they may have learned not to express themselves except in the presence of friends in the department. The department is still the victim of its own past and of its refusal to deal with the problems of its internal prejudice and discriminatory practices.

The LAPD's prejudice against Negroes and Mexican-Americans was found not only in the department's internal institutional arrangements, which excluded Negroes and Mexican-Americans from many normal police duties and normal promotions, but also in the influential though ostensibly private semi-official organizations to which the members of the LAPD give their allegiance. Police officers generally feel a sense of separation from the civilian world: unlike civilians, their off-duty status is anomalous, for they are permitted to carry their guns. Police officers believe they are more vulnerable to criticism for their private behavior, and so feel constrained in their public behavior off-duty: a known police officer, for example, is hesitant about drinking in public and certainly about getting drunk in public, lest someone complain about him. As a result, they are much more likely to spend their off-duty hours with each other than with non-police groups, and their private lives are much more linked, through police organizations, than is true of non-police groups. The LAPD officers give their allegiance to a whole range of organizations: in addition to the military groups, which have posts of officers, there are a police Masonic lodge, police religious groups, shooting clubs, and the FIPO, a right-wing political group of the Fire and Police Departments. LAPD officers' wives have two organizations, one for the wives of white officers and one for the wives of Negro officers, and so the separations between whites and Negroes are maintained informally as well as officially.

It is also characteristic of the LAPD that despite all the department's public assurance about how free it is from prejudice, the white inspector assigned by Chief Parker to head the community-relations division was sarcastically and resentfully described by his peers and superiors as "our nigger inspector." Yet many police officers, especially some of the younger ones, wish that their superiors were less prejudiced. Unfortunately, institutions like the police change very slowly, often so slowly that they are incapable of dealing with such new developments as the emergence of militant voices among minority groups.

To all these problems of the relations between the police and the minority groups, one more must be added: the deep sense of frustration felt by anyone on the outside, Negro or Mexican-American or Puerto Rican, because the citizens of Los Angeles lack effective control over the police department. "A strong protective feeling has always existed among policemen," states the Board of Rights Manual of the LAPD. "Many policemen will jeopardize their own positions to protect a fellow officer. One of the principal reasons for policemen believing they must 'stick together at any cost' is the prevalent opinion that the public is generally opposed to them personally. This protective belief is shared by many supervisors as well as rank-and-file policemen."

Nominally, a Los Angeles citizen can make a complaint against a police officer to the Police Commission, to any superior officer in the department, or to the department's Internal Affairs Division. Charges against a police department employee of "criminal action" may also be made to the City Attorney, the District Attorney, or an appropriate state or federal agency. If a complaint is lodged with the Police Commission, it is either referred to the police chief for "information, investigation, action or report," or the commission can order a hearing to be held. During 1964, 709 complaints were made against police department personnel, of which only 133 were filed initially with the Police Commission; the commission adjudicated 83 of these 133 complaints and referred the remaining 50 to the chief for investigation and report. Thus, the department itself, and not the police commission, had judged 626, or nearly 90 per cent of all the complaints made against its personnel, either from outside the department or from inside it.

No matter how the department gets the complaint, it eventually goes to the Internal Affairs Division. The division defines its role as one which "removes internal discipline from the pressure of partisan politics, special interest groups and other influences detrimental to a professional police service. The division is the central control for the processing of all matters pertaining to personnel complaints." The Internal Affairs Division can make an investigation, which it does when the complaint involves more than one division or where the investigation requires a great deal of time and resources. But in the majority of cases the Internal Affairs Division refers the complaint to the police officer's division commander, who makes his own investigation. The divison or the commander then recommends what action should be taken; that recommendation is reviewed by the commanders of the Internal Affairs, the Bureau of Administration, and the chief. If a police officer is dissatisfied with the recommendation, he can request a hearing before a board of rights, appointed by the chief from among the high-ranking officers; at the board of rights the department is represented by a lieutenant from the Internal Affairs Division.

The military parallel is obvious, of course, and it is clear that when Parker established this procedure, he took the court-martial procedure as his model. But unlike the military establishment, which uses courts-martial almost exclusively to judge charges emanating from within the system, the LAPD's procedure must also handle charges from outside the system, from the civilians who complain about some aspect of police behavior. This double role presents the department with a special problem: it must keep its ranks free of what it believes to be corruption, i.e., the taking of bribes, sex crimes involving officers, etc.; but at the same time it must protect its officers from civilian charges of additional offenses, *i.e.*, the specific charge of excessive use of force and the more general one of "conduct unbecoming an officer." But because the department believes, no matter what it says, that it is better to use more than less force, it is convinced that if it did not back up its officers for what they do in the performance of their duty, the department's morale would suffer greatly.

A striking commentary on the LAPD's view of what is important enough to require an investigation of a police officer's action is that for many years there was an automatic inquiry whenever an officer damaged a department motor vehicle, but not until March 1965 was a board of inquiry ordered set up whenever an officer inflicted a wound on a person. Before March 1965 the only department investigation of shootings by police officers were those conducted by the Internal Affairs Division, which prepared reports on the shootings "to keep the Chief of Police and other concerned command personnel informed regarding these incidents."

The key to the judgment a police department will make about the behavior of its officers seems to be whether the action was taken "in the performance of duty." An officer who commits an offense totally unrelated to his duty or in direct contravention to it will be subject to severe penalties—severe by the department's standards but very often not as severe as if the offense had been committed by a civilian—because of the department's belief that it must protect its public image. If the department believes that the officer's behavior does some *public* damage to its reputation, the penalties may even be more severe than would be meted out to a civilian. Thus, an officer who doesn't pay his debts or who makes a public spectacle of himself is likely to be reprimanded or even suspended for a few days, when no such penalty would be assessed against him if he were a factory worker or even a corporation executive.

When an officer is accused of committing a wrongful act in the performance of his duty, there is a feeling that he must be protected publicly, even if it is agreed privately that what he did may have been wrong. There were some LAPD officials who believed Officer Samaniego should have gotten more than a 180-day suspension for participating in planting a knife on the man shot by mistake; some thought that Anderson should have been removed from the force for shooting at the men in the car because of the bumper strips. The internal pressures in the department kept them from speaking out, however, for they are part of a closed world which feels beset by outsiders who don't understand the true import of their mission.

The cities, too, have a direct financial stake in providing a sanctuary for their officers even when they commit wrongful acts. The city is held legally responsible for the actions of its police officers, and so it provides the legal services required when a citizen sues an officer for an act committed allegedly in the performance of duty. In addition to the legal stake, the city officials also feel that police morale must not be allowed to drop because of the city's failure to back up the men who are protecting its life.

But even assuming that aggrieved citizens know of the channels of complaint open to them, there is great hesitancy about their use: the minority groups usually believe that making a complaint against a police officer does no good and subjects the complainant to possible police harassment in retaliation. And while this alleged condition may not be true, it is believed to be so, just as widespread police brutality is believed to be a fact.

Quite apart from whether or not the police use harassment and retaliation against complainants, the LAPD's record in handling complaints doesn't justify much confidence in its procedure. As noted above, 709 complaints were made against police personnel during 1964. Of these, 243 were initiated by the department itself, and of the 466 complaints that came from outside the department, 412 were made by aggrieved individuals, 50 by government agencies, and 4 by organizations or businesses.

There are some revealing differences among the kinds of complaints made against the police. From outside the department 121 complaints were made about the use of excessive force; from inside only one. "Conduct unbecoming an officer" was the source of 169 complaints from outside, but only 23 from within; "neglect of duty" was the subject of only 87 complaints from outside, but 184 from inside the department. Taken together, the three major sources of complaint represent 82.5 per cent of all the complaints;

taken separately, they show the differences between what the citizens see as their grievances against the police and what the department sees as its grievances against its own staff. The two major complaints from the outside against the department are the use of excessive force and "conduct unbecoming an officer"; these make up 44.3 per cent of all the complaints. Inside it is "neglect of duty"; into this category go 184 complaints, representing 38.2 per cent of the total.

The disposition of the complaints is equally interesting. Of the 121 complaints about the excessive use of force, only 21 (17.4 per cent) were sustained. Further, no officer found guilty of excessive use of force was dismissed, though twenty-three officers were either removed or allowed to resign as a result of other offenses.

The resignation in lieu of disciplinary action is a characteristic device by which an institution seeks to protect itself from internal corrosion of its standards while still preserving an outward appearance of purity. Of the officers allowed to resign in 1964 five were charged with sex offenses, three with dishonesty, one with making a careless report on the discharge of a firearm, one with firing a gun at another officer and slicing the tires of his car, one with an off-duty murder, one with failure to pay child support, and one with committing a burglary. (There is a discrepancy between the number of resignations the division reports in its publications and the number told me by its commander, who listed thirteen resignations instead of the twelve given in the report.)

The department's rationale for allowing officers to resign even though they may have broken the law is that it doesn't necessarily have enough evidence on the men to warrant criminal prosecution, and that sometimes the evidence it does have is hearsay or is taken from a polygraph test or wiretaps, which cannot be used in court. A similar rationale is used to justify not beginning criminal proceedings against officers removed from the department by a board of rights. But the effect of the department's attempt to keep quiet its own internal problems is to provide a sanctuary for those officers guilty of serious enough offenses to warrant the most severe penalty the department can mete out—removal from the force by resignation or firing. It is especially relevant that not very severe penalties are invoked by the department even when an officer is found guilty of planting evidence in order to cover up shooting a civilian without cause.

By now the police animosity toward any "outside" interference in their internal affairs has become an integral part of their view of themselves as a "professional" group. Like any professional group, the police insist that they alone have the right to set the standards by which their members will be judged. Lawyers judge other lawyers, doctors set the standards for excellence in medicine; so, too, say the police, only they should have the right to judge their own behavior. But what this argument fails to take into account is that the discretionary authority of the police extends far beyond that of any other group, the police power to do permanent damage is far greater than that even of a surgeon, and the ability of the police to manipulate situations to justify their correctness extends into levels not open to any other group in society. Yet when a department believes that one of its officers has seriously violated its internal standards, no expense is spared in the effort to bring the culprit before the internal justice system, and tape recordings or other illegal devices are used without hesitation. The case of Officer Michael Hannon is a demonstration, in detail, of how the LAPD responds to what it considers to be improper conduct on the part of a police officer.

Hannon joined the LAPD in 1958, and followed the normal, routine pattern of his fellow officers for a few years. Then, while assigned to patrol duty, he became interested in the civil rights movement. Eventually he joined the Socialist Party and became extremely active in the Los Angeles branch of CORE, participating openly in its picket lines and demonstrations. His public support of CORE quickly came to the attention of the department, and "his activities were followed all along," according to an officer in the Internal Affairs Division. He was observed on a picket line at a sit-down demonstration, where he allegedly "aided and abetted the sit-downers in committing a misdemeanor." In addition, during this period, he was involved in CORE demonstrations around the Federal Building in Los Angeles, where, the department charged later, "he exposed a police undercover agent who was on the scene to gather intelligence information." At the same time, the department says, he helped direct CORE pickets who were trying to stop a bus carrying off arrested demonstrators.

During the period in which the department kept Hannon under observation an undercover police "operator" was assigned by the department to become friends with him. The "operator," pretending to be a Latin-American student, began participating in Socialist Party peace demonstrations; he met Hannon and became friendly with him. At about this time Chief Parker, who had taken an active interest in the Hannon case, decided that the department had to move against Hannon because of his criticism of the President and his open opposition to the war in Vietnam.

One important step in the department's attempt to bring Hannon to trial was to tape-record, without his knowledge, a telephone conversation between him and the police undercover agent. The agent spoke to Hannon from a police department office in the presence of other police officials, pretending that he wanted Hannon to advise him on how to export CORE techniques to his own country, where they could be used to create difficulties for the government. But Hannon, though unaware of the attempt to trap him, refused to give the agent the "revolutionary" advice he was trying to elicit.

Because what Hannon said during the tape-recorded conversation was in no way damaging to him, the department decided not to use it during the trial. But Hannon's civilian attorneys discovered the existence of the recording during the trial and got a court order forcing the department to produce it.

Hannon's ten-day trial was the longest ever held by the department, producing a fourteen-hundred-page transcript. Hannon's defense was to admit freely to membership in CORE and the Socialist Party and participation in the demonstrations; he maintained that he was always off-duty when he took part in CORE demonstrations. In addition, Hannon attempted to prove the existence of prejudice and discrimination within the department and to demonstrate that many officers of the department were openly and avowedly either members or supporters of the John Birch Society.

In effect, Hannon was asking why he was being penalized for his participation in the civil rights and socialist movement, while no LA police officer was prosecuted for participating, just as openly, in right-wing politics. The department's rationale for bringing Hannon up on charges was not that he was a supporter of civil rights, but that he was guilty of "conduct unbecoming an officer." And, of course, the department attempted to deny the charges of discrimination and prejudice.

The result of the Hannon trial was the expected one: the trial board recommended that he be removed from the force. But this trial was unlike others in another aspect, for it had received a great deal of publicity and wide press coverage. With all this public attention focused on the department, Chief Parker, who, like any military commander, had the authority to lessen but not increase the penalties ordered by a trial board, decided that Hannon should not be removed from the force but suspended from it for six months.

At the end of the six-month suspension Hannon reported for duty. Instead of being reassigned to a patrol car, he was sent to guard the City Treasurer's office, where he sat in a glass cage in full view of the public. He was not allowed to leave the cage nor smoke while on duty, and it was obvious that the department hoped he would quit rather than continue in such a boring, routine task. But Hannon refused to quit, since he was studying for the bar (like Parker, he too wanted to be an attorney) and he continued to fight his case, hoping to get back pay for the time he had been suspended.

The question of the relationship between a policeman's off-duty beliefs and his on-duty conduct was raised sharply in the Hannon case. He maintained that his strong feelings against discrimination, including discrimination in the police department, were the impetus for his taking part in demonstrations. But to the department, participation in demonstrations, no matter how well-intentioned they were, was reprehensible if the demonstrations resulted in illegal activity of any kind. In addition, a very large percentage of men in the LAPD believed that Hannon's mere participation in civil rights demonstrations was proof by itself that he was unfit to be a member of the department, for despite all rhetoric to the contrary, they believe civil rights demonstrations are evil and are sponsored by groups who are critical of the department.

Inside the department there is great bitterness directed toward these critics. The department's 1964 Annual Report states scornfully: "In Los Angeles, the detractors of law enforcement stepped up their pervading accusations of police misconduct and pleas for an independent review of police practices in an attempt to create an atmosphere of apprehension, predicting that the streets of this city would also become an arena in which the issues of the civil rights movement would be settled."

The LAPD is also the active, articulate voice of those people in police work throughout the country who have resisted civilian police review boards, attacked judicial rulings against the use in court of illegally obtained evidence, and resisted the general pressure from the courts for extending wider protections to the rights of those accused of criminal acts. The voice of Chief Parker, clear and forthright, was heard throughout the land, for he made speeches by the hundreds and perhaps even thousands to every type of audience that might respond to his message.

In 1956, speaking at the Annual Conference of the California Peace Officers Association, he stated: ". . . A dangerous custom has arisen in America wherein the helpless police officer is a defenseless target for ridicule and abuse from every quarter. It is a dangerous custom because our society is destroying its ability to protect itself by discouraging those qualified from taking up the police service as a career and creating such an uncertainty in the mind of the police officer as to what is appropriate action to the extent that inaction may become the order of the day. This is a situation long sought by the Masters in the Kremlin. The bloody revolution, long the dream of the Comintern, cannot be accomplished in the face of a resolute police."

In 1960 he told the Women Lawyers Club of Los Angeles:

"The philosophy of brotherhood which we began spreading over the world carries with it an indulgent attitude and a lack of self-discipline."

In 1964 he warned the Sherman Oaks, California, Rotary Club that ". . . In another thirty years, we will have primarily a socialist government . . . The drift to socialism is caused by the Supreme Court giving out social philosophy in the guise of legal opinions."

Predictably, too, Parker described civil disobedience as a "revolutionary tool to overthrow existing governments," and rejected the demands of civil rights leaders for police review boards as devices "to break the will of the police and get them out of the way of the social revolution they, 'the civil rights leaders,' choose to call civil disobedience."

Parker's rejection of a police review board was closely tied to his view of himself as the commanding officer of an elite corps, the police, who, he said, "are the real guarantors of freedom in America." Thus, he tolerated virtually no criticism of the department from outside and only a limited amount of it from inside. "I didn't come here to be lectured to. I am going," he once told a meeting of Negro ministers and community leaders who were complaining about certain police practices. Parker's view of himself as paramount authority inside the department was shared by most of his subordinates: an order given by him was carried out without question; indeed, some high-ranking officers seemed so fearful of the chief's possible displeasure that they did not even ask him to explain an order they didn't understand, and tried instead to find out from other officers what he might have had in mind.

The LAPD exercises a great deal of open and hidden influence in the life of Los Angeles: the Mayor, City Council, County Board of Supervisors, juvenile courts, Probation and Parole Departments, coroner's office, and the District Attorney are all considered legitimate objects of LAPD pressure. The department believes few aspects of life in Los Angeles to be legitimately outside its purview: when a professor at UCLA was conducting a study of which the department disapproved, it went directly to a high university official to have the study ended; its undercover agents infiltrate civil rights organizations; it has a secret squad which compiles dossiers on those people whose political beliefs the LAPD considers subversive.

Typically, too, the department responds to any criticism by using its resources to investigate the critics while denouncing them as enemies of law and order whose motives are the destruction of the social system. Since the LAPD is convinced of its own moral rectitude and the overwhelming importance of its mission, every attempt is made to discourage any criticism as being destructive of its public images: even when a complaint against the department is discovered to be justified, its importance is always minimized and as little publicity as possible is given to it.

The LAPD's overall posture is approved by many influential Los Angelenos who are more than satisfied with the role the police play in their city. This powerful group sees in the LAPD the embodiment of their values and the expression of their concept of how a city should be run. They believe in a police department which will act as an efficient, productive, paramilitary establishment, for they, too, believe that only in that way will crime be kept down, property protected, and order preserved. But in a period marked by grave internal racial tensions and the emergence of new social forces, the very efficiency and productivity of which the LAPD is so proud serve to aggravate rather than diminish the tensions in the city. By themselves efficiency, productivity, indeed, even incorruptibility are *not* adequate qualities for dealing with racial conflicts; understanding and compassion are required as well, and those qualities are in short supply among the five thousand men of the LAPD.

There are, of course, as in any organization of this size, obvious variations in its personnel. Still, some general characteristics of a Los Angeles policeman do emerge; he is the result of the department's recruitment policy coupled with the training given the recruits and the socializing process through which the recruit becomes a member of the police world. Although the material is available, no complete or accurate data have been made public by the department concerning its men. Detailed records are kept of every Los Angeles police officer, but they have not been processed in any thorough way for use outside the department, and the department displays a typical police reluctance to reveal to the outside world any more about itself than is absolutely necessary: the internal secrecy and suspicion of outsiders, a common characteristic of most police departments, is present in the Los Angeles Police Department as well.

Like most police departments today, the LAPD finds it difficult to attract recruits who meet its standards. "The somber outlook afforded by the discrepancy between the growing criminality in our society and the scarcity of police applicants has improved only slightly," according to the department's report on its 1963 activities. During that year the department was unable to "achieve an enduring manpower level sufficient to meet the needs" of the community, despite "an intensified recruiting effort" and the help of private industry. "The shortage of qualified applicants" was "the most critical problem" faced by the department that year.

The next year the same situation prevailed: "Filling vacancies to maintain the department's strength required a continuous effort . . . ," the Annual Report for 1964 states. That year 4,816 persons applied for a policeman's job; less than 10 per cent of that number finally graduated from the Police Academy as probationary officers. Thus, "despite all efforts, 148 vacancies for policemen existed at the end of the year."

Chief Parker was probably correct when he explained the difficulty in recruiting police officers as resulting from scandals in the police forces and the fact that Americans tend to view the police as "inhuman": "When you join together the deeply rooted concept of individual liberty with an abiding sympathy for the underdog, you have the basis for a cleavage between the public and the police. When it becomes necessary for a police officer, wearing the badge of authority of the state, to deprive an individual of his liberty, perhaps remove him from his home by legal process, those who witness this legal invasion of personal liberty are inclined to allow their innate sympathy to turn the resentment towards the police . . . The misdeeds of the arrested person are often overlooked, as has frequently been the case, even though the most serious criminal case has been involved." According to Chief Parker a policeman's work often places him in an adversary or hostile relationship to the general public; as a result, police work is not viewed with much sympathy.

There is a good deal of merit in Parker's explanation for the unattractiveness of police work, but other factors also hinder the efforts of the police to recruit applicants to fill vacancies. The conflicting and inconsistent demands made upon the police by the American community weaken the attractiveness of the job. While being a policeman used to be viewed as an avenue upward (to a political career, for example) or as a safe job during the Depression, few people able to meet police standards worry today about an economic depression, and they have found that new avenues of personal mobility have opened for them.

The police officers in Los Angeles do not serve as a very active recruiting corps, either, partially because once they become officers, they tend to live inside the police world and have less contact with people in other occupations than do most other groups in society. In addition, despite any preconceptions about the nature of his work a man may bring to the department, he quickly learns that most of the job is actually monotonous, dreary, and boring, that advancement is comparatively slow, that inside the department the highest status job is that of a detective who does not wear a policeman's uniform, and that the pay scale is usually insufficient to allow his family to live in the way society insists is proper—as continually spending and accumulating consumers. One important indicator of how unattractive police work is in Los Angeles, even to those doing it, is the comparatively small number of policemen's sons who follow their fathers into the department.

Other characteristics peculiar to the LAPD act as additional barriers to recruitment. Minority groups have long considered the department to be prejudiced against non-whites. In spite of Los Angeles' large Spanish-speaking population, the LAPD has never had much success in recruiting from that community, because the department has reflected the white community's denigration of the Mexican-Americans. To many Mexican-Americans the "zoot-suit" riots of 1943—when any dark-skinned person was likely to be arrested and physically mistreated by the police—were symbolic of the treatment Mexican-Americans could normally expect from the police. In addition, the LAPD requirement that applicants be at least five feet, eight inches tall automatically rules out a great many Mexican-Americans, who tend generally to be shorter than that. Negroes have also avoided joining the Los Angeles Police Department, for they, too, have been correct in their belief that the department is biased against them.

Faced with the community's uncertain views of the police role and with a continually growing community needing more and more police services, the LAPD has to carry on an intensive recruiting campaign. The bulk of the recruiting is done through the Civil Service Commission: a police sergeant is assigned as liaison to the commission to make contacts with all kinds of groups and display LAPD exhibits at fairs and other public community activities. The department also sends officers to other parts of California, and to Nevada and Oregon, to make background checks on applicants from those areas. While the officers are in those places, they visit military bases, schools, and employment offices to make contacts for possible recruits. They are also given tips on potential applicants by teachers, like the one in an adult education course who had a class which included a number of Marines facing discharge from the military service; they ultimately went into the LAPD at the teacher's suggestion. A good many Western junior colleges offer courses in police work, taught by police officers, and they serve as a recruiting pool for the LAPD. Athletic-scholarship students at these colleges who cannot meet the academic requirements or young men who can't finish college because of financial problems are also sources of recruitment.

The recruiting standards are set by the Los Angeles Civil Service Commission and the department: an applicant must be between twenty and thirty-one years old at the time of application; he must have a high school diploma or its equivalent; he must be at least five feet eight inches tall, show physical agility, and be in excellent health. In addition, recruits must pass a psychiatric examination administered by the department's psychiatrist; but this is rather brief, and although the department insists that it attempts to weed out anyone with psychiatric problems, the shortage of officers undoubtedly allows for overlooking marginal deviations which might eventually become more serious. In addition, because the department places so much stress on physical bravery, its stress tests are geared to determining how a recruit will stand up under difficult conditions; but not as much emphasis is placed on the emotional problems a police officer might encounter.

The character of the police department's recruits has changed considerably, reflecting the changes in the character of the city. When Los Angeles was incorporated in 1850, its population was 1,610 persons, with one city marshal who could deputize citizens to keep order. In the city's first year he found it necessary to deputize a hundred people; three years later, despite the help he got from such volunteers, the marshal was assassinated in the midst of an especially bad outbreak of violence. Twenty years later there were only six police officers in Los Angeles, but from then on the number grew rapidly. The biggest expansion took place in the 1920s, a period in which 50 per cent of the police were ex-motormen or conductors from the Los Angeles railways, although no one today is certain why.

In the post-World War II period, thirty-five hundred officers were recruited from the military services; by 1951 they represented 83 per cent of the force. According to the department, recruiting from the military dropped off as the Armed Services diminished in number and as better economic opportunities were offered to returning servicemen; but most of the higher-ups of the department today are from that 83 per cent.

What happened to those young men recruited from the military services after a period of years in the LAPD? Ample evidence exists that a great many members of the Los Angeles Police Department are politically conservative or even reactionary, cynical, privately contemptuous of and hostile toward the civilian world, racially biased, defensive, self-protective and secretive, and convinced that they are members of an elite group, misunderstood and even persecuted by the very society which they and they alone are protecting.

The recruits' value system was influenced by their families, schools, peer groups, and occupations. As police officers they began to absorb a different set of values: however they may have regarded Negroes, for example, too many of them have come to believe that Negroes are "studs" and "black motherfuckers"; whatever view they may have had of themselves as civilians, too many of them have come to think of civilians as "stupid assholes"; too many of them accept and justify wiretapping, lock-picking, and other illegal methods of gathering evidence. They learned, too, that because their work is judged on the number of arrests they make or citations they issue, making a "good pinch" becomes more important than how it is done or preventing a crime, and "a greenie a day keeps the sergeant away" (a "greenie" is a policeman's duplicate copy of a traffic citation).

The recruit's entrance into the police world begins once he has passed all the tests and his background check has yielded nothing detrimental. He starts work at the Police Academy, located in a park a few miles away from the headquarters. "There's a public misconception about the academy," says Deputy Chief Noel A. McQuown, who heads the LAPD's personnel and training bureau. "The Police Academy is a training school, not an academic institution. We only teach the recruits how to do it."

"How to do it" is taught in 529 hours in 12 weeks. The curriculum, reflecting accurately what is considered important in the LAPD, emphasizes the technical aspects of police work: only a few hours each are devoted to the background of law enforcement and to race and human relations—although the department states that such questions are discussed in other classes, too—and the major emphasis is on such subjects as criminal investigation procedure, the care and use of firearms, physical conditioning and control tactics, and patrol procedures, which includes approximately two hours on race relations, two on press relations, and eight on public relations.

The Academy's syllabus description of the official instruction in race relations is extremely interesting: "Conversations and terminology that cause misunderstanding and friction. The department's efforts to reduce tension. Class develops an adequate social perspective, an awareness and understanding of the multiple factors which cause individual and group differences. Avoidance of any activity by an officer which could be interpreted as showing racial intolerance or bigotry."

Significantly, the newly enlarged community relations program proposes that six days be given to the study of race relations.

The real education of a Los Angeles police officer begins after he leaves the academy and is assigned to a division. Separated from the other recruits with whom he went through training, he learns a different set of standards and discovers what it is to be a "working cop." The gap between what he has learned in the academy and the reality of police work is frequently enormous and even terrifying. His "on-the-job" training quickly convinces him of the need to conform to the standards of those officers who are more experienced and of higher rank than he is, for it is this group, not the academy instructor, who judge him during his probationary period, and it is their judgment which will determine his acceptance into the police world. And so he seeks their approval, and in doing so, learns to accept their standards as his own.

After graduation from the academy the new police officer is usually assigned to one of the department's patrol divisions scattered throughout the city. For the first half of his probationary year he works with a training officer selected by the division commander. Theoretically, these training officers are chosen for their ability to teach; in practice, they are sometimes those policemen whom the division commander believes he can most easily spare from what is thought to be more important work than teaching probationary policemen. Since the training officers receive no formal instruction in teaching techniques except for a few classes sometimes held at the divisional level, the new officers, in effect, get their training and are judged by the less capable men in the division.

The only other formal training programs directed to the probationary officer are specialized training in specific aspects of police work (if he is assigned to beach duty, he will be instructed in how to solve beach problems; if his duty is in the city parks, he will be taught about park problems) or occasional instruction at roll call when he reports for duty. Roll-call training isn't taken seriously by the watch commanders who read the lessons or the officers who listen perfunctorily to them. One watch commander in a division located in the ghetto gave roll-call training by reading three pages from a new manual and then saying to his men, "Those book-worms uptown are bending over backward to coddle those people. You men know how to do police work. Go out and do your job the way you have to."

At the end of his first year the officer returns to the academy for two more weeks of training; between his fourth and fifth year he takes a short refresher course. Senior officers may attend seminars, as do the top-ranking officials. (At a recent seminar for the top department officials, held at a lake near Los Angeles, the military hierarchy order was even used to assign living accommodations: the deputy chiefs were given the best cottages, high on the hill over the lake, and the lower ranks put up in the less desirable cottages in descending order down the hill.) But this type of training is al-most exclusively technical, and the LAPD's real values are learned in the locker rooms, over cups of coffee at gatherings of the de-partment's social clubs, at the parties to which very few ousiders are invited, and inside the police cars.

It is in such situations that the new officer quickly learns the real standards he is expected to meet. At the academy, for example, sixty-seven hours of instruction are given to the recruit in "Traffic Functions," of which seven are devoted to "Citation Issuance" and two to the department's traffic-law-enforcement policies. But no matter what he learns at the academy about these policies, once on the job and assigned to traffic-law enforcement, he learns about "greenies." He begins to exercise his discretionary powers—*i.e.,* to give or not to give traffic citations, not only when a clear offense has been committed (when he observes a car doing ninety on the freeway) but also in marginal situations (a broken taillight)—in response to his need to produce citations, the product by which the LAPD judges officers assigned to traffic-law-enforcement work.*

* "You never know when it will happen," begins a typical article in *BEAT,* the LAPD's house organ. "According to Officer Gary Lee, he was riding along minding his own business and trying to stay out of trouble when he happened to observe a minor traffic violation. Not

Traffic-law enforcement in Los Angeles reflects the same basic view of the police function as the department: it is mechanical, impersonal, and basically repressive. Anyone driving ninety miles an hour on the freeway will get a ticket, whether he is a white corporation president who lives in Beverly Hills or a man who sweeps out the corporation's locker rooms and lives in Watts. Traffic tickets cannot be "fixed," and everyone in the city knows that clear and flagrant violations of the law which endanger lives will be cited.

But it is in the marginal cases that the repressive traffic-law-enforcement policies become a source of tension. Every officer is aware of the pressure on him to produce citations as an indication that he has not been asleep in the back of the car, parked behind a billboard alongside the highway. Once on the job, the officer learns to use for his own purposes the academy's principles of "selective traffic-law enforcement," because he knows in advance at what locations it can be statistically predicted that traffic violations will take place—the boulevard stops, where no buildings obstruct the view of the intersecting highways, or the thirty-five-mile zone where drivers customarily do forty-five are known as an "apple orchard," "duck pond," or "cherry patch." The traffic-law-enforcement officers know that many people do not make a complete stop late at night at the intersection, and that they drive forty instead of thirty-five during the day. "So," as one officer says, "if the end of my watch is coming up and I need a greenie because the sergeant has been on my back, I go on over to the 'duck pond' and write me a fast ticket."

Ordinarily, the motorist thinks of the occasional "fast ticket" as one of the hazards of driving—he may complain to the officer who caught him on Monday driving forty in a thirty-five-mile zone that he didn't get a ticket for doing the same thing on Friday—but at

---

that he needed a 'greenie' or anything like that, but he felt it was his duty to proceed as any good policeman would. So he turned the red lights on and proceeded to stop the violator . . ." The article then described how, when the officer saw the driver trying to hide something in the car, he investigated and discovered sixty-five hundred pills of an undisclosed nature.

most it is a minor nuisance, and the fine is likely to put only a temporary dent in his purse. Under precisely the same circumstances a poor person, especially a poor Negro, suffers considerably more—indeed, if he cannot easily pay the fine, he may ignore the citation and eventually end up with a warrant out for his arrest—and if the poor person is also a Negro already resentful of the police, he may attribute the citation to police prejudice against Negroes. If his resentment about getting a ticket instead of a warning for a marginal offense (like a flickering or dead taillight) spills out in his response to the police officer, he may end up by getting arrested for failing to pass the "attitude test."

The new police officer assigned to patrol duty discovers that pressures for production are exerted upon him at an even more potentially dangerous level. Although patrol work, according to the police, "is the traditional and basic police task," the officer soon discovers that being on patrol duty does not have high status inside the department, despite the fact that the "Patrol Bureau is the largest subdivision of the Department," with "2,738 officers (54.5 per cent of department strength) augmented by 621 civilian personnel of whom 285 were crossing guards and 11 were correctional officers."

The bureau's "broad duties" consist of "crime prevention, juvenile delinquency control, crime repression by means of twenty-four-hour uniformed patrol, protection of life and property and providing service, information and assistance to the public." But in the tradition of modern police work most patrol work is viewed as only a steppingstone to a better police job, and not the most important police function. The reward to a "good" patrolman in a patrol division is transferral to a "felony car," where he does not wear a uniform on duty, or promotion to plainclothes detective status.

Even on the job the patrolman has second-class status. If he is called to the scene of a crime, he makes the preliminary investigation, collects whatever evidence is available, interviews the victims and the witnesses, and if it is possible to do so, arrests the criminals. But if any of these actions present difficulties—*i.e.,* if the witnesses have disappeared or the crime is old, complicated, unique or serious—detectives in plainclothes are dispatched to the scene to take over from the uniformed officers. Thus, patrol officers are continually reminded that they are not judged to be competent at solving crimes or following through with investigations. And if they need any further reminder of their inferior status, they get it when they see that the punishment meted out to a detective who has performed badly or has violated departmental rules is relegation back to patrol duty.

In practice, then, the police patrol force is simultaneously a pool from which the best men are promoted to other status and into which are deposited those police officers who have failed to meet the department's standards in other assignments. Inevitably, the patrol officers are not the men thought of within the department as being the best, and they begin to reflect the department's internal opinion of their lower status, with the result that they seek every opportunity to get away from patrol work into higher-status jobs.

Yet these are the police officers who have the jobs which bring them most often into contact with the poor and the minority groups at a time of great tension in the community. Even worse, these are the men who affect, in the sharpest and most profound way, the attitude of the minority groups toward the white world, for very often they are the visible symbol of the white world as seen by the Negro or Puerto Rican or Mexican-American. It does not matter that Parker maintained that his men are not educators; they are, and whether they will be educators for better or worse is what must concern the entire society.

One way a patrolman can raise his status in the police department is to demonstrate to his superiors how zealous he is as an officer. Just as the test of a traffic officer's work is the number of citations he has given, so one important standard for judging a patrol officer is the number of field interrogations he makes on his watch, or how many "good pinches" (arrests) he makes. "How many shakes did you get tonight?" is a question the patrol officer very quickly learns to anticipate on his return to his divisional headquarters; and to ward off having to give an unsatisfactory answer, he sees to it that he always makes the recognized informal quota for the area.

That quota is based on the anticipated amount of crime in any given area, just as the incidence of traffic violations at certain locations has become a matter of predictability. One lieutenant in the LAPD devised his own method of maintaining a high level of "efficiency" among the men on his watch: he issued "report cards" each month. The top line on the card gave the overall monthly watch "average" for "shakes" (broken down into such categories as adult, juvenile, vehicle, and pedestrian) and citations (moving and non-moving, and arrests, subdivided into felonies and misdemeanors, and traffic and non-traffic categories). Under the line of the overall watch averages, the individual officer's record was kept: if he exceeded the monthly averages, the figures were written in blue; if he went under, they were written in red. The lieutenant used the report cards as the basis for judgments concerning the patrol officer's efficiency and to determine whether he should accede to an officer's request for special duty, change in days off, or assignment to a special watch partner.

There are also more subtle pressures than this for increasing the numbers of arrests, shakedowns, etc., as indicators of efficiency and productivity. The pressure on the officers to make field interrogations or misdemeanor arrests as an indication that they have been working acts as another of the elements to build up the self-fulfilling prophecy that the minority groups produce more crime than other areas of the city. Tragically, too, neither the police nor the white community at large seems to understand the real consequences of misdemeanor arrests for members of minority groups. For Negroes or Mexican-Americans or Puerto Ricans a single misdemeanor arrest, even though no conviction may follow it, is a bar to civil service employment, a terrible handicap to private employment, and a license for future arrests: the single most important determinant for the typical police officer who is uncertain about making a misdemeanor arrest is whether or not the person involved has been previously arrested. If so, and even where there has been no conviction, the scale is almost automatically tipped in favor of another arrest, for now the arrest can be justified not only by the person's actions in the present case but by a prior action which was at least suspicious enough to have justified arrest in the past. And it is of little consequence that the prior arrest may have been made, as it often is, only because the person failed to be respectful enough to satisfy the arresting police officer.

Too often, also, the doubtful misdemeanor arrest is made on the assumption that the adversary system will give the prisoner adequate opportunity to defend his innocence in court. But the poor Negro or Mexican-American or Puerto Rican has very little real opportunity to defend himself, since he cannot afford proper representation and the state does not provide it, either. If he cannot afford to make bail, he loses time from his job and must explain to his employer that he didn't show up for work because he had been arrested. If he loses his job because of the arrest, his only alternative may be to become the criminal that he wasn't when he got arrested initially.

The misdemeanor arrest is occasionally used by the police as a device to "clean up" a troublesome area, just as it is used against those the police believe to have a hostile attitude. If the arrested person protests and complains, it is always possible for the police officer to scan through the "wanted" file to find someone who looks vaguely like the arrested person and thus justify making the arrest on suspicion.

In May 1964, more than a year before the riots broke out in Los Angeles, Howard Jewell, an Assistant Attorney General, made a report to the State Attorney General, Stanley Mosk, predicting the outbreak which occurred in August 1965. He listed some of the incidents which had taken place between the police and minority groups, and in the course of his reports made an observation directly relevant to Parker and the LAPD's true feelings: "Chief Parker does not dislike Negroes because they are Negroes, but because they dislike the police department. This, in Parker's book, is the only unforgivable sin." Jewell discusses elsewhere the LAPD attitude toward civil rights demonstrators, pointing out that

Chief Parker "has made it clear that the struggle *is* between the police department and the demonstrators."

". . . the struggle *is* between the police department and the demonstrators"—that is the key phrase, for it sums up the LAPD's view of the present situation in California. If the police department is no more than representative of the population, for every member who did not favor repeal from the state constitution of an anti-discrimination-in-housing law there were three who did, for it was by that ratio that the law was repealed in a referendum election. But when a police officer in uniform stops a woman in a car for a driving violation and tells her that she ought to remove the bumper strip opposing repeal, he is expressing his true feelings about those who favor non-discriminatory housing.

Along with proponents of housing integration and civil rights demonstrators, the LAPD also sees as its enemies those forces in the city who stress crime prevention as a solution to the crime problem rather than the apprehension, arrest, and conviction of criminals. Specifically, in 1963 the LAPD was successful in bringing to an end the operations of the Group Guidance Section of the Los Angeles County Probation Department.

The Group Guidance project had been in operation for eighteen years, establishing contact with gangs of Negro and Mexican-American youths and attempting to direct their activities into more constructive channels. But the LAPD, which believed the program encouraged juvenile delinquency by "coddling" the youthful offenders, ultimately put enough pressure on the Probation Department, as well as other agencies, first to kill it and then to begin it again in a form more acceptable to the department.

The supporters of Group Guidance, especially those from the minority groups, charged the LAPD with continual harassment and arrest of gang members even when they had done no wrong; with exerting pressure on schools to expel known gang members; with trying to get employers to fire youths from jobs because of gang membership; with unnecessary surveillance of gang youths' houses; with forcing the Park and Recreation Department to deny facilities to the youths; with pressuring the Probation Department to transfer the probation officers working with the gangs; and with both verbal and physical abuse of gang youth members.

The LAPD credo is simple: "Great strides have been made in improving the technical ability of law enforcement officers to perform their daily tasks. Highly sophisticated electronic data processing equipment, greatly improved communications, swift and reliable means of transportation and modern administrative techniques have all contributed to more efficient use of police personnel. But the beneficial effect of these advances has been largely negated by the fetters of legal technicality by which the officer of today finds himself bound. He performs his duties amid a maelstrom of conflicting legal theory and changing rules of law, trying to maintain the public security in an adequate and precise manner."

But a veteran officer, who served for many years in the juvenile division, believes he was able to do his work better in past years, when he was able to establish some kind of relationship with a juvenile and spent time getting to know the family background and the problems the juveniles were facing. Today, he says bitterly, the laws do not allow juvenile officers enough time for the slow effort required to develop the kind of personal relationships with juveniles that will keep them from becoming adult criminals.

To this view a Negro lady in Watts adds, "The police is brainwashed that every colored person is a criminal. In the old days the police were better. They were on the beat and the parents cooperated good with the police. The police would come to the house and talk to the kids if they did something bad. Now they just talk to you on the phone, and the kids hate them and they got no respect for them. The police used to have band groups and boy and girl clubs but they stopped all that. Now they just give out tickets and arrest you. That's one of the reasons we had the trouble here."

"The Welfare Bureau"

I began to get some true perspective about welfare on the day I applied for welfare myself, just to have the experience of being processed. I sat in the waiting room for hours, along with a hundred other people, mostly women with their children, who were crying, wriggling, restless on chairs, or racing up and down aisles. Even I, just pretending to be in need of help, felt humiliated, perhaps because the experience brought back memories long suppressed of those days, years ago, when I too had really needed help.

A few days later I went to lunch with the official who was then in charge of the office and asked him about the processing, without telling him that I had already been through it. He assured me that no one waited very long, and as he took me on a tour of the building, kept pointing out how businesslike an operation he was running. I asked him why he didn't provide a little space for a nursery and find a couple of women to take care of the children while their mothers were being interviewed. He looked at me as if such a notion could never have occurred to a rational person. Obviously, it hadn't occurred to him that applicants for welfare might be humiliated by having to answer questions in front of their children.

One afternoon a week later, when I was talking with a group of Negro high school students and I asked how many of them had been arrested, almost every hand went up. But when I asked how many of them came from families getting welfare, not a single hand went up. And yet I knew that at least 75 per cent of the kids in that room were from families whose sole income was the twice-monthly check from the county.

People for whom humiliation is a condition of life find it hard to admit its existence or to organize themselves. Yet over and over in studying the welfare system, I saw that very few people in government have any notion of what effects their agencies are having on those unfortunate people, upon whom the constellation of separate government forces bears down inexorably.

Instead, each government agency operates under its own rules, impulses, and drives, responsible not so much to the citizens' needs as to its own internal organizational modes. These modes commit the staffs and especially the welfare staffs to never challenging the status quo, never taking risks, and never listening to voices that question.

Until recently the county agency administering the public welfare program in the city was called the Department of Charities. And the still implicit attitude of the department toward the program was explicit in that name: the welfare program is considered to be a "charity," something to be given only to the very poor and needy in Los Angeles who must first prove and then continue to demonstrate that they are "worthy" of being helped.

William Barr, County Superintendent of Public Charities, described the Bureau of Public Assistance as a "huge monster, an octopus, a monstrous thing which spreads out everywhere."*

He is correct.

Ellis (Pat) Murphy, who under Mr. Barr has direct responsibility for supervising the LA welfare department, says, "The police and the welfare system are the two agencies that touch the lives of the most people in the Los Angeles ghetto but the welfare system doesn't fit the needs of the people who are the recipients. The grants given by the bureau are cut off below the physical needs of the people, and the system is so involved in administrative detail that 50 per cent of the social workers' time is taken up with filling out papers instead of doing social work."

Mr. Murphy is correct, too.

* The bureau is now called the Department of Public Social Service and has been reorganized administratively. But nothing fundamental has been changed. Most recipients still describe it as the BPA or "the welfare."

But what neither Superintendent Barr nor Mr. Murphy says is that they, their subordinates, and the County Board of Supervisors to whom they are responsible are deeply involved in creating the situation they seem to deplore. If the administration of the "monstrous" welfare system is a source of tension in Los Angeles, and it is, a great deal of the fault must be attributed to the County Supervisors and officials. If the grants are below the physical needs of the people, and they are, the County Supervisors and officials can be held accountable, for they have lobbied successfully for many years to keep those grants down. And if the system is as involved in administrative detail as they maintain, part of the blame rests directly on them.

A forty-year-old Negro woman, whose sole income is an Aid to Families with Dependent Children grant, is much more accurate than Barr or Murphy in her description of the program: "The main thing, too, is that from the very word go the income is based on the barest necessities. There is no such thing as an extra income, so say something—an accident or something else—happens that you've got to have extra transportation money; there's no such thing as there being a fund that can be an emergency fund that can be sent to you, you know, on the spur of the moment.

"Like, for instance, if you get a check on the first of the month, okay, that's our rent, utilities, phone, and so forth, and the kids have to have shoes. Then the next one is for the fifteenth—we get a little groceries on the first, enough that'll hold us until the fifteenth—then we do our heavy shopping. But you still got another bill or the kids need something or something is going on somewhere. You better believe there's always something, especially when it gets cold weather. And we can't live without necessities for ourselves—our personal necessities and our house necessities. Like I told my worker, my children have to take baths, my children have to have clean clothes to put on—and I can't clean up the house with the food I eat. All you can buy is food, and you can't buy much of a meal anyway because of the prices you got to pay.

"And another thing is that the caseworkers is falling under such a caseload that they don't have the time to give to the personal problems of the people that they're dealing with. They don't have time to listen a lot of times. This is where it is—a person will have a problem or a person will have a particular need to know something, and his social worker is sometimes his only contact with professional, educated-type people that could give him advice, and he's busy, and he's busy, he's had a lot of cases like this, he's tired, he's cranky, he doesn't want to be bothered. This causes quite a hassle, quite a feeling of insecurity."

The number of people in Los Angeles who suffer from a "feeling of insecurity" is staggering: the staff of the Los Angeles County welfare department is larger than that of many state governments; the number of family aid cases handled by just one office of the department is greater than similar caseloads of twenty-eight states; 40 per cent of all the welfare payments in California are made in Los Angeles County; the amount of money disbursed by the department just to families with dependent children in Los Angeles County is larger, by far, than the grants made in similar programs in forty-eight states. There are 7,500 people on the welfare staff; its total annual budget is half a billion dollars!

The sole or major source of income of 300,000 men, women and children in Los Angeles County is from public funds. More than 150,000 of these receive public funds through the Old Age Security, Aid to the Blind, Aid to the Needy Disabled, and General Home Relief programs, while nearly 175,679 families with a total of 218,425 children are the recipients of grants from the Aid to Families with Dependent Children program, the single most controversial program. But the average monthly payments to these AFDC families are only $174.55, nearly $1,000 per year below the federal government's poverty line; each recipient in an average family receives only $43.26 a month.

In August 1965, the month in which the events took place that shocked the country, $5.5 million in public assistance payments of all kinds were made to nearly a hundred thousand people in the Negro ghettos, a population larger than that in thirty-six of California's fifty-eight counties. But while that monthly $5.5 million is portrayed as a tremendous sum by the taxpayers' associations and the supervisors, it averages out to only $55 per person per month —far, far below the barest minimum for the essentials of life.

In that same month the south-central Negro section of Los Angeles alone accounted for more than a third of all the payments made in the whole county to families with dependent children; BPA offices located in the ghetto areas account for nearly 68 per cent of all the cases aided and 84 per cent of the total AFDC expenditures. Forty-five per cent of all the Old Age Security program cases in the county and more than 60 per cent of the General Home Relief programs are also located in the ghetto. And despite the sanctimonious attitude of those who portray the $5.5 million as a drain upon the *local* taxpayers by lazy people who refuse to work, 84 per cent of the money comes from federal or state funds, and most of the people receiving it *cannot* work because of age, disabilities, or dependent children.

Other facts about the welfare population in Los Angeles must be emphasized, for they have generally been obscured and distorted, either deliberately or from ignorance. The commonly held notions about hordes of people coming to Los Angeles for the specific purpose of getting on welfare and then remaining on the welfare rolls for the rest of their lives are false. More than half the people who receive Old Age Security have lived in California for twenty-nine years before applying for help; more than half the families receiving Aid to Families with Dependent Children have lived in California for sixteen years before applying for help.

And while the size of the welfare population in Los Angeles may remain constant or increase, its individual components are changing continuously. Even such programs as Old Age Security, Aid to the Blind, and Aid to the Needy Disabled have changing populations as death cuts some off and age brings others to them. In the most controversial and, to the taxpayer, most aggravating program—Aid to Dependent Children—the population is continually shifting. Families grow desperate and go "on the county," leaving when they can, to be replaced perhaps by ones who had been on it previously. On the average, families remain on public assistance for only two years. Thus, the welfare recipients are not a fixed population of the very poor who remain in that condition for the rest of their lives; instead, they are only part of a larger group of people who lead marginal lives, marked by periods of unemployment, underemployment, working at very low-paying jobs, and entering or leaving the welfare system.

So to the millions of poor whites, Negroes, Mexican-Americans, Indians, and Puerto Ricans in the U.S., the welfare system is only one element in the economic structure of their lives, albeit a far more disagreeable and abrasive one than the unemployment insurance office or the badly paying job as a dishwasher in a non-union restaurant. And it is not a lack of motivation that brings most families without fathers or with longtime unemployed ones to the welfare department offices for help: it is a lack of opportunity for the family head to get a job. But while the local authorities who control the program cannot be held responsible for creating an economy with no employment in it for the unskilled, they cannot evade their share of responsibility for *keeping* the unemployed and unskilled in their condition of dependency.

The Los Angeles County Board of Supervisors and their subordinates are not alone in this role, for the board seems to mirror accurately the sentiments of many people in the community. It is with generalized community approval that the welfare administration in Los Angeles forces humiliating, punitive, and tension-creating conditions of life upon the recipients as the price they must pay for receiving a meager amount of financial aid. The recipients, in turn, are forced to lie, to cheat, and to try to circumvent the rules of the administration in order to survive. One recipient writes about the amount of money allowed a family for rent and clothing:

SAFE, HEALTHFUL HOUSING

How can a welfare recipient have safe, healthful housing when the rent allowance is so low that it covers only about one-half of what he is now paying for rent—unless he lives in a housing project, and there, every time he gets an increase in his budget the rent is raised. He can not afford to move to a better residence because then he would use the food allowance—he can't afford the amount of rent he is now paying for the high-rent, run-down house or apartment he's in now, designed for three or four people, which he has to stick three or four children into each bedroom or bed, and if he's lucky, he ends up in the living room—if he is not lucky he sleeps in the bath tub or maybe the family sleeps in shifts . . . How! How can you rent a three or four bedroom house on a NO-bedroom rent allowance—$55 per month (monthly rent allowance for most welfare recipients—some even less). This large amount will get you an unfurnished single on the lower east side— NO CHILDREN— but CATS allowed; because the RATS come pretty BIG and the CATS aren't allergic to RAID and BLACK FLAG used to try to kill off the roaches. How can a sardine-can be safe and healthful????? For a sardine—yes—but he's dead and nothing matters then anyway . . .

MINIMUM CLOTHING FOR HEALTH AND DECENCY

For an example we shall take a six year old school student . . . $6.15 per month is allowed for clothing per child through age six (6) . . . $6.15 per month totals the grand sum of $73.80 per year. With this large amount you are able to purchase for this six year old the following items:

4 pair of shoes—(1 pair every 3 months) at $3.99 pair

($4.15 incl. tax)................................$16.60

Note: $3.99 shoes last three to four weeks, child without shoes seven to eight weeks before it is time to buy a new pair.

10 used dresses or pants at the "Good Will" for about $20.00

5 shirts or blouses at $1.59 each on sale (IRR's)...... 7.95*

48 pairs of socks—4 pair per month if they are

4 for $1.00................................12.00*

1 new—but cheap—coat at $10.00 (everything can't

be used)................................10.00*

1 sweater................................ 5.00*

	71.55
*Sales Tax	2.25
	$73.80

Now let's see just what we have here—4 pairs shoes, 10 used (and I do mean used) dresses or pants—what is so healthy about USED clothing—I bet GOVERNOR BROWN thinks "Good Will" is an attitude and doesn't know it is a welfare recipient clothing store—5 shirts or blouses, 48 pairs of socks— you say why so many socks, well baby with those cheap shoes with those big holes after only a few weeks, the cardboard, book covers and sidewalk wear out the socks (and that weak bleach we use ain't going to get them clean), I coat, the nicest thing on the list, for it covers all those used things underneath, one sweater, it will last if it doesn't get lost—and that is all for that six year old. Oh, you say I forgot underwear? No I didn't, but as some people say, welfare recipients are usually second and third "welfare generations" and "illegitimacy is a way of life" so if this is the case underclothing would only get in the way . . .

Even though most of the money distributed by the county comes from federal and state sources, the welfare department exacts a heavy price for the funds it distributes. It demands, first, that anyone seeking help prove in detail that no other means are available; specifically, the administration of the program is based on the assumption that whatever the people seeking aid say about themselves must be checked, exhaustively. The parallel would be if the Bureau of Internal Revenue were to investigate, exhaustively, every single taxpayer's income tax return rather than make spot checks. The Internal Revenue Service assumes that most taxpayers tell the truth in their declarations of income, even when they ask for tax relief or refunds; the Department of Public Social Service assumes that most of the people asking for relief lie in their declarations of need.

Next, the county assumes that in exchange for the financial help it gives it has the right to determine the essential conditions of life for those who receive any assistance. It determines not only the amount of income for each recipient or family of recipients, it also says how much of that income shall be spent on rent, food, clothing, and furniture. And because of this policy it forces a family of recipients to pay a larger portion of its income in rent to a public housing project than would be paid to the same project for an identical apartment by an identical family with identical income derived from unemployment insurance! Yet the man drawing unemployment insurance who can spend his money as he pleases has not contributed a single penny directly to the fund—unemployment insurance is wholly paid for by the employer. And no one in government told a single person receiving assistance under the GI

Bill how the monthly check was to be spent, although every penny of that money came from the same public funds that supply most of the money administered by the welfare department. In fact, the closest parallel to the way in which the local government operates the welfare department is Mr. Bumble, who beat Oliver Twist when he asked for more porridge. The department beats its recipients, too, and even though the beating is psychological rather than physical, the consequences are just as filled with hate and tension.

The analogy between the welfare department and Mr. Bumble is not so far-fetched, for public assistance programs in America have evolved basically from the English Poor Laws. These laws were fundamentally "paternal, custodial, coercive and punitive," as they are described by Jacobus TenBroek, an outstanding authority on the subject. Poor Laws were based on the assumption that only the indigent poor, those not physically capable of working at some job, were to be helped, for idleness was considered a vice. And the Poor Law tradition, still the basis of all public welfare in America, also assumes that in exchange for assistance given to them the recipients must give up control over their lives and subject themselves to a series of controls and regulations of any work they do, any movement or travel arrangements they make, their living arrangements, family relations, and how they spend the money they receive. Above all, too, the taxpaying public believes that the recipients must somehow demonstrate how "grateful" they are for what they get.

Yet, California's Welfare and Institutions Code asserts: "The purpose of this code is to provide for protection, care and assistance to the people of the State in need thereof, and to promote the welfare and happiness of all the people of the State by providing public assistance to all its needy distressed. It is the legislative intent that assistance shall be administered promptly and humanely, with due regard for the preservation of family life, and without discrimination on account of race, religion or political affiliation; and that assistance shall be so administered as to encourage self-respect, self-reliance, and the desire to be a good citizen, useful to society." The code also indicates that the welfare programs should be administered liberally, but in actual practice the manner in which the programs *are* administered is precisely opposite to the stated legislative intent.

While the federal government, too, advocates progressive and rehabilitative policies, it does not release funds to states without systematic requirements for eligibility that govern each category of assistance. Los Angeles County gives admirable attention to those sections of the federal handbook outlining eligibility requirements, but hardly notices the sections that call for actual services. The multitude of forms produced and insisted on by the federal and local bureaucracies cripples any social worker's efforts to obtain the funds and services for recipients that the law entitles them to.

Theoretically, welfare policies are supposed to help maintain and strengthen the family life of the recipients; in fact, the welfare department weakens family life by, for example, pressuring recipient mothers of youngsters to work, without making adequate provisions for proper child care or providing supplemental allowances for travel or clothing which would make the job more attractive: "Like the social worker might come in and say, 'Get a job,' and maybe I got kids from the ages of two months through twelve years old, and then on the other hand they will say, 'You need to be at home with your children.' So what do you do? Do you get a job or do you stay home with your children? So, okay, they tell me, 'This job is important,' and if I want my aid to continue, I have to go. Okay. But we don't have a day-care center here, so what am I supposed to do if I can't hire me some kind of a decent babysitter?"

Theoretically, every AFDC family is entitled to detailed help from the caseworkers; but because of understaffing and consequently heavy caseloads, the welfare workers rarely have enough time to sit down with the recipients and discuss with them all the advantages and disadvantages of a work situation. Thus, instead of being able to plan for the future, the recipients merely drift from day to day, from welfare check to welfare check.

Theoretically, welfare administrations should encourage recipients and their children to become self-supporting; in fact, the typical welfare bureau robs them of any incentive to do so by deducting, under most conditions, whatever is earned from their meager grants. In Los Angeles, it also permits the public housing authority to increase the monthly rent automatically when additional income is brought into the family: "Every time the Bureau of Public Assistance gives us a raise in our money—a small amount that they do—the housing authorities get it. So we still don't have anything, you know, and it's just like not getting it. Okay. Well, then they tell us we're getting a raise; all right, well, we figure that it can go to our food and so forth, but when we look around and get our rent statement, then they took the little nickel we get."

Recipients are urged to maintain physically decent homes, but the welfare department sometimes attempts to force the recipients to sell items of furniture and use the money to cut down on the grants: "If you come in with a nice record player or a living-room set, you get these things for a good reason—you're showing an interest in your own home. You know a woman can't help that. That's nature you know. But if your worker sees this and comes in, she wonders, 'Where did you get the money?' or 'How could you afford this?' Or if it's nice and so it looks expensive, she says, 'You could sell this and live off of this for certain months, for a certain length of time.' They'll stop your check or cut your check until you sell it. Now not all the caseworkers do it but some of them do it. Another thing about that, too, when I went down to apply for aid, they asked me did I have any kind of insurance policy, any money in the bank, some kind of property. I told them if I had all that I wouldn't be applying for aid, but if I did, in other words, you get explained that if I had any kind of insurance policy, I don't care what amount it was, I would have to sell it. And *live* off that money, *live* off it without any aid from them, *live* off that until it runs out!"

A welfare program should seek to help relieve family tensions, but the Los Angeles welfare department often tries to pressure wives and husbands to remain married even if the marriage is causing great distress in the family: "When the situation is so bad where a husband and wife cannot live together, I don't want a caseworker coming in and telling me, 'Well, try to make it, try this, try that.' When you been trying so many number of years, embarrassing the children and still going through the same thing and everything is getting worse and worse and worse. And especially somebody's going to end up hurt, dead, or in the hospital. If you say two words, he's down your throat; if he says two words, you're down his throat. So there's nothing left in a marriage. You're just there because of the kids, see, and that makes it bad, that makes it awful bad on the kids, because I do have that problem and I do see it right now. If I didn't, I wouldn't even apply for BPA, I would try to make it on the little money he makes right now. But I couldn't. I couldn't because it was affecting my oldest son very badly, he had to have therapy at school. I've been at school a number of times where maybe he have a mental block because he won't learn; it's something in the home. And it's still—even with the little money they're giving me now, it's not helping my problem because that stuff is too late now. When I needed it, they wouldn't give it to me. They wouldn't help me when I needed. But when they did give it to me, it was too late."

Finally, the welfare department and the recipients clash over whether or not sexual relationships outside of marriage should exist; the bureau attempts to force any unrelated man living in a household either to contribute to the family's support or leave, lest the family's grant be terminated: "If you have a boy friend or your ex-husband and they're going to come in, good enough in their hearts to give you enough to get junior a pair of shoes when you can't see getting them until the first or the sixteenth, and they got to go to school, they got to have those shoes or pants or what have you, I feel they need this extra money. And what we do in our private lives is our business. I don't feel that anybody from the Bureau of Public Assistance or anybody else should pry into a woman's private life, because that is private. You know, so I mean why suppress a woman of being able to release things, because they have to be done. Now our social workers, they got husbands, and if they don't have a husband, they got boy friends that they're going to do it, so how are they any better than we are? They're no better than we are; they have to have their release and we have to do the same thing. Unless they want us to just stay women and then go with other women, and then that's no good, then you're jeopardizing the children."

The AFDC program is the most costly *to the county* and the most abrasive to the people of the ghettos. Thus, while nearly $15 million a month is paid out to the aged in cash grants or medical care, only 10 per cent of that amount comes from *county* funds; the remaining 90 per cent is supplied by the state and federal governments. But of the approximately $8 million paid out each month in Aid to Families with Dependent Children funds, more than 21 per cent comes from county sources. It "costs" the irate taxpayers as much to support the 175,679 families (with 218,425 children) dependent on public funds as it does to support more than 100,000 of the aged. And at the same time that society, under pressure from the lobbyists for the aged, has come gradually to accept the notion of its obligations to the aged, it only grudgingly concedes that it must also take care of children who have at least one parent.

This grudging attitude begins to make itself felt the moment help is sought and the citizen becomes a "recipient." Two offices of the welfare department serve most of the city's Negro population, although they are located so inconveniently to the ghetto that it is both difficult and expensive to get to either without a car. Sixty per cent of the caseload of the Southeast I office is in the Watts area, but in the past fifteen years the office has been located in Cudahy, a town six miles and an hour-and-a-half busride away from Watts. (Typically, the policy determining that the county establish the office in Cudahy had no relation to the reality of the recipients' lives; the decision was made on the basis of greatest geographic convenience from the bureau's administrative viewpoint.) It was only after the tragic events of August 1965 that an office was opened in Watts.

At Metro South, the largest office in the department, located at the intersection of Grand Avenue and Adams Boulevard, the people seeking aid walk into a large, cheerless room, give their names at a window, and sit down to await being called over a public-address system. On an average day more than seven hundred people go to the offices to apply for some form of help. A large percentage are women with children, children who become so restless that eventually they leave the protection of their mothers' presence and begin running around the room, kicking at wastepaper baskets, scowling at other kids, fighting with their brothers and sisters, and occasionally breaking out into a wail that brings their mothers to them. There are no nursery facilities in the building where mothers can leave their children while they wait, although ample physical space exists, and there are not even facilities for the mothers to heat up bottles for their small babies. Caseworkers go in and out of the room, separated from the clients by their neat clothes and the papers they always seem to hold. Finally, after a wait of a minimum of an hour and a half to much longer periods of time, the applicant's name is called and he is told to report to Door C.

"I went down there early once so I could get out early," says a woman recipient, "and I sit there and I sit there until about twelve o'clock, and they just hadn't done anything for me—hadn't called my name or nothing—so I went over there and I asked her, 'Well, I mean, I've been here since eight. I mean, do I have to sit there all day waiting for someone to help me?' So the lady told me, she said, 'Well, our workers are so tied up.' And other times I have got up and went to the desk and asked them, you know, could they call me now because my kids are hungry and they're tired and they're restless, and they tell me you have to wait your turn, and I explained to them my appointment—you know when they told me to come in—and they say, 'Well, we tell everybody to come in at that time; you just have to sit here and wait.' And I have had them tell me that and I got so discouraged at times I felt like walking out, forgetting the whole thing, but I need it, you know, so I couldn't walk out. And I have went out to get my kids some milk and so forth, and by the time I got back they had called my name and I was back at the end. That particular day I sat there until five with my kids."

The most fateful decision in the initial interview determines whether or not the applicant is eligible for aid. Residence standards must be met (at least a year in the state), severe financial need must be proved, and it must be demonstrated that: "The employable parent of the child is available for and seeking employment or is receiving training for future employment."

In addition to these qualifications, an AFDC applicant is told that she must also institute legal action against the father of the child or children if he is not contributing to their support. This provision, adopted by the legislature under pressure from the County Supervisors, is difficult for applicants to understand, a traumatic experience, and a bar to getting help for the children.

If the intake worker, often the least experienced employee in the agency, believes the applicant seems eligible for help and is willing to file suit against the absent father, the investigation process is started; if no difficulties arise, there is a reasonable assumption that the applicant may become a recipient within thirty days. But 50 per cent of all the applications are rejected by the intake workers, who are supposed to give an explanation for the refusal. Theoretically, a rejected applicant has the right to appeal the intake worker's decision to the State Department of Social Welfare; in practice, very few such appeals are ever made, partly because of the applicants' uncertainty about their rights and partly because the appeals process always takes a very long time.

No one knows how many eligible people are turned down incorrectly by the county welfare department. "When I got pregnant with my oldest child, his father and myself, we weren't married. We couldn't make it, and anyway it turned out we just split up. And my mother sent me to this home. Then, later, I got married but I had to apply for aid. When I went to apply for aid after I married—now all this time, mind you, I hadn't seen him, I had no kind of way of getting in touch with him, didn't know where he was, didn't even know if he was in the city— when I went to apply for aid, they told me I would have to find him. And I asked, 'Well, how am I going to do that? It's been a long time—five years—what should I do, where should I go to find him?' Well, they couldn't put me on unless I come up with some kind of information, that's what they told me."

Theoretically, too, at the time applicants are turned down, the intake worker is supposed to inform them of other programs for which they may be eligible. But in practice, the inexperienced intake workers may not even know of the existence of other such programs or they simply may not be disposed to inform the applicants about them, especially if the programs for which the applicants seem eligible are supported by county funds.

If the intake interview has established a *prima facie* case of eligibility, the normal next step is a house call made by the intake worker within a few days; but in a dire emergency a cash order may be issued to pay for food, rent, utilities, or medicine. Each district office has its own informal standards for determining under what conditions these emergency orders shall be issued: in some the would-be recipients are required to make two or three visits to the agency office to prove that they have made every effort to exhaust all possible help from relatives and friends. In other, more liberal offices, emergency orders for food and rent may be issued much more quickly. In either case it is assumed that emergencies occur only between Monday and Friday from eight A.M. to five P.M., for the offices are closed evenings and weekends.

The purpose of the house call is to check further into eligibility requirements; it may have to be repeated, too, before all the essential information is collected. Almost all the responsibility for getting the information is placed on the recipient, who may not be able to collect it. When a final determination of eligibility is made and the case approved for help, the intake worker computes the amount of the grant to be made.

The basic computation is a simple mechanical process: the State Department of Social Welfare has set up a county-by-county table of basic minimum needs for every possible combination of family group; it takes into account such items as the cost of food, clothing, personal needs, recreation, household operations, education and incidentals, utilities, transportation, housing, and intermittent needs.

But the state *legislature* sets the maximum allowances for family units, and they do not take into account that the basic cost of living is different in different places. For example, the legislature allows a maximum of $300 to a family of five children living with their mother; in Los Angeles, that is *$52 less than the amount the State Department of Social Welfare says is necessary for a minimum standard of living in the county!* And no way exists to force the county to add the $52 the welfare department says is required.

Such contradictions are found not only between county standards and what the State Department of Social Welfare asserts is needed: even within state government the same disparities exist. Thus, the State Social Welfare Board, whose ostensible function is to advise the governor on how to improve public welfare programs, states flatly that while the typical housing allowance granted recipients is about $46 a month, the typical payment a welfare family must make is about $85 a month. But that $46-a-month figure is one set by the State Department of Social Welfare, the very department over which the board is supposed to exercise some influence.

Obviously, then, the standards set by the state legislature, the State Department of Social Welfare, and the county have little or no relationship to the daily financial realities faced by the recipients. It is true that additional funds may be expended for a one-time outlay, such as the purchase of bedding or the repair of a stove; but even though the family may be getting less than the state maximum, it takes a great deal of justification on the part of the caseworker to get approval for such expenditures. Indeed, it is characteristic of the LA department that a cut in a recipient's grant or a "hold" on the check requires only the routine approval of the caseworker's supervisor and can be done immediately, while a proposed increase for any reason requires the signature of at least the director of the office or the person to whom that authority has been delegated. Increases always take much longer to get approved than decreases.

Once the amount of the grant has been computed, the caseworker informs the recipients and explains the conditions under which it is granted. This marks the official entry of the recipients into a world of dependence in which their lives are controlled and dominated from the outside, in which personal decisions are limited to the most trivial matters and personal choices open on only a narrow set of options, and in which every change in their life conditions must be reported, lest they lose their grant.

And the recipient is told: "You are required to notify us when there is and [*sic*] change in your income, your needs, or financial circumstances. Should you fail to report the facts regarding these matters you might not receive the full amount of aid to which you are entitled. On the other hand if you fail to report promptly you may receive more aid than you are entitled to receive under the law. If you do receive aid to which you are not entitled because you failed to report the facts to us we must demand repayment from you.

"The following statements may help you to understand the kind of facts which you are required to report:

> Notify us if you buy or sell any real property, or if you sell any of your personal property.
>
> Notify us if someone dies and leaves you some money or property, or if you receive money or property from any other source.
>
> Notify us if you begin to receive income from earnings, relatives, social security benefits, rent from any property you may own, or income from any source.
>
> Notify us if you begin to receive free rent in the place you live. Even if you have already notified us that you are receiving income from some source, let us know if that income increases. You should also let us know if that income decreases or if it stops.

"When there is any change in your need, your income or property holdings, notify us immediately by letter, by calling at our office, or by telephone. DO NOT DELAY until someone from our department calls on you. That may be too late."

The consequence of this reporting procedure is that in the course of a typical year approximately five hundred thousand changes in grants are processed, apart from new claims, restorations of old ones, and discontinuances of grants. The administrative cost of increasing or decreasing recipients' grants, often by the most nominal of sums, in response to changes reported by recipients is approximately $5 million. And to record such changes there are literally *thousands* of different forms on the shelves in the stockrooms, forms that must be filled out in the hundreds of different situations involving even the most trivial changes in the life conditions of the recipients.

The concept of local control over assistance programs has been so integral to the American public welfare system that from the start of the New Deal's social welfare legislation even the federally financed programs were given over to the local authorities for administration. The result of this unhappy compromise can be seen now in the Los Angeles welfare department, Superintendent Barr's administrative "monster," in which federal, state, and county funds are all administered by county officials under varying degrees of control by the state and federal authorities. Thus, the county supervisors exercise effective administrative control not only over the General Relief program, which is totally paid for from county funds, but the federal programs—OAS, ADC, Aid to the Blind, Aid to the Disabled—as well, even though they are financed almost completely from state and federal funds.

Since the agency is administered by the county government, the chief administrative officer of the Los Angeles County Board of Supervisors exercises the effective controls over its operations. He "acts as overall manager of County government operations"; sets the budget for agencies like the LA welfare department; fixes the number and salaries of its professional and clerical personnel; and, in general, acts in the name of the County Supervisors in overseeing the day-to-day administration and establishing the day-to-day character of the welfare department. Under the present chief administrative officer, that character is oriented toward "administrative efficiency" and productivity—clerical rather than social work procedures are emphasized.

The Board of Supervisors, the chief administrative officer, and the men who run the welfare department have for years been a dominant force in the County Supervisors Association, an extremely powerful lobbying group. It has always been the voice of county government in the state, pushing as hard as it can against any social welfare legislation that might increase the cost of the programs, supporting the kind of punitive measures against welfare recipients that are exemplified in "midnight raids" on recipients' homes, and generally acting as the voice of those who believe most strongly in the Poor Law view of social welfare.

It is not accidental, either, that most of the top personnel in the welfare department come from the office of the chief administrative officer and lack any training in social work. Their expertise lies in areas of administration, and their philosophy is basically cost-oriented. The necessary qualifications for appointment to the job of director, deputy director, or program supervisor, for example, in a welfare department district office do not include any social work training, despite the fact that these jobs are the most important in setting the tone for the agency's operations. All that is required is graduation from college and three years of experience in: "(1) the supervision of social work, or (2) a staff capacity analyzing and making recommendations for the solution of problems of organization, procedure, program budget or personnel." And until very recently another possible qualification for the delicate work of dealing with thousands of recipients was experience "in the administration of a very large public assistance *clerical* unit" (emphasis added).

Theoretically, all promotions within the Department of Public Social Service are governed by civil service regulations; actually, the system can be and is manipulated so that promotions go to those the top officials want advanced. The qualifications are initially set by the Civil Service Commission in consultation with department officials, thus accounting for the fact that directors, deputy directors, and program supervisors are not required to have social work backgrounds. An important element in determining promotion is the "Appraisal of Promotability," which is made by the applicant's superiors and is given weight of 25 per cent in determining who shall fill a vacancy. So, too, the oral interview in which the potential promotee participates is given enough weight to disqualify anyone the top officials do not want to promote, no matter how high he may score on the written exams.

Those the county administration want promoted may even receive help in getting a high grade on the written examination, for sometimes "acting" promotions to higher posts are made. Since these are *not* governed by the civil service regulations, such promotions can be given to the favored ones so that they are enabled to learn on the job the answers to the questions that may be asked of them weeks or months later on the written examination. Finally, another subtle factor operates to make certain that promotions go to those the hierarchy want promoted: "the word" goes out in the agency about who is scheduled for the promotion, and anyone wishing to get ahead who is not scheduled simply refrains from applying for the job.

The importance attached by the top county officials to the values of businesslike efficiency as compared with social work is made clear to everyone in the department.

One typical brief example of how the administrators' stress on productivity creates a conflict with social welfare practice is in the intake interview for single men who are applying for general relief. In this interview, conducted in one of the department's grimmest offices, the applicant goes through a fairly lengthy questioning by the caseworker, who requests that the applicant sign the application form before he asks the applicant a question that is decisive to whether or not general relief will be given: Is the applicant willing to go to a work camp? In Los Angeles, as in many other cities, any help given to single able-bodied men is conditional upon the applicant's willingness to enter a work camp; if he refuses, no aid is extended. Of course, that question could be asked first, and if answered in the negative, the interview could be terminated immediately, without putting the applicant through the stress and anxiety associated with a long interview which may end with no help being given. But the question isn't asked first because the size of the staff at the office is established by standards of production, by the number of single applicants processed, not by the number of men who come in looking for aid and leave without signing an application.

Procedures like this one, petty as it is, serve to create tension between the administrative staff and those caseworkers concerned with social welfare problems. "Tension does exist between the administrative staff and the caseworkers," states Ernest Koucky, the Director of Districts, to whom all the district directors are responsible. "The caseworkers want to spend their time with their clients and not fill out papers, while the administrators are more interested in setting up orderly procedures for the control of funds."

An "approved caseworker" takes over the case once the budget is set. Theoretically, the recipient should be visited at least once a month and the caseworker is available to the recipient at other times for assistance and information. In practice, the caseload is so high and the amount of paperwork so enormous that very few recipients are seen that often; except in emergencies, the workers may not be able to make a visit more than once every three or four months, with even once every six months not uncommon, despite all the regulations to the contrary.

While the family is receiving a welfare grant, the social worker *is* often the only representative of society, except for the police, with whom they have contact. To the children the caseworker may be the only sign that a larger world does exist outside of the poverty-stricken home in which they live. Unfortunately, the picture of the world that evolves from this relationship is often a very grim one: "I would start with the orientation of the caseworker," says a recipient, "and I always say this and feel this way—a person's eligibility is not determined by a snobbish answer or a look-down-upon attitude or snappin' a person up or makin' him feel inferior in any kind of a way. I think you can determine a person's eligibility with a smile, and it still makes the person feel good inside if you explain to them why they're not eligible instead of doing a lot of things the way they do them and then turn them down and make them feel they— I think a certain amount of the person's dignity is already taken out of them when they come in through the simple fact of having to ask for aid."

The responsibilities of a social worker, according to a state welfare study commission, "require a high level of human understanding, mature judgement, self-control, initiative and originality. Furthermore, a worker is required to maintain a delicate balance between public interests and the rights of the recipients while authorizing the expenditure of public funds which in some instances total more than $300,000 per year per worker."

But, says the commission, "the employment specifications for these positions do not now reflect the seriousness of these responsibilities, and most persons coming to these positions for the first time are unprepared to carry them out effectively . . . A majority of the public assistance workers in California lack the professional education to meet the demands of their assignments."

There are only two absolute requirements to be met by a potential caseworker for LA's welfare department: he *must* have a bachelor's degree from any college in any subject, and of equal importance, he *must* have a driver's license. If he meets these two standards, he fills out a civil service application and is given a written examination immediately. The exam takes about three hours and is then graded by a computer. In most cases, the exam is given and graded and the applicant is interviewed all in the same day. Two interviewers, one from the Civil Service Commission and the other from the welfare department, question the applicant for about twenty minutes in the most general terms.

Very few of the caseworkers have had experience with poverty groups and they may have little or no sympathy for the problems of the recipients. Indeed, like the general population of which they are a cross-section, a large percentage of caseworkers may even resent the recipients, and although the department maintains that it attempts to screen out such workers, it concedes that perhaps 15 per cent are unsympathetic to the clients; estimates by professionals outside the system run to as high as 85 per cent.

One department official, who works in the ghetto area, says: "The majority of social workers in the BPA are *not* professional in terms of their education being in the field of social work. Their educational background is just about every field that you can think of, but when they are interviewed, an effort is made to determine what their feelings are regarding people. Basically, they are going to have to deal with people, not with administrative problems. They are going to have to be working with people in the community with various backgrounds, ethnic backgrounds, educational backgrounds, all types of people. And so an effort is made to try and determine in the oral interviews whether or not they are able to deal with this variety of problems."

Of course, this official understands the limitations of an oral interview conducted by a Civil Service Commission representative and a welfare representative. As she says, everyone comes to the bureau with a lot of preconceived ideas and opinions about ethnic groups, about poverty, about unwed mothers, and about deserting fathers, but "naturally, they're going to say what they feel you want them to say at these interviews."

It is not just the serious shortage of professionally trained social workers that accounts for the tension in welfare departments. The entire welfare system creates the tension. For within the world of social workers, public welfare jobs draw very few trained people because the jobs have very low status, derived from a combination of factors: lower salaries than those paid probation officers, large caseloads, rigid promotion systems, emphasis on efficiency and productivity rather than social work practice, plus the vulnerability of public welfare programs to political manipulation and attack; all of these make such jobs unattractive, and the result is a very high turnover rate.

The turnover rate inside the welfare agency is one of the best illustrations of how the basic cost-oriented view of the county supervisors and administrators results in short-term savings and long-term losses. By June 1965 low salaries, heavy caseloads, and job frustrations had created an annual turnover rate of more than 35 per cent. In 1966 the New York City Department of Welfare, with a similar rate, released a study of turnover. It showed that those with the highest scores on the written examination tended to be the first to resign, while those who almost failed tended to make a career of welfare and, through seniority, rise to authority. Native New Yorkers, also, quit the department much faster than out-of-towners.

In the two offices serving the ghetto the annual turnover rate is nearly 40 per cent in one and close to 44 per cent in the other. The overall quit rate in the first eighteen months of work is estimated at 70 per cent, and the waste of public funds involved in the replacement of these social workers, hard to calculate, is estimated at from $600 to $1500 per worker. But the human consequences of this very high turnover rate can be even more disastrous: a woman recipient had six different workers assigned to her in one year, two of whom she never met or even talked with on the phone!

Heavy caseloads are not only a cause of the high turnover rate but the result of it as well. Theoretically, the BPA assigns no more than sixty cases to any AFDC worker, for if the caseload goes any higher, the county loses a sizable federal subvention based on the sixty-case maximum; if the worker's load goes above the sixty, the subvention is cut proportionally. But because of understaffing it is impossible for the BPA to keep the caseload down to sixty, and it gets around the federal requirement by setting up what case-workers call the "phantom" or "uncovered" files. These files may have in them up to a thousand cases which are assigned a number but no caseworker. Sometimes, too, the cases are put into a "transfer" or "suspense" file, so that they never show up in the total number of cases assigned to the caseworkers.

A recent audit by the federal government of one office in the LA welfare department disclosed that 70 per cent of the services claimed to have been administered by the office had never actually been performed. To the department this kind of manipulated bookkeeping may be just a device to keep the county costs down, but to the recipients who are not receiving the service to which they are entitled, it means that only rarely and perhaps never do they see the caseworker who might help them out of the poverty in which they are caught.

Until recently the newly employed caseworker received practically no training of any kind before beginning his actual work. In some cases as little as one day was allotted to him for reading a manual before being assigned to such sensitive tasks as being an intake worker. In other cases, depending on the character of the district director, training programs may have been held for a week or extended to a few months. Today that has changed somewhat, and a training period of 160 hours plus job orientation is required in order for the county to receive federal funding.

But the real training of the caseworker is done on the job, and therefore varies enormously in character and quality. If the caseworker is assigned to a district office where the district director insists that all regulations be applied strictly, that very careful checks be made into eligibility, and that people aren't to be certified for any help, including even emergency help, unless they meet every requirement, it becomes very difficult for the newly hired caseworker not to adopt this set of attitudes.

Until very recently the director of Metro South, which has such a high proportion of recipients in the ghetto, was a man who describes himself as a "conservative" in his approach to welfare problems. He speaks of the work done by the agency as "our business," which is understandable since he joined the staff after his retirement as business manager of a large dairy. His rise within the department was very rapid; quite clearly, he was the kind of man the administration felt fit their image of a director. The turnover rate for staff in his office was the highest of any district office in the county. He accounts for it by saying, "Nobody wants to work in this area because it's deteriorating. Ninety percent of my clientele are Negro, and that's a big factor in the turnover, too."

Today, that man has been promoted to an even higher post in the agency.

On the other hand, if the worker is assigned to a more "liberal" office, where the orientation is directed toward a more realistic interpretation of requirements and a wider view of social work, those attitudes will tend to prevail among the staff. Unfortunately, no matter how idealistic the new social workers may be about their jobs, the very organization and functioning of the BPA drives them eventually into a state of frustration; no matter how oriented to rehabilitation they and their superiors may be, the amount and character of the paperwork they are required to do does not allow them to work with their clients for the purpose of rehabilitation. And for this situation the county officials, with their clerical and administrative orientation, must bear prime responsibility, because even though the state and federal regulations are also overburdened with paperwork, the forms manual has far more county than state or federal forms combined in it!

"The workers themselves should let the recipients know what they need," says a woman recipient. "They should let them know how much they are allowed for so much, this, that and the other, you know, and then let them know the things they're supposed to have, the things that they are entitled to. Your workers are not going to tell you unless you ask them. I have one situation where a girl that I know, she had applied for a home training course. Well, her worker sent her a check, twenty dollars extra for this course because this is how much they charge. Well, I wanted the same thing because I had wanted to go back to school, too. I called my worker; my worker told me that she had never heard of it, didn't even know nothin' about it, didn't know *nothin'* about it. Then I found out later that they do this."

It's not hard to understand why the worker "didn't know nothin' about it": the handbook for just the AFDC program has nearly eight hundred pages! One result of this fantastic number of complicated regulations is a total lack of communication between the department and the recipients. Imagine, for example, the reaction of the recipient who received the following letter from the LA welfare department concerning her AFDC grant:

A breakdown of your allowance is as follows: according to our cost schedule, the total monetary needs of a family of your size and age group (this does not include Mr. X) is $337.00 per month. This figure is arrived at as follows:

Individual Allowance/Mo.	Age Group	No. of Members	Total
$25.25	1-6 yrs	3	$75.75
$35.30	7-12 yrs	2	$70.60
$48.00	Boy 12-17 yrs	1	$48.00
$41.60	Adult Female	1	$41.60
		7 members	$235.95

Total, plus a monthly allowance for utilities,
rent, household operation for your family of   91.35

TOTAL $327.30

Effective January 1st, this agency recognized a
cost of living increase of $10.00 per family
bringing the monthly needs to   10.00

$337.00

Rounding this off the agency recognizes your need, if your [sic] were not going to school, to be $337.00

However, since Mr. X is working we deduct part of his income from your total needs.

Even though Mr. X has a gross monthly income of $412.00 we recognize only $219.89 of it as applicable toward meeting your needs.

Therefore our basic monthly allowance is

$337.00
— 219.89
$117.11
or
($117.00)*

If you did not have special needs such as school, etc., this $117.00 would be your monthly grant. However, we recognize the following school expenses in your case—per month—

Tuition	$90.00
Child Care	54.12
Transportation	6.49
Standard Allowance	25.00
Total School needs	$175.61

Therefore your total needs are recognized as being

$117.00
+ 175.61
$292.61

However, the maximum that the state will pay to a family with three *eligible* children, regardless of need is $221.00

Since we wish to allow you the money for school in some way, the difference of $71.61

$292.61
221.00
$ 71.61

must come from some other source than state funds. In your case it comes from Federal EOA Funds. (There was a prior error in computing the budget of $1.00) so you are now receiving EOA Funds of $ 72.61 and therefore you will continue to receive this amount.

The reason for the increase in EOA funds from $54.61 to

---

* This figure is as of Jan. 1, 1966.

$71.61 is *mainly* due to a *decrease* in the amount of Mr. X's earnings that were deducted from your needs. Since the amount that Mr. X earned, which could be deducted from your family's needs decreased, the amount of our basic allowance to you had to be increased to $117.00 from $92.00. However your total needs remained the same. Therefore the money which is the difference betwen your basic grant and the state maximum had to be decreased because:

Basic Grant + Special Needs = State Maximum

If you increase the grant the special needs money must be decreased. The state maximum remains fixed. However your total allowance still remains at

because of your school expense and since

Basic Grant+Special Needs+EOA Funds=Total Allowance

and

Special Needs+EOA Funds=Total School Expense

If the special needs allowance decreases because of the increase in the basic grant, and the limit imposed by the state maximum, the rest of your *total school expense* must be made up of *increased* EOA funds.

Presently you are getting   Basic Allowance $117.00

+ School Needs   175.61

TOTAL allowance $292.61

However only $221.00 of this figure can be made up of state funds. The rest must be taken care of by EOA funds.

Therefore you can see that the closer your basic allowance comes to $221.00, then the more EOA funds must be increased. If your monthly basic allowance were $221.00, all of your school expenses, ($175.61) would have to come from EOA Funds.

I hope this information will be of help to you.

Very truly yours,

————, District Director

By————, Social Worker

File Number ————

Not even the most skillful and professionally trained caseworker could explain the contents of that letter to a recipient in any way that might fit into a pattern of rehabilitation, the supposed purpose of the welfare program. And the district director who signed the letter, or at least whose signature appeared on it, has the reputation of being one of the "better" directors in the entire agency!

Another example of how clerical orientation cuts down on the amount of time the caseworkers might be able to spend working toward rehabilitating their clients developed when the federal food stamp program was started. The welfare department insisted that the social workers fill out forms that were not required by the federal government. At a meeting with the Board of Supervisors to protest the amount of paperwork involved in bringing clients into the program, the president of the Social Workers Union told the Supervisors:

"I am referring to locally designated form, PA Form No. 1810, which is titled 'Application for Food Stamps.' And I am referring to the form titled 'Food Stamp Program Work Sheet and Certification,' PA No. 1811, which has as a part of its preparation four parts divided into various sections, running alphabetically all the way from A to Z twice.

"These forms, gentlemen, are to be prepared every time there is a budget change in the budget needs of the family, every time there is a change in rent, every time there is a change in a child being eliminated or a child being added. If they are a working family, every time there is a change in their income, their net income; every time that there is a change in the amount of utilities; every time that there are medical expenses; every time there may be some catastrophe within the home; any time that the working family decides to subscribe to a health or welfare plan; any other unforeseeable change in the budget requires a new set of forms; whether it is once a month or it is once a day, these forms are required—and this is absolutely ridiculous."

He was right: it *is* absolutely ridiculous for caseworkers to spend their time filling out these forms. But it is characteristic of the welfare administrators to have set up such requirements, for behind them are the assumptions of the County Supervisors and most of the public about the welfare program; assumptions that still rest, in the twentieth century, upon the punitive bases of the Elizabethan Poor Laws. (Characteristically, all over the country, welfare administrators are more likely to resist those proposals by welfare workers' unions dealing with methods and procedures than demands for wage increases. Attempts by the welfare workers' unions to modernize or eliminate welfare procedures are usually met with the reply that such matters are solely the prerogative of management.)

Another reason for the high turnover rate of caseworkers in public welfare is that the field is so infused with the contemptuous spirit of the Poor Laws that caseworkers genuinely concerned with their clients' welfare inevitably become so frustrated they leave for other jobs: "I find that I am first, a county investigator; second, a budget and filing clerk and last, a social worker," wrote a caseworker who left public welfare work in disgust. The letter of resignation continued: "If there is any time left after investigating for evidence of fraud, filing and doing budgets, I am allowed to do some 'social work' provided it is not of too great a benefit to the client. So much time is spent searching for fraud that little time is spent actually helping the recipients . . . It would be naive to assume that fraud does not exist but the relationship between the actual cases of fraud and the number of recipients is almost negligible . . . the vast amount of time spent on investigation could be put to better use in helping the client become a responsible and self-supporting citizen through the encouragement of retraining and education."

In fact, the "welfare fraud" turns out to be another popular myth with grave consequences, for it reinforces the widespread public contempt toward the poor. The investigation of alleged welfare fraud cases is done both by the county welfare department, which has its own agents, and by the District Attorney's office, which has a Welfare Frauds Squad. Cases of supposed fraud are reported to the department by caseworkers or perhaps a neighbor of the recipient, often someone with a grudge against the client.

According to the District Attorney of Los Angeles County, welfare fraud investigations are undertaken against those recipients who, it is charged, "fail to report income from employment, social security, unemployment insurance or support payment from the natural fathers. It is also fraudulent, of course, for the recipient to report children who are not living in the home or to fail to report the presence of a man in the house. The most frequent violations occur when a man is in the house and whether his income is not reported or he has no income at all and is living off public funds being paid the mother for the support of children." (In 1964 the State Attorney General's office ruled that if a man living with an AFDC family had no regular income, it was *prima facie* evidence that welfare funds were being illegally spent.)

Once a charge of alleged welfare fraud has been made, continues the District Attorney, an investigation begins that includes "such techniques as checking social security, motor vehicle and unemployment records as well as interviewing friends, relatives and neighbors and conducting all night stake-outs—not to be confused with night raids, which we never employ."

The recipients' description of "stake-outs" are somewhat more vivid than those given by the District Attorney. One woman described, bitterly and resentfully, her experience: "They came out early one morning, about six. I hadn't even gotten out of bed. They knocked on my door. I got up. I went to the door. The man just pushed me, the officer just pushed me and came right into my home.

"So he comes in and he—I had two doors, one was here and one was here—so he comes in and looks around a while. I guess he figured somebody was going to run out the other door or something, you know. Then he looked around under the beds, in the closets, in the bathroom and everything to see if my husband had been in the home, to look for a razor or a hairbrush, and I'm still half asleep. So then, you know, he tells me, 'Well, we have to make this investigation,' and I'm still half asleep. By the time I wake up, the man is gone."

The county's Welfare Fraud Squad consists of "nine expert investigators" and a supervisor "who is himself a veteran of twenty-one years as a fraud investigator." The squad arrests approximately 220 persons annually, and if all of them are convicted, says the District Attorney, "we will have saved the taxpayers $396,-000." But he did not comment on how many of the 220 arrests made in a year do result in convictions.

In fact, according to the State Department of Social Welfare, less than 10 per cent of all the "suspected fraud" cases reported end in convictions. The total of all the alleged cases of fraud reported represents only one half of one per cent of the total number of AFDC families in the state, and the total of the "established fraud cases, resulting in convictions by the District Attorney actually amount to a fraction of one thirtieth of one per cent of the total Aid to Families with Dependent Children caseload."

But statistics like these and the hostility generated by these investigations, 90 per cent of them dismissed for some reason, seem to be of no significance to either the general public or the District Attorney's office. The county's expenditure in salaries and expenses for the BPA investigators and the Welfare Fraud Squad may equal or even go beyond the $396,000 that might be saved if all the arrests resulted in convictions, but the public morality, as the county officials interpret it, would be preserved. The money that might be saved the county is not really the important issue to the administrators; rather, an ideological principle is involved.

It is ideology that creates the context in which the homes of AFDC mothers are entered in search of a man. At present there is no provision in law to prohibit payments to the 2 per cent of AFDC families in which the the adults living together are unmarried, although at least one member of the Board of Supervisors believes such laws should be passed. But in 1963 the state legislature rewrote the laws to require that a man not married to the woman with whom he was living be required wherever possible to help support the woman's children from a previous relationship. In addition, the senate made it a crime for a mother to use any welfare funds for the expenses of the man living with her.

In passing this legislation, the senate ignored the fact that the AFDC program is designed to help the *children,* and that when a check is held up or canceled because the mother has a man living with her, it is the children who are being severely penalized. And it is the ghetto children who are most penalized, for not only have they been born with the wrong color skin, not only do they not have a family life which includes the presence of a father, but the welfare law discourages a common-law relationship, which might bring a masculine influence into the home.

Tragically, too, this kind of Poor Law ideology, as expressed in the AFDC program in California, places a heavier financial burden on the family in which the unemployed father is at home than on the one from which he is gone; although the monthly grant is increased when the father is present, the amount of the increase is as low as $16 and no higher than $19, hardly enough to meet the expense of an additional adult in the house. Thus, the AFDC program *contributes* to the broken family situation which it is designed to alleviate.

The same kind of ideological principle was invoked in some states when persons over sixty-five who applied for Old Age Security were refused help unless their relatives contributed to their support. The amount contributed by the relatives was very small—only about 3.4 per cent of the total OAS outlay—and the expense of investigating the relatives' financial resources was very large. But the amount of money it cost to administer the "relatives' responsibility law" was of less consequence to the administrators than was their commitment to the belief that the aged in our society ought to be taken care of by their relatives, as a sacred obligation, rather than by society.

That belief, which is also part of the tradition of Elizabethan Poor Laws, was shared neither by the aged themselves nor by a large group of social workers, but it took a determined campaign on the part of the pensioners' lobbyists to erase the relatives' responsibility law from the California statutes.

The grim picture of how the AFDC program is administered in a typical county is duplicated in all the other important programs as well. Caseloads in the Aid to the Disabled Program, for example, go as high as 275 to 300 per caseworker, which means that it is impossible to carry on any rehabilitative work. In fact, only the blind receive any semblance of proper social work services, and only because they have created a vociferous and effective lobby to speak on their behalf. But the vast majority of people in the welfare system have had no voice in determining the conditions of their lives.

It is hardly surprising, then, that 34 per cent of all the juveniles arrested in the August 1965 events came from families whose major source of income was the welfare department; that an additional 5 per cent were from families to which the department was making some contribution; and that another 2 per cent were graduates of welfare.

The top department officials are correct when they admit that their agency has been one of the two major sources of tension in the cities. And it will continue to be a source of such tension until the whole investigation system is abolished and replaced with a simple declaration; until the recipients are given specific services they need, such as day-care centers and proper job training; until eligibility is no longer the unilateral prerogative of intake workers; until welfare recipients are given some voice in determining the conditions of their lives; and until the general public realizes that the social welfare program need not be the kind of abrasive institution it unfortunately still is.

```
IIII
≡ IIII
─────────
IIII IIII  IIII≡
IIII
```

Employment

The tall young Negro was very well dressed. He was wearing a white shirt, regimental tie, three-button suit, and polished shoes. He spoke in an educated voice to the Negro woman interviewer at the state employment office. He seemed an ideal type for some professional or semi-professional job except for one thing—he had the damnedest "Afro" haircut I'd ever seen: his hair grew out high and straight from his head in all directions.

Yet to me he looked both natural and of a piece—the haircut suited him admirably—but not to the interviewer, for I heard her tell him he should cut his hair if he wanted to get a good job. He refused and the next day, when he was back again to talk to the personnel officer of a large utility company, his hair was still "Afro" style. He didn't get the job, of course.

I took him outside the office and we sat in my car, talking about what had happened.

"What do you people want from me?" he asked bitterly. "You tell me I should be proud of my descent, so I let my hair grow instead of getting it processed. I spend a lot of money on this haircut. It costs me six dollars to get it fixed like this, and I have to put hair spray on it every day to keep it neat. I try to keep neat

*and clean. This morning I took a shower, used a deodorant, put on
a clean white shirt, had my mother press my pants, and came
down to look for a job. But all they want me to do is cut my hair.
Mister, I'm the only one in my whole family who graduated from
high school. I even have a year of junior college. But I'm not going
to cut my hair. I'm going to wear it 'Afro' even if I don't get a
job."*

"What will you do?"

*"Hustle. I'll get a couple of girls working for me and a few other
hustles going. I'll make out. Screw the job if I can't look the way I
want."*

*When I talked with the employment service interviewer about
why she hadn't argued with the personnel man when he said he
wouldn't hire the kid because of his haircut, she got angry. "He
should cut his hair. He should look like everybody else, like the
employer wants him to look. It's not my job to argue with employers."*

*A week later I sat with a group of young Mexican-American
kids in another office of the employment service. To them I was
just another "Anglo" looking for a job, and so they talked among
themselves, indifferent to my presence in their midst. I found it
hard to follow their rapid Spanish, filled with Mexican slang words
and "chicano" references, but still I heard and understood enough
to follow their general thoughts about the jobs. Evidently, none of
them expected to get any decent jobs.*

*Their English is poor and heavily accented. Their mechanical
skills are minimal, and that is the primary criterion for employment. Their education is limited, and that is another sizable handicap.*

*As I talked with unemployed, underemployed, and low-paid
workers all over America, I began to see how wrong it is to let
the fixed categories of "skilled," "semi-skilled," and "unskilled"
worker become the determinant of how people shall live. Does the
label "skilled" tell what sort of husband, father, citizen, and human
being a man is? Does "unskilled"? If some unskilled man is a good
father, husband, citizen, and human being, should he and his*

family be condemned to a miserable life because he can't handle a welding torch or operate a computer?

The more I asked that question, the madder I grew with how the kid with the "Afro" haircut had been treated. Maybe by this time he's become a successful hustler, but he got a bad deal from the employment service and the employer.

"Whenever I'd see some Negro walk in with a 'do-rag' on his head, I used to give the girl at the desk a signal to keep him away from me," admits the well-dressed Negro official, high in the California State Employment Service. "I knew I couldn't do anything for him and I knew that if I told him to get rid of his 'process,' he'd probably have told me to go to hell. I guess maybe I was ashamed of him too."

("Processed" hair flares up in front, in a tuft, often dyed.)

"I shouldn't have been ashamed, either, because I was born here, right inside the ghetto. I grew up in the ghetto, went to school in it, and didn't leave until I was an adult and married. I left at twenty-two and after being gone for five or six years I discovered that I'd lost my feeling for it. Maybe it gave me an advantage that I left and could come back and realize what I'd gotten out of, but still I left it, and even though I work there now I don't ever want to live in it. So you can imagine how difficult it must be for someone who's never had to live off Central Avenue to know what the problems are."

But even if all the officials and staff of the employment service were to know "what the problems are," they would still be unable to solve them within the framework of the agency as it operates today. As it is, federal and state intervention into employment relationships in the United States has been of such a minor character and so dependent upon the market system that little or nothing has been accomplished to help those who most need help. Getting those Americans working who are not now employed demands far more from the employment service than it is capable of doing, for solving the problems of unemployment requires, among other things, that a whole value system, hitherto considered a fundamental part of American life, be junked as useless. This is true because apart from the continuous financial distress which is a consequence of continuous unemployment, another problem associated with it has now assumed disaster proportions.

"The first time in my life I felt like a man was when I was burning down that store," said one of the Negroes arrested during the August 1965 upheaval. And he had never felt like a man before because chronic unemployment denies access to one of the single most important routes to manhood in America.

To become an adult in America means to have graduated from high school and gone on to college, or to have left school, perhaps before graduation, to take a job or learn a trade. To be an adult in America means to have work, to hold down a job, to have an occupation, to be a professional, or to be married to a man who fits into one of those categories. Work, a job, an occupation, a profession, are central to American conceptions of masculinity; it is as true for the whites in America as it is for Negroes and other minorities.

But in the case of the Negroes, and to a lesser extent the other minorities, the cities are now truly paying for the sins of the fathers. Since racism kept non-whites from decent jobs or the prospects of decent jobs for hundreds of years, the nearly permanent absence of employment has created an increasingly large pool of men and women unable to meet the standards of adulthood because they do not have the basic requirement of adulthood—a job.

The young men and women, searching for some other identity to substitute for their lack of occupation, turn to devices which make it even more difficult for them to get jobs. The young Negro's "do-rag," which makes the employment service official turn away from him in disgust, is there to protect his "process," the hair style he has adopted to give him some sense of individuality. Since the young Negro has no identity derived from work, he uses another means of establishing his identity, a means which in turn keeps

him from getting a job and so further deepens his sense of bitterness toward society. And all of this is happening at a time when
society's technological advances make scarcer and scarcer any
kind of unskilled or semi-skilled job at which the young man might
begin a life of working.

This is the dilemma confronting the Employment Service official; its dimensions are enormous and frightening. Every few years
another generation is produced of young men and women who
literally cannot speak or write English, though they may even
have graduated from high school. Their perception of the world
is so limited that events outside the narrow confines of their
own lives have little or no significance for them. To get up in
the morning, get dressed, go to work, come home, work in the
garden, visit friends, earn enough money to buy a house in the
Valley, spend a weekend at Lake Arrowhead, have babies who
grow up to become teen-agers attending the senior prom, visit
Hawaii for a twenty-fifth wedding anniversary, and never get arrested, never go to jail, hear about venereal diseases but never
know anybody who gets them, have credit cards and play bridge,
shop downtown before going to the PTA fashion show, learn to ski
at Sun Valley, take scuba-diving lessons at Hermosa Beach, and on
and on and on—these, the life patterns of middle-class Los Angeles, and comparable patterns in other cities, are unknown to
these generations of unemployed, underemployed, and low-paid
workers.

One link between them and the world outside is the TV. The
TV is on all the time, its sounds a continuous undertone to the life
of the house. While they are very young the TV is a combination
pacifier and babysitter; as they get a little older it becomes a device
for inducing euphoria, and so the kids watch the cartoons for
hours. Everything they see reinforces that hatred of themselves for
being born black which was once so widespread but which is now
being replaced by hate of Whitey: they are exhorted to buy a
certain detergent and "Think White! Go White! Stay White!" or to
buy "flesh-colored" Band-Aids like the one being put on a little
white boy's scratched white arm by his blond, beautiful, white
mother.

The TV teases them, too, with its visions of what they as adults should have—the new cars, watches, dresses, electric shavers, ✓ sewing machines, radios, freezers, and all the other goods that pour out of the American cornucopia—but since they are without jobs, none of what they see on the white American TV is available to them. The only way they can get the newest-model anything is to steal it; and in their truncated society there is no strong moral sanction against theft, only the fear of getting caught.

So in place of any other occupation, some learn about crime. As kids they start by stealing from the dime store or supermarket. Then they serve an apprenticeship in purse-snatching. After that, perhaps, they try muggings and stickups, attempting to "score" at a gas station or liquor store out of their own neighborhood. Or perhaps they opt for the career line of the hustler, beginning with selling marijuana to their schoolmates. From that they can graduate to pushing narcotics or handling stolen goods, specializing in the accessories stripped from cars in the housing project parking lots, and possibly developing this business so well that after a time they can take advance orders for specific accessories and make delivery within forty-eight hours. They can also expand into other areas of hustling, like buying cheap merchandise from jobbers in downtown Los Angeles and selling it in the ghettos as guaranteed stolen goods. (After the events of August 1965 the Los Angeles ghettos were flooded with allegedly looted merchandise; but much of the "loot goods" had actually been bought in order to cash in on the high demand for loot goods.)

The unskilled young men who do not become criminals take the menial jobs, which is all they can do, but reluctantly, for they know they will be sneered at by their peers. They know, too, that they will not keep the jobs, for they never had or have lost long ago the discipline of a daily routine. Perhaps they will pick up a smattering of some trade, but more often their hands and minds will be completely untrained in the skills needed in the cities today. The white newspapers' fat want ads sections, imploring aircraft engineers to come to Douglas Aircraft, electronic engineers to look at Litton Industries' pension plan, and chemical engineers to report tomorrow to Shell Oil mean absolutely nothing to them. After all, eight of the ten jobs most short of workers in the cities require either college graduation, some kind of special license, or more training than is obtained in four years of high school.

Many of the unskilled become parents very young, but the young men, unable to cope with their wives and families in a state of permanent joblessness, will drift off into some other section of the country, to repeat the same set of actions again and again. The mothers of their children know from their own childhood how to "get on the county," and soon the welfare department pattern becomes the life history of another generation.

The streets of the minority ghettos are filling up with these men and women, caught in a trap from which there is no escape.

Computers can predict, within fractions of a second, the time at which two space ships will rendezvous, but no one knows the exact number of totally unemployed men and women who live in America. No one knows how many men, women, and teen-age Americans work only part of the time, or how many are working at jobs that pay them so little that even when they put in forty hours or more, they still don't earn enough to bring them up to the basic poverty minimums set by the government. And no one knows how many Americans do get jobs but seem incapable of keeping them for more than a few days. All that is known about the number of unemployed, underemployed, low-paid Negroes, Puerto Ricans, and Mexican-Americans is that it runs into the many thousands. Estimates of the Negro unemployment rate range from a minimum of two and a half times to six times that of the whites; for Mexican-Americans the range is somewhat narrower but still very high.

A great many people know how widespread unemployment is among the minority groups and even understand something of its awful consequences. What is not understood is how ineffective such institutions of government as the state employment services have been in changing the situation, and why they have been so ineffective.

The failure of the California State Department of Employment to deal with this problem has been massive. The least disturbing analysis of this agency, federally-financed and state-operated, must acknowledge that its operations have been unimportant to the ghetto dwellers and thus irrelevant to their lives; the most disturbing must make clear how the agency has helped to perpetuate the very conditions of unemployment it was designed to overcome. As a result the number of unemployed, underemployed, low-paid, and anti-job Negroes in Los Angeles has increased while their chances of finding and keeping work have diminished.

"A fundamental need of humankind is economic security," states a handsomely illustrated brochure designed to recruit staff for the Bureau of Employment Security, the U.S. Department of Labor agency that supervises the state employment service operations. "Employment security gives men and women the confidence to plan ahead, to prepare for the future with some reasonable assurance that they will not be taken by surprise by what the future will bring.

"Thus, Employment Security is the program that relates the basic need for economic security to the world of work—jobs, careers, employment."

But to the many thousands of men, women, and children for whom economic security is non-existent, the Bureau of Employment Security has been one of the last places to go to find "jobs, careers, employment." Less than 6 per cent of the *employed* people in the Los Angeles ghettos got their jobs through the State Employment Service. To those without work for long periods of time, the agency is even less meaningful as a source of job referrals.

"Sheet, man, that unemployment ain't worth shit. If you want to find you a job, you don't go to the unemployment. There ain't nothin' there for you. If I ever wants to find me a job, I'm goin' someplace else."

The trouble is, there isn't "someplace else" where that eighteen-year-old Negro can look for a job and find it. If he ever wants work, he must go to someone, not someplace else: he is most likely to find work by hearing about it from a friend—someone he knows who knows someone else who heard that maybe they need someone down at the carwash on LaBrea Avenue. Maybe. And so maybe the eighteen-year-old borrows carfare from his older brother, puts on his tight pants, pointed boots, yellow shiny shirt, covers the stocking "do-rag" protecting his "process" with his "stingy" hat, the hat with a brim so tiny it hardly exists, and struts his way to the bus stop, carrying the cheap transistor radio that helps keep intact the fantasy world in which he lives. Perhaps he will get the job, for at the wages offered the carwash operators cannot afford to be very choosy about whom they hire. And none of the car owners pay any attention to the young kid in his hip-length boots and raincoat sloshing their cars and then perfunctorily scrubbing the hubcaps with a brush as the cars are pulled through the mechanized washing process.

But even in a city as car-oriented as Los Angeles only a limited number of carwash jobs are open and only a limited number of Negroes want them. So the unemployment rate among Negro teen-agers continues to climb, just as the unemployment rate among Negro adults continues to be at least twice that of the white; Mexican-American teen-agers and adults also have a much higher proportion of unemployment.

Although nothing is more important in America than a job, the market system and free enterprise no longer are able to offer work opportunities to the unemployed ghetto dwellers. And the unemployed have no status in modern society because a man's "skill" is taken to be the test of his basic worth, as if a human being could be regarded as a machine whose value could be determined by its capacity to perform its mechanical function. It matters not, in the American city of today, whether the unemployed are decent human beings, conscious of their obligations to other human beings; if they are unemployed, they are seen as surrounded by an aura of unworthiness, and they begin to accept it as being true. In this kind of atmosphere it is inevitable that the government institutions charged with the specific responsibilities of helping people find employment will fail to help those most in need of it.

.   .   .

The basic assumption on which the employment service functions—that it is part of a "nationwide network of public employment offices that find jobs for people and people for jobs,"—is useless to the task of solving the unemployment problem of the "unskilled," especially the minority "unskilled." In fact, it does *not* find jobs for people or people for jobs if these people are the unemployed who have never worked. Indeed, as it has been operating, the service *cannot* perform that function. Instead, it has been helping those people find work who least need help and who might have found jobs without any assistance.

The failure of the California State Employment Service is not due to lack of good will either at the top levels in the federal government, which supplies the funds and the over-all direction, or at the high state levels, which direct the administration of the program. Many of the program's top administrators know that the way in which the organization has operated is wrong; many know that their institution has not been responding to the new demands upon it, especially at the lower administrative levels, and some of them even know what ought to be done. But even if they know, they cannot do what needs doing, for what needs doing lies outside the area of possibilities for the employment service as it is today. Whatever merits it once had as a social tool, it is no longer a useful instrument, because today's unemployment problem has dimensions and qualities that did not exist when the service was created.

The employment service, naturally enough, originally reflected in its internal organization and psychology the dominant views of a laissez-faire America about jobs and unemployment: a willing man could find a job, and unemployment was a sign of laziness or vice. The first public employment offices in the United States were municipal ones set up during nineteenth-century recessions; by the early part of the twentieth century the federal government had entered the field through the Immigration Service, which tried to spread immigrant workers all over the country. In World War I the federal operations were expanded, only to die out after the war, when it was again assumed that anybody who wanted work could find it without assistance. It was not until the Depression that Congress passed the Wagner-Peyser Act (1933) establishing the

United States Employment Service. In 1935 the Social Security Act, which financed the unemployment insurance program on a federal-state basis, was tied into employment service operations; and in 1936 the state employment services were established, to work cooperatively with the United States Employment Service but with local control as a basic concept.

Over the years, in and out of the agency, its primary function—employment placement—became subordinated to its providing of unemployment insurance, especially during recessions, when it had to compete with private agencies for the few available jobs. And so the operation became known as the "unemployment" rather than the employment office, a name it still has to most of the unemployed today.

And since unemployment insurance, which is paid for by a payroll tax on the employer, is given only to those people actively seeking work, the "unemployment" became an often formidable barrier, which had to be got around in order to receive the benefits. First, the applicants for unemployment insurance benefits had to prove that they were unemployed through no fault of their own. Then they had to prove that they were continuing to seek work in order to continue receiving their weekly checks. Since the two functions of job placement and unemployment insurance were carried out until 1960 in the same physical location, it was easy for the unemployment insurance personnel to learn from their colleagues in placement whether or not the applicant was actively seeking work and therefore entitled to receive the benefits.

"The unemployment insurance system was always based too much on a worker's ability to get a job from the employment service," says one official of the agency. "A man would come in and the placement people would talk to him about taking a job. Then the unemployment insurance personnel would know about it and would disqualify the man if he didn't take the job. If he went out and applied for the job but didn't get it, there was always some question about whether he really tried for it. The heavy concentration of the offices was always on trying to get the man off unemployment insurance by getting him any kind of a job, instead of trying to help him get the best kind of job."

The federal government's method of financing the employment services long ago became another handicap to their being of use to the unemployed, unskilled worker. Basically, financing is determined by the *number* of placements. If fewer placements are made by an office, its staff is cut, and so the managers inevitably tend toward making fast and easy placements. And since placements in short-term jobs can be made more quickly than permanent placements, which require more interviewing and counseling time, the long-term jobs get neglected.

The unskilled workers' attempts to find jobs through the state employment services are also hindered because the size of the grants made by the federal government to the state offices is based on the unit-time system, a method of judging productivity borrowed from industry. Fixed amounts of time are established as the norms for the employment service personnel to carry out various assignments. Thus, in 1959 and 1960, 162.9 minutes were allowed for making a professional or clerical placement, while only 52.7 minutes were allocated for getting an unskilled worker a job, and a mere 22.8 minutes for making a placement in day or casual work. Forty-five minutes were allowed for each counseling interview.

This system of administrative piecework obviously went against the interests of the unskilled and minority workers. Helping such workers to get jobs which might raise their skill levels obviously demands a great deal more counseling and interviewing time than does helping a worker with readily salable skills and appearance. But because the federal policy emphasized making skilled, professional, and clerical placements by allowing them more time per placement, the people seeking work in those categories were favored over all the others.

In addition, the norms became maximums; the staff learned how to beat the system, as workers always learn how to get around piecework standards; the operations became routinized, and the need for filing daily reports on the filling of the unit-time quotas also helped to sacrifice the minority workers' interests to the piecework quotas. The forty-five minutes allocated for counseling is an apt illustration of how useless such a system is if the norms are actually used: the California State Employment Service discovered that proper counseling of a single unemployed teen-ager took at least fifty-eight hours!

Naturally enough, too, the prejudice patterns of American life existed within the service, and so for many years discrimination against members of minority groups was widely practiced. "Everybody in Los Angeles had heard or everybody assumed that there was a certain amount of prejudice with the employers and that the state was no exception," states a Negro official of the department in describing his experiences when he entered the employment service in the 1950s. "And frankly, when I took the written exam, I passed it and I honestly believed that I would be flunked on the oral. And I was. It was given by an all-white panel. Now maybe the reason I flunked was because I believed I was going to when I went into the orals, and so I failed. But anyway I appealed, and when I took it again, I passed it.

"One thing I noticed right away was that in the office where I worked the few Negroes who were there had been on the job for five or ten years. They were very quiet and some of them told me that I was on trial, that I shouldn't talk up, that I was marked because I had appealed from being turned down for the job."

Over a period of years the discriminatory practices of American business and unions were not only accepted within the state services but were translated into discriminatory placements. And even though some of the personnel may have doubted the correctness of these policies, they believed they had to accept discriminatory job orders in order to compete with the private agencies, which could more easily serve prejudiced employers even though they might be prohibited legally from doing so.

"Let's face it," states the manager of an employment service office. "In the past, employment service was completely employer-oriented. An employer would call me up and tell me that he wanted someone and that he would pay him a dollar an hour. I didn't question this. If he said he didn't want any Negroes, I wouldn't argue with him. I just assumed that if we wanted that employer's business, we had to do business his way."

During the late 1950s the employment service began to change its policies at the top federal and state levels, but it encountered internal resistance from many of its older staff. The personnel were primarily lower-middle-class white people attracted by the stability of civil service. Like most members of civil service bureaucracies, they learned quickly that the road to advancement was to take one step at a time and above all not to rock the boat. This group had been joined by a considerable number of ex-military personnel who brought with them organizational concepts learned in a completely hierarchical system. Together they represented a considerable barrier to internal change, a great lump of inertia, resisting any movement in a new direction.

The department's old recruitment policies also made it almost certain that it would not attract the kind of idealistic people who might go, for example, into social work organizations. To qualify for the department, an applicant must have graduated from college within the past five years or be a high school graduate with 'appropriate business experience in employment interviewing, personnel administration or labor relations . . . at a level of responsibility indicating ability to perform the duties of an employment interviewer."

Applicants who pass the written exam and oral interview start their work as Employment Service Trainees. A year later, after completing their classroom training and working at various jobs in the offices, they become Employment Security Officers. From then on they move up in grade from ESO I to ESO VI by taking exams. Some people entered the department by working three years as an Employment and Claims Assistant, which is a temporary status established to allow offices to hire high school graduates part-time to help out in rush periods. As the skills of this group increased, they learned the office routines and how to use the manuals, the Bibles for everyone in the department.

The consequences of the department's past recruitment policies are still visible in almost all of the offices. The staff is primarily middle-class, conventional in appearance and behavior. They have none of the physical or social qualities associated with civil rights militants or VISTA volunteers, and in the past the department seemed pleased that this was so. From its early viewpoint the ideal employees for carrying out its functions as a labor exchange and unemployment insurance office are people who have been out of college for five years and are ready to settle down at a job whose career line is certain if somewhat slow.

Ideally, from a bureaucratic viewpoint, these people should follow orders well, not care that their work is often boring, get along with fellow employees, not promote wild or radical notions, be interested in getting periodic raises through taking periodic exams that raise their professional status, and not become objects of either public or legislative attention that might raise doubts about the agency's sobriety.

Characteristically, too, the professional organization of Employment Security Officers in the state refused continually to take positions on any "controversial" questions, especially those involving discrimination or prejudice; and during the fifties, when the department's top staff attempted to break with the concept of accepting discriminatory job orders, they met resistance from some senior staff people. "We were told by our staff," states a top official, "that if we denied an employer service because he gave us a job listing that was discriminatory and we hadn't been able to persuade him to change it, we'd lose half our placements. Well, we did it anyway and didn't lose enough placements to put in a thimble. Now we don't worry about it any more.

"But unfortunately, some people on our placement desks, maybe one of our employees, likes to make placements and he has a good rapport and working relationship with an employer, and when he sends an employer an individual who has an arrest record or something else or the wrong color skin and the employer says, 'Well, hell, you know I did have that old thing but I've decided now I don't need to hire anybody for it,' well, then, our employee is human and our employee worries about not making that placement. But officially, we don't worry about it; I couldn't care less if placements drop from half a million to two hundred thousand a year because of this reason."

Officially, the top personnel may not worry about losing placements, but some people in the lower echelons still do, especially since many people on the staff share the employers' prejudices. Even though since 1958, more and more training has been given to the staff, both newcomers to the service and the older personnel, the problems of staff prejudice still exist, to the detriment of the minority unskilled. "I'd be less than candid," says one of the high officials, "if I said one or two or three cycles of the sensitivity training we're giving are going to orient every member of the staff in the right direction. We're trying but we haven't got it licked."

And although the unit-time system has not been used by the state officially for about four years in the placement services, old habits die hard and the service continues to be handicapped by its past practices. "I still get reports," states a senior official, "that some of the counseling people say, 'I'm sorry but I couldn't do that because I can only spend an hour on this case.' This attitude is a carryover from the past, from the time when we did have a work-load unit-time problem. And the office managers are still very cost-conscious because their resources are still leaner than the total job for the community really requires.

"Another problem is that if we go to the counselors and say, 'We've looked at your schedule and you've got seven appointments today; now, these people are coming in and we want you to serve them,' the counselors will think, 'What are they trying to get over to me? See, if I divide that seven into the time I've got, I can only spend so much time per person.' And so they say, 'Well, this is the old unit-time deal back again.' But I think gradually our people are learning that we really mean it when we say we aren't judging our offices on the basis of how many placements they make or how many counseling interviews they do in one day."

Unfortunately, though, no matter what the top officials say, the inadequate size of the employment service staff means that every manager must be conscious of how the workload is distributed.

"It depends on the manager of the office to determine how much time he's willing to put into a certain category," points out a manager. "So, whereas I might put a person on a desk and say, 'take as much time as you need to handle the job,' then I might have to cut down on counseling time or cut down on the special program the welfare department is running. I know we're not supposed to be going on unit-time any more—this is always being told to me by the administration all the way up to the top—but nobody has come up with a budgeting system where we can actually tell what we're doing in terms of production other than this unit-time. So, in reality, while maybe we're not being budgeted on unit-time, when it comes down to the interviewer on the desk, he knows he's on a time basis."

But in the past five years, there has been a gradual change taking place in the employment service, beginning at the federal level and seeping down into the state agency. With the rise in minority unemployment and the growing gap between white and minority workers came the realization that the service could not perform much of a role for the minority workers if it continued to be only a labor exchange, a place to bring together employers looking for workers and workers looking for employers. The change sometimes served to work against the best interests of the unskilled minority worker even though the intent was just the opposite. Thus, for example, the "heartland" concept, developed to help the minority workers get employment, actually hindered their efforts.

Prior to the development of the "heartland" notion, the employment service had at least a few offices on the periphery of the minority communities where unemployed workers went to make unemployment-benefit claims and to find jobs. But in 1960 the placement services in the neighborhoods were discontinued, although the local offices remained open for the unemployment insurance benefits, and the job placement functions were centralized in a downtown office on the theory that applicants would then have available in one place all the job possibilities in the area. But the unemployed couldn't afford to look for work at the office in downtown Los Angeles since they either had to travel by bus, which was costly, or if they drove, had to pay for an expensive parking lot.

And, too, the concept that workers must prove that they are not responsible for their unemployment has remained an integral part of the service's operations. In Los Angeles until very recently, for example, a man could be refused benefits if he had been arrested and subsequently fired because while in jail he had not been allowed to inform his employer he would not show up for work that day; the fact that the arrest may have been improper and the charges against him dropped made no difference. It is true that when an applicant for benefits is turned down, either because the employer says he quit rather than was fired or because the interviewer decides the applicant is not eligible, that decision can be appealed. But the appeal process is so long and difficult that only a tiny percentage of the refused applicants avail themselves of it.

When the "heartland" policy was initially proposed, the state office opposed it. "We pointed out to the Feds," says a high official, "that from the job-seeker's viewpoint there are certain ethnic boundaries that don't get crossed. Then we told them there are some very tough questions of how much transportation a job applicant can afford to look for work, to go from here to there. From the employers' standpoint, we pointed out that certain employers want to hire people as much as they can within the general area in which their plants are located because of the transportation problem.

"But we had to compromise. Instead of closing all the offices, we closed just some of them. But unfortunately, one office we did close was the one in the area near where the Negroes live."

Then the job placement and unemployment benefit functions were physically separated in order to change the image of the service from that of the "unemployment" office. This physical separation of the facilities was part of the realization at the federal level that special efforts would have to be made in order to reach minority workers and assist them in getting jobs. The "heartland" concept gave way to the "outreach" office, which would reach out to the minority workers by serving them in their own areas.

At the state level it had also become apparent that the older ways of doing business were useless. A Negro official explains how he changed his view of what was required of the service: "I went to set up an employment service in a primarily Negro community. This was to be the first one in the state that was in a neighborhood community to serve a particular population. First, I had the idea that it should work like a youth employment service office, where you find after-school or Saturday jobs and concentrate on getting the kids for them. I thought it meant getting jobs like washing windows or cleaning up a store on Saturdays or moving laundry, all just for a little pocket change.

"But when I began sending kids from this Negro neighborhood out on this type of job, I began to get calls from irate parents saying 'What do you mean sending my kids on a job like this?' And I would explain that it was just a temporary job, just to make pocket change, and their retort would be that 'My uncle or my brother or my husband started at that kind of a job thirty years ago and he's still on it and I'm not sending my kids to school to be a janitor.' I couldn't understand this attitude at first, and not being able to understand it bothered me. So I started to find out why this attitude prevailed in the community. I went to all kinds of community meetings and I asked all kinds of questions, and that's how I became aware of what was going on inside the ghetto."

At about the same time as these shifts in focus were taking place the concept of manpower training began to evolve at the federal level, culminating in 1962 in the passage of the Manpower and Development Training Act. But despite its desirable objectives— teaching the unskilled and upgrading the semi-skilled—the program initially gave the least opportunity to those who needed it most and the most to those who needed it least.

Politically, the sponsors of the program believed it was essential to build up a good record for the program so that Congress might approve additional funds for it; thus there was a tendency to screen from the program those people who seemed to have the least chance of either finishing training or of getting jobs if they did complete it. In addition, the program had a built-in limitation—the Act required as a condition of admission to the program a "reasonable expectation of employment." But in most cities it was very difficult to demonstrate such a "reasonable expectation" for any jobs other than those which had traditionally been filled by Negroes, especially since the skilled trades were normally closed to new admissions of Negroes.

Still another built-in limitation prevented minority groups from entering into the program: initially admission was restricted to those who could read and write. Training funds could not be used to teach literacy either, and so once again those on the bottom of the heap were shoved still further down into it.

The results of the Manpower and Development Training Act policy were clear in Los Angeles in August 1965: in that tragic month the only on-the-job training program operating in the south and southeast ghettos was a program to train janitors! Four MDTA training classes in institutions in the ghettos were running at the same time: in them 176 people, mostly women, were learning clerk-typist work, and 31 men were being taught to be service station attendants. But at the same time 173 MDTA classes were being operated *outside* the minority areas, training thousands of men and women in nursing, electronics, stenography, office work, sales, lens grinding, stationary engineering, welding, machine operating, animal keeping, coin-machine servicing, and automobile detailing.

The small number of classes being taught inside the ghettos is the result of more than just the prejudices of some people allocating the training funds. Low attendance from ghetto areas in adult vocational schools has always been characteristic of the cities, partly because the tuition fees and costs of materials keep the low-income working groups from trying to upgrade their skills. The holding of classes late at night in locations distant from people's homes is another handicap to attendance, for many of the women do not want to travel alone at night or depend on the inadequate public transportation system.

The poor participation of the minority groups also reflects the fact that most unemployed minority people, unconvinced that they will find employment even after they take training, aren't strongly motivated to attend. In addition, the physical and psychological atmosphere of the classes acts to hold back attendance as well as encourage absence and tardiness in those who do come. Almost always the classes are given in the very schoolroom location and milieu the students associate with their past failures. Here they are, back again, so to speak, in the same kind of place which had failed to meet their needs once before. But now it is worse, for while in their own minds they are adults, they are treated as children. The classes are conducted in the traditional classrooms; there are homework assignments, and the teachers seem to have little or no understanding of what is required for proper vocational education.

One area in which the lack of understanding is especially serious is attendance and tardiness. Because the schools persist in treating the students as if they were children whose only problem in getting to school on time was having their lunchboxes ready when they go out the door, the teachers complain bitterly when their adult students are late or absent. But very rarely does the school make any attempt to discover the reasons for the lateness or absence, to find out whether they were related to a lack of interest, problems at home, or the feeling that the school isn't meeting the students' needs.

Perhaps, too, the students are "insubordinate" or steal materials. Then they get dropped from the class while the school administrators bitterly complain that "what we get here is the bottom of the barrel and that's why they behave the way they do." But evidently it has not yet occurred to the vocational schools, especially the commercial ones, that their job is to relate, somehow, to the people at the "bottom of the barrel" and that to do this requires not routine administration but social inventiveness.

In 1965 the Department of Labor began to train its own staff and recruit new staff for "youth opportunity centers" to function on an "outreach" basis. At these centers, which were to operate primarily for the benefit of minority youth, trained counselors were to advise the jobless teen-agers of training opportunities under the Manpower and Development Training Act and of such anti-poverty projects as the Job Corps for which they might be eligible.

But in order to function effectively the employment service staff has to learn to deal differently with the minority unemployment crisis; it must operate inside a rigid organizational structure imposed upon it by federal regulations and state civil service requirements. When the University of California at Berkeley was asked to conduct a special training program for counselors in youth opportunity centers to be operated in the ghettos, the university staff did not succeed in persuading the officials that people with arrest records ought not be barred from participating in the program.

Indeed, one trainee, highly qualified by her educational background for such work, was even rejected by the federal officials because she was a spastic, and regulations prohibited hiring people with such a "handicap." No attempt was made to ascertain how she might function in the new situation. And the University of Southern California, which in July 1965 was conducting a training program for employment service personnel assigned to work in the ghettos, encountered opposition *within the service* to holding sessions in the Watts area. A few of the key administrators involved in setting up the training program resisted having sessions in a community center in Watts, and only the determined push of the university personnel kept the sessions in that area.

Characteristically, too, many of the state personnel attending the discussions obviously were so uncomfortable in the Negro section that they came to the area only reluctantly in the morning, went outside it for their lunches, and left as soon as the sessions were over. The discussions revealed, too, that many staff members, including those from the minority groups, had very strong feelings of antagonism toward those unemployed who do not fit the standard American notion of how a worker should look and behave and are unwilling to emulate the pattern.

In staffing "outreach" offices, the state service was and is prevented by its own civil service regulations from hiring the natural leaders of the community, who may lack formal education or have arrest records, to work in any but the lowest jobs. They can be hired as "community workers," but they cannot be promoted for the same reasons or because they lack the work history that would qualify them for the better jobs. And so these people, who play an important role in persuading the minority communities that it is possible for one of "theirs" to work for government, are doomed to remain at the lower-paid jobs, no matter how competent they turn out to be.

Even if it had been more successful than it was in breaking through its internal structure into a more flexible kind of operation, the employment service would still have had to face the political consequences of taking other affirmative actions to bring the unskilled unemployed into the world of work. The unions in California, for example, are a powerful political force controlling the state apprenticeship program. And the record of this program reflects precisely the same kind of past failures that are found in the other government agencies: in December 1964 only 3.8 per cent of all the apprentices in Los Angeles County were Negroes, although Negroes represent more than 8 per cent of the population. And in thirteen of the twenty-nine trades in which the programs were being conducted less than 2 per cent of the apprentices were Negroes. Indeed, in four of the occupations—boilermakers and blacksmiths, ironworkers, asbestos workers, and telephone installation workers—there were no Negro apprentices.

Another illustration of government agencies' cooperation with a union to perpetuate discriminatory anti-Negro policies was the $1 million training program of the International Union of Operating Engineers, financed in 1964 and 1965 by the Federal Manpower and Training Act. The union was given the grant to upgrade its members' skills, using other members as instructors at $5.23 per hour pay. Since less than 1 per cent of the apprentices in the union were Negroes and the union has only a tiny percentage of Negro members, there were only a few Negroes among the more than a thousand union members who went through the program. Despite this visible fact, however, the inspection reports of two Department of Labor officials stated "Ethnic Composition Good."

Incredibly enough, too, given the great stress placed by the Department of Labor on the need for upgrading skills, other government agencies are still trying to discourage those in minority groups from learning the modern techniques of an industrial society. "I wanted to get into the IBM field," says a woman receiving aid from the welfare department, "because I want to get off the county. I have to raise my children by myself, and the county doesn't give me enough to send my children to school, feed them, dress them properly, and have them go out decently. So I told my worker, 'I want to get off the county, I want to get me a job that is well worth getting me off the county. So I want you to send me to school.'

"So they told me, 'What you're going to have to do is go down to the employment office, make an appointment to get an aptitude test.' Well, okay, I had to spend fifteen cents going, fifteen cents coming back to make an appointment. Okay, I got down there and I made the appointment. I come back home. That's half a day making an appointment. Well, then they gave me a date making an appointment. I got down there and then they had to write up my papers. There's another fifteen cents going and another fifteen cents coming back. I still hadn't taken my test. So, then I had to go back down there for the third time to take my test. Okay, they said that they would call or let me know when to come back, and so they gave me a date. I went back there, I didn't find out nothing. They didn't give me the results of my test, I had to go back again. So all in all I went five times before I found out. Then I found out that I didn't qualify to go to school for IBM.

"They told me that I had an excellent vocabulary and that I have a lot of speed in my hands, and what they told me is that I should be a clerk-typist or a nurse's aide. But I don't want that kind of a job. That's not going to be much more than what the aid is giving me anyway. Then they told me that I could do assembly work. Well, all right, but this is not what I want. Why should I take a job that I'm not going to be satisfied with? I'm not going to do my best anyway.

"So then after all of this, I still didn't get nowhere, you know, get what I wanted. So then my worker sent me a letter, they told me that in order to continue getting my aid for me to be down there to talk to some lady down there at the employment office where they wanted to talk to me. Well, all right, when the time came, I had forgot about it, I didn't think about it until a couple of days later, so then I talked to my worker about it. They were supposed to give me another appointment for another test, but they haven't yet."

In recent years the character of the aptitude tests given by government agencies and private employers has been coming under more and more serious questioning. As a general rule much larger percentages of people from minority groups than from the white community fail these tests. And even though the people giving the tests to applicants for training or employment insist that they do not discriminate consciously against the minorities, the tests themselves are discriminatory: members of minority groups are less prepared than whites to deal with the questions, which are drawn from the experience of the white people who prepare them.

Take the Wonderlic Test, for example, a standard "personnel test" used by many large employers in America even for jobs at the common labor level, on the theory that the companies always want to hire "potential vice-presidents." The Negroes taking the test are asked to place answers to fifty questions (which they don't understand, in any case) inside parentheses, when they may not even know what parentheses are.

A bitter commentary on the Wonderlic Test circulates inside the ghetto in the form of another test prepared by an official of the state employment service. Its counterpart for the question on the Wonderlic Test which asks: "Silver is more costly than iron because it is (?)— 1, heavier, 2, scarcer, 3, whiter, 4, harder," is: " 'H' is more costly than 'Pot' because it is (?)— 1, Whiter, 2, Prettier, 3, Scarcer, 4, Gooder, 5, Cleaner."

The Wonderlic Test says: "A man who is averse to change and progress is said to be (?)— 1, democratic, 2, radical, 3, conservative, 4, anarchistic, 5, liberal"; the other puts the question as: "A man who is against progress is said to be (?)— 1, Conservative, 2, Radical, 3, Fool, 4, Tom." Where the corporation asks the Negroes: "Darkness is to sunlight as (?) is to sound— 1, noise, 2, brightness, 3, air, 4, echo, 5, quiet," the satirical test poses the query, "Bull is to Connor as Chief is to (?)— 1, Indian, 2, Cow, 3, Calf, 4, Tribe, 5, Parker." The personnel test queries: "A hotel serves a mixture of 2 parts cream and 3 parts milk. How many pints of cream will it take to make 15 pints of the mixture?" and, bitterly, the Negro-devised questionnaire asks: "The new Jewish clothing store (Men's) announced a policy of 'easy credit,' which turned out to be a rate of 68.5 per cent plus carrying charges. How long will he remain in business?—1, He'll retire, 2, ten years, 3, Forever, 4, Next riot."

But even those welfare mothers who do know how to take "aptitude" tests must first overcome other restrictions placed on them by the government before they're permitted to start job training. "I talked to my worker about studying clerk-typist," says another mother, "because I thought, once you get into the clerk-typist field, then you can always work yourself up to where you want to be. So anyway, he told me that what they would have me to do; they would have me working in one of the schools, doing clerk-typist-filing and all of this. Then he said, but the thing of it is, they're not going to pay me to work. They're just going to give me the money that they give to me, that the county sends me; this will be my pay.

"Well, all right, this is what I'll do if this is what they want me to do, because I want to get the experience where I can get off the county, where I can get me a good job where it's worth it for me to get off. But they haven't called me and told me nothing, and it's been over a month ago since I called and asked for an appointment. They haven't called or nothing."

Even if "they" do call, even if the mother does get an appointment and passes the aptitude test and begins her on-the-job training, her troubles aren't over. In order to get to school she needs extra funds for transportation and for babysitters, funds not easy to get from the county. If the request for the extra allowance is approved, she must then find some way to take care of her children while she's at work.

"If somebody called me up tomorrow," points out another in just that situation, "and said, 'Well, we have a job for you,' and if it's what I want, then quite naturally I'm going to take it. But what am I going to do with the kids? If you have anyone you know you can trust to do it, you have to wait on a waiting list to get them. I'd like to get my kids into a nursery school but there isn't one anywhere near where I live in the city. There isn't even a day-care center, and if there was one for working mothers, I wouldn't be able to afford it. I know one lady, they charged her nineteen dollars a week to take care of her child. She had to stop working because she couldn't afford to pay the nineteen dollars a week."

Paradoxically, too, considering all the emphasis placed by the employment service and employers on the need for job applicants to look as if they were already in the middle class, no provisions are made in the welfare allowances for helping them acquire such an appearance. As a result, says one woman, "half of the women don't even try for work because they don't have the money to dress or keep their hair up to get the kind of jobs they want to take."

A man with a family who becomes unemployed and seeks training for new skills must hack his way through the same kind of administrative jungle to get into a training program. There is a training program in Los Angeles, for example, to upgrade the skills of long-term unemployed fathers whose families are dependent upon public assistance funds. Ostensibly, this federally sponsored program is designed to bring the unemployed father back into the labor market by having him work on projects where he will be trained for useful skills. In practice, many of the men are used by the county as replacements on low-paid menial jobs where they receive little or no training. The county saves money twice by its subversion of this program because it does not have to hire people for the menial jobs, as it might otherwise have to do, and because the father never actually receives any pay for his work—the amount he earns is merely deducted from the family's grant.

Five supposed work-training projects were being carried on in Los Angeles in the summer of 1965: the hospitals, parks, clerical projects, the road department, and the toy-loan project. Of the six hundred fathers assigned to work projects, only eleven were receiving any on-the-job training. The largest number of men in the program were assigned to the hospitals to carry out such menial tasks as washing walls, making beds, laundry work, kitchen work, groundkeeping, morgue work, etc. In the parks the men were doing only clean-up work or sitting on benches. In the clerical project many did no more than filing or loading. Only the toy loan required the use of any skills or offered any on-the-job training and even here very few of the men were trained enough on the job to get other jobs outside the welfare system.

In addition, the amount of time a man is required to spend on these menial projects handicaps his search for any other employment. The father of a family with two children receiving $185 a month in aid must work on these projects 18.5 days per month; if the family is larger, as most are, and the grant is larger too, the father must work 19.5 days. Even a 31-day month will have only 20 to 22 working days; the result is that the father will never be able to seek any other job.

This subversion of the program's stated purpose is recognized by some of the caseworkers and project foremen who do allow the men time off to look for other jobs. But sometimes, even though the man is told by his caseworker to seek another job, he is canceled from the program for his absence. And then he must seek to get back the help for his family which was conditional on his continuing to work on the project. The effect of this program, financed by the federal government as a "training" device, is to provide the county government, through its welfare department, with a continually filled pool of perpetually unskilled slave labor.

The problem of unemployment in the ghettos will remain unsolved, a festering sore that will continually erupt, unless a totally new approach is taken to deal with it. If the unemployed men and women are to work, they will have to unlearn the habits begun when as little kids they stayed away from school because the classes didn't meet their needs or were too difficult for them. They will need to be given special, preferential treatment until they are able to compete on a somewhat more equal basis. They will have to be held by the hand on the jobs they get while their families' hands are held, too. The "normal" patterns of education will need to be discarded, and new techniques devised to meet their special problems. They must learn what will be useful for at least a few years rather than develop a skill which has become obsolete by the time they have finished training.

A change in the viewpoint of employers and unions must be combined with a totally new, individualized approach to the problems of unemployment. If this is not done, then America can resign itself to more and more upheavals in which young men with "do-rags" will again try to assert their masculinity by burning down a store.

Housing

I don't know how many Mexican and Negro homes I visited in Los Angeles, but it was a sizable number. And once inside the houses and apartments, I got the full impact of the tragic physical separation between the whites and non-whites. Indeed, before the visits I sensed the separation in the hesitancy of the responses when I would ask for a chance to talk with people in their own homes rather than in places like the waiting room at the welfare office, the interviewing desk at the employment service, or the corner restaurant.

The hesitancy had its origins, I discovered, in the fact that in most cases I was the first white person who had ever come to the homes of these poor Mexican-Americans and Negroes on a non-official basis. All had been the objects of visits, of course, from welfare officials, police officers, parole agents, or bill collectors, but very, very few of them had ever participated in an exchange of social visits with whites. So they would sit uncomfortably at first but gradually growing less and less self-conscious at my presence.

The homes varied widely in style, furniture decoration, and cleanliness. In some of them the children stared at me openly and with hostility; in others they peeked at me shyly from behind the door of the bedroom from which they wouldn't venture. Some of the houses were so filthy I could hardly bear to sit on the sofa, while others were so neat I was hesitant about smoking a cigar, lest I drop ashes even in the ashtray. There were two items almost every house had in common—a television set and a telephone. In even the poorest and dirtiest homes there was always a TV set and it was always playing, with a group of kids clustered together on a dirty, uncovered mattress, their eyes glued to the presentation of a world about which they knew nothing.

The housing projects were the places I liked least because a feeling of tenseness hangs over them, a feeling that someday soon the buildings will burst apart, spilling their human contents into the streets in a boiling, screaming mass. When the next outburst comes, it may start in a housing project, perhaps with a fight between two tenants which the police will try to break up.

Yet not once did I encounter any overt hostility in the projects— on the contrary, I was always received politely, offered cookies and soft drinks in the Negro homes, tacos and frijoles in the Mexican ones. But I always came to the projects under special circumstances, with someone who knew the people and could act as my sponsor until I got to know them better. I don't know how I would have been received if I had simply gone into the projects as a stranger and knocked on doors.

Yes, I do know. I would have been turned away—because in Los Angeles, like everywhere else in America, we are strangers in each others' houses.

"Do only colored people ride on buses?" a small boy asks his mother as they sit in their car at a bus stop waiting for her maid to arrive. "No," she answers, "it just looks that way. The colored ladies all live away from here and if they haven't got a car, the only way they can get to work is on the bus. I'll take you for a ride to Los Angeles and you'll see lots of white people on the bus, too. Oh, there's Zelia now, getting off the bus. Now, you don't say anything to her about what you asked me."

"I shop downtown," says the Negro woman who lives in a very neat house with a beautifully kept lawn on 99th Street in Watts. "I do all my shopping downtown, even for groceries. We're lucky we can do it instead of having to buy from the bad stores down here. I have my own car and my husband has his that he uses to go to work. He's a guard at North American and he's worked there ever since he's retired from the Navy. We bought this house while he was in the Navy. I'd like to shop out in Beverly Hills, but I won't. I tried it once. A friend of mine and I drove out there, all dressed up. We wanted to go to Magnin's but while we were on Wilshire Boulevard, out in Beverly Hills, we got stopped by a couple of policemen. They wouldn't believe us when we told them we were going shopping. They kept asking us why we'd come so far from Watts, where we lived, just to shop at Magnin's. They acted as if we were prostitutes."

.   .   .

"Living in the projects, it's suicide, it affects you mentally," states a tenant in one of the all-Negro public housing projects in the city, "and when one has a mental problem, you can have it so long before it will hurt your body and become a physical illness, you know. So this is where it is in the projects—it keeps you nervous, shaky, you know, this kind of thing. They got a lot of rules and regulations that need tearing down. They need to do it like they did Tobacco Road, take a train and dynamite, you know, and blow it up and do it different. That's what it needs. You got so much to cope with when you live here in the project. Like I said, it's suicide."

The university professor was in his office when the phone rang. The department secretary told him the police wanted to talk to him. When he answered the phone, a police sergeant said that three teen-age Negro boys had been picked up, just outside the university grounds, driving a very old car and claiming to be on their way to the university for an appointment with the professor. "The officer who spotted the kids thought there was something suspicious about them, so he stopped them. When they ran a make on them, they found out that one of the three had a record. But they say they were coming out to see you. Is that right?"

"Yes," answered the professor wearily. "They're helping me with a project and usually I meet them not far from where they live. They're all right."

"Well, I'm sorry if we've caused any trouble," apologized the officer. "It's just that those kids were in the wrong part of town, and so naturally our men are suspicious."

The "right" part of town for Negroes in Los Angeles, in which it isn't considered "naturally" suspicious for them to be, is the area lying in the southern and southeastern parts of the city. The outside borders of that area are expanding continuously, spreading out like an inkblot, growing larger and larger each year, frightening more and more whites into hasty flight to the suburbs. But despite the outward expansion of the quarter, more and more Negroes are

living inside it, making the area into a potentially explosive magazine of frustration, bitterness, and anger.

Segregated living is central to the existence of Negroes in all
America, whether they are very poor or upper-middle-class; no
matter how far away they work—as a drugstore clerk in the central part of the city, as a porter at the county general hospital in the northeast section, a welder at the automobile plant in
the southeast, an assembler at the new toy factory in the southwest area, or as a maid in the rich section directly west, where
a curious little boy waits with his mother at a bus stop—they live
together. Whether or not they want to, the overwhelming majority
of Negroes in the cities live within the confines of the Negro
ghetto. They shop in the ghetto and their children go to schools
there. Only the very rich, those who can afford $65,000 houses,
can escape the ghetto.

The poorest Negroes in Los Angeles live in public housing projects in the Central, Watts, and Avalon districts, all in the east and
southeast; the richest live in private homes in Baldwin Hills, up in
the hills at the western boundary of the areas. There, every
Christmas, the middle- and upper-class residents decorate the ex-
teriors of their homes, keeping up the tradition begun years ago by
middle-class whites. The brilliant beads of lights outlining the
houses can be seen from all over Los Angeles, and people come
from miles away to drive slowly through the curved and hilly
streets, oh-ing and ah-ing at the expensive ways in which the
houses have been converted into Christmas decorations. But the
people who live there know the neighborhood is slowly becoming
all-Negro.

The lives of the Negroes in the big houses up in the hills have
very little in common with the lives of those jammed together in
the flatlands. Over on Central Avenue the markets sell chitterlings,
chicken necks, and grits, and the teen-age boys sit for hours in the
"process" shop, getting their hair processed; in the Baldwin Hills
district the shopping centers are hardly distinguishable from those
in the San Fernando Valley, where hundreds of thousands of white
middle-class people live. The recreation and social life of the poor

Negroes who live in Watts and Avalon center around the store-front church, the drive-in or hamburger joint, and the pool hall, while up in the hills the richer Negro girls and their boy friends in three-button suits drive off to tea dances in the old mansions on Adams Boulevard, now converted into Negro versions of white country clubs.

Yet suddenly in August 1965 all the Negroes in Los Angeles, the few rich, the larger middle and working classes, and the very many poor, everybody who lived in the ghetto, were linked to-gether: the police and the National Guard drew up boundaries for them, describing what was inside the lines as the "curfew area." For five days it mattered very little whether a man who lived inside that curfew area was the owner of a store or its unemployed looter, whether a woman was a social worker or a social welfare recipient, whether a high school kid was an honor student or a dropout—all were Negroes, and color was the single test of what they could do and where they could go. And the same thing has happened after upheavals in Newark, Detroit, and other cities.

The "right" parts of town for most of the Mexican-Americans in Los Angeles are the sections east and northeast of downtown. They are not as large as the Negro city, since it's somewhat easier for a Mexican-American to live outside the "barrios," as the Spanish-speaking residents call the three sections in which they live. The larger barrios were once the sections where the working-class Jews of Los Angeles lived, and there are still signs of the earlier inhabitants to be found. But the kosher symbols on the butcher store windows have grown fainter and fainter, covered over by the sign advertising *menudo,* the non-kosher tripe soup that is a staple of the Mexican-American diet; the synagogues, once crowded with the Orthodox Jews laying their *tefillim* every morning, are deserted, and the *iglesias,* where the black-shawled women come to cross themselves before Our Lady of Guadalupe, have become the focal point for the religious life in the area.

What the church is to their elders, the taco joints and drive-ins may be to the younger Mexican-Americans. Generally bilingual from birth, often with Spanish as the primary language in the family, the kids begin to grow up in a white "Anglo" city, which rejects them and their use of Spanish despite all the rhetorical flourishes made toward California's Mexican and Spanish traditions. And the tensions between the Mexican-American barrios, the Negro ghettos, and the white communities of Los Angeles grow worse each year.

Overcrowding and ghettoization are on the increase in Los Angeles. In 1960 only 70 per cent of the people in the south and southeast areas of the ghetto were Negroes; by 1965 it was 81 per cent, and in the Avalon section, with its nearly forty-four thousand population, 96 per cent. Ninety out of every hundred in Watts are colored, as were seventy-six out of every hundred in the Central section.

So, too, today, in the three Mexican-American barrios, an average of seventy-six out of every hundred people have Spanish surnames; in the East Los Angeles barrio more than 81 per cent of the seventy thousand people are Mexican-American: one elementary school in Boyle Heights, the largest of the three barrios, has more children from Spanish-speaking homes than any elementary school in Mexico or South America! Yet five years before, only 66 per cent of the people who lived in the barrios were Mexican-Americans.

Thus, even though the *total* population of these minority areas has diminished slightly in the past five years as the whites have left, the proportions of Negroes and Mexicans living in them increased every year.

The racial and ethnic housing segregation of Los Angeles is probably no worse, however, than that of most other large cities: in 1960 Dr. Karl Tauber's "Segregation Index" gave Los Angeles a segregation index of 81.8 per cent, New York, 79.3 per cent, Chicago, 83 per cent, and Detroit, 84.5 per cent.

By now it is clear that in Los Angeles, as in other cities, there has been no voluntary breakdown in the patterns of segregation in housing. If anything, housing segregation has grown worse, especially for the poor. The separation of the impoverished minority groups from the white world has become almost total. And this dividing process, exacerbating to everybody, destructive of all possibilities of decent relationships developing among the groups, goes on without any or at best only a feeble, half-hearted attempt made by government to change its direction and so stop the destruction of the cities' internal life.

It has been characteristic of America that among some minorities even those who can afford better housing must still live either with the poor of their group or at best in a better ghetto. In Los Angeles, as in most American cities, the poor and lower-middle-class Negroes live next door to each other, while the middle- and upper-middle-class Negroes live in other sections of the city, but still directly contiguous to the poor areas. There is no way out of the ghetto for Negroes unless they are very wealthy; the only possibility for escape is to move to the edge of the ghetto and wait there until the poor Negroes catch up. This is the pattern set by private enterprise in housing, a pattern in which government has helped private enterprise in barring the exit doors.

The personal consequences of the government's support for the restrictive practices of private housing were described recently by a tall, well-dressed Negro presiding at a discussion meeting held by a small civil rights group in a high school. He listened politely as the white representative of a local bank ended his speech about the opportunities open to all Americans: "In our country any American who gets an education and works hard can go as high as he pleases and live where he pleases. That's what makes America great."

When the bank official had finished and sat down to a slight murmur of applause, a woman panel member arose to take the microphone. But before she had a chance to start, the chairman interrupted her: "I'm not supposed to do this," he said softly, "since I'm the chairman, but I think I must tell you a story before we go on to the next speaker. It's a true story. When I was in high school here in Los Angeles, I believed what the gentleman from the bank has just told us about the opportunities open to anyone with an education. So I went on to college, and it was a struggle to get through because I had to work to pay for my tuition. But I graduated from college, got married, and then, because I still believed in opportunity, I decided to go on and do postgraduate work in architecture. So my wife worked as a schoolteacher while I kept on at the university and graduated with honors as an architect.

"Then I got a job with a good firm of architects. It wasn't easy because there aren't so many firms of architects that hire Negroes in Los Angeles. But I got the job. I began to make a decent income and my wife was still working as a schoolteacher. So we decided to buy a home, and instead of trying to find one inside the Negro section, we looked outside it. Finally, we found one we could afford, over in the Eagle Rock section. Some friends of ours, white people, bought it for us and we were going to buy it from them. So we went to a bank to get an FHA loan, a government loan, but when we told the bank where the house was located, they refused to make us a loan. They told us they wouldn't make loans to Negroes who were trying to move into white neighborhoods. And do you know which bank that was? It was the same one this gentleman works for, the same one that pays his salary to get up here to tell us that all Americans can live where they please if they work hard and get educated. Well, I can tell you I know it's not true."

No one in the audience thought it was true, either. They knew it wasn't possible for them to buy a house anywhere they pleased. Over the years they've seen some breakdown of the barriers that have kept them from jobs they were qualified to fill, but they are convinced that unless they can spend $65,000 and up for a house, they must live someplace inside the Negro ghetto.

Yet the pressure for opening up new neighborhoods to minority groups is inexorable as the minority populations continue to grow. All the salients of the Negro ghetto, for example, respond to that pressure: in the west, where the houses are newer, first the higher-income Negroes move in and then the exodus of frightened whites begins, with the brokers buying the remaining houses at cheap prices from the whites and selling them at expensive prices to the Negroes who are so desperately seeking new homes.

To the north, south, and east the ghetto grows, too, but in those areas the houses taken over are the old ones of the city, the homes already on their way to dilapidation, the leftovers the whites no longer want. But in these sections more white families remain until the family dies off, for unlike the whites to the west, these families are too poor to move elsewhere. So the Negro ghetto expands, its borders extending closer to downtown, further west, more to the south, and out to the east, its progress marked initially by a probing finger of Negro homes which quickly becomes an all-Negro neighborhood. And the schools respond to the new residents by having only a few Negro students at first, then 25 or 30 per cent, and finally, in a rapid transformation, becoming all-Negro.

In general, any government intervention into or regulation of land use and housing has always been and still is resisted bitterly. The private market in land and housing is an integral characteristic of American society today, entrenched in the country's legal and political systems. And since white Americans fear and look down upon non-whites, the operations of the housing and land market reflect those attitudes and thus reinforce them still more.

It is always assumed, too, that any undue or substantial interference in or competition with the operations of the private market will destroy the "American way of life." As a result government has always lagged in asserting any sovereignty over the private market, and in almost every instance of the private market's failures forcing government to act, it has done so only very reluctantly. The apologetic view of the Los Angeles City Housing Authority about its function is typical of most such agencies: ". . . low rent public housing in Los Angeles is not an end in itself but only a temporary refuge for the needy and in most cases eventually the gateway to private housing and the American way of life."

Yet in America's very early days public regulation of property and housing was considered normal: in Colonial America there were laws about how chimneys were to be maintained and prohibitions against unrestricted stripping of the woods to build homes. The first colonists made legally certain that the houses being built had the proper kind of roof coverings, the right size kitchens, and the correct construction. As far back as 1658 the New Amsterdam Council insisted that vacant lots be improved by their owners, and the penalty for refusal was a tax or the surrender of the lands to the city for sale to the public. They planned, too, with some sense of community and neighborhood needs, knowing that a city was more than a collection of houses built haphazardly near a water supply. After the American Revolution, Washington understood the need to plan the capital city. But the cities were tiny places, then, and the country was basically rural. None of the Founding Fathers ever conceived of America as a society dominated by urban metropolises like New York, Chicago, Philadelphia, Detroit, or Los Angeles.

Post-Revolution America began to change very quickly in its attitude toward the use of land. The private landowner was supreme during the period of American expansion, and society was committed to the notion that government land should be turned over as quickly as possible to individuals. Once the land became the private property of individuals, it was assumed to be free from even the minimal amount of regulation which government exercised over state-owned property. The freedom from regulation and control over the use of private land was also extended to the buildings on the land, and in absence of any regulation, landlords and landowners sought the maximum profits possible from their properties.

In the cities the most profitable housing market was the tide of immigrants flooding the country—men, women, and children needed for the factories, most of them unable to speak the language and having no choice about where to live—and so the city tenement developed, a building designed to hold as many people as possible in the smallest amount of space possible. The tenement idea met with only a few scattered protests in America, for the people jammed into the tiny dark rooms with hardly any toilet facilities or running water were not considered deserving of anything better. It was not until well after the Civil War that agitation began for tenement reform; agitation resisted bitterly by such landlords as Trinity Church, which fought against a law in New York City that would have forced Trinity to supply running water on each floor to the tenants who lived in the slum buildings it owned. The belief was generally held that if deplorable conditions existed in the slums, the fault was that of the immigrants who lived there, just as during that period factory workers were held responsible for any accidents that happened to them on the job. The concept of unsafe working conditions or unsafe housing had not yet entered the American legal system: a factory or a tenement was private property, and the owner's rights to use the factory or tenement without regulation were inviolate, above the human rights of the workers and tenants.

Public regulation of tenement structures did not come into existence until the very end of the nineteenth century, and then it was only of the most minimal nature. Meanwhile, speculation in land began to drop off, and even the large fortunes made in real estate began to turn toward industry as a source of wealth. But still no one paid any attention to how the land was being used, so that new housing was built without any attempt being made to control its quality or its location in the community. The slums continued and grew, until finally enough pressure was generated to bring about the legislative introduction of zoning laws, construction and building regulations, and control over landlords.

But low income public housing was always anathema. After World War I a Senate committee denounced public housing as an attack upon American democracy, and it was not until the Depression that large-scale public housing came into existence.

In Los Angeles real estate and housing development followed the national pattern. The city had begun to boom during the 1880s, when the westward migration to southern California was reaching its height. Until that time northern California with its goldfields had been the focus of the restless westward push, and San Francisco had been the urban metropolis, housing the Chinese and Italians who provided the chief source of cheap labor for the mines and railroads. As the migration wave shifted to southern California, the Mexicans—those who had lived in Los Angeles when California was still a Mexican province and the newer immigrants from Mexico—became the counterparts of the Chinese and Italians, the cheap labor needed for the railroads and fields.

Initially, the Mexicans lived on what were the outskirts of the city, in small compact communities made up of jerrybuilt houses constructed hastily in the 1880s. But the city quickly grew up around these communities, leaving them as blighted islands surrounded by white areas. By the early 1900s living conditions were so deplorable in these slums and those in which the very poor whites of Los Angeles had to live that the mayor and City Council set up the first Los Angeles Housing Commission to deal with the menace the slums had become to the city.

Negroes, too, began to arrive in Los Angeles, although not in anywhere near the number of Mexicans. But from 1900 to the early 1920s the population of Los Angeles shot up from a hundred thousand to more than half a million. Real estate prices were shooting up, too; rents were very high, and even the middle-income groups were having difficulty in finding adequate places to live. More and more the low-income families, especially the minority groups, were forced into the older slum areas, converting them into even more crowded slums. And in the face of these problems, the Los Angeles Housing Commission was totally inadequate.

The situation became so bad that in 1925 a new City Charter included a provision that the mayor appoint a municipal housing commission to construct and operate low-income housing. This charter requirement was the result of the pressure put on the city government by a wealthy landowner, William Mead, who was appointed the commission's first chairman. (One of the few re-maining signs of Mead's attitude about public housing is the project named for him which stands isolated in a sea of deserted factories near downtown Los Angeles. And certainly very few, if any, of the people living in this public housing slum know or care about the man for whom it was named.) But William Mead died before the Housing Commission could do anything, and the slum ghettos of Los Angeles continued to increase in size, without any significant regulations by local government.

In 1933 the Depression brought about an attempt to revive the commission, this time to seek state and federal help to build low-income houses. By that time the federal government had been forced to intervene actively in the housing problem. But no at-tempt was made to break up the segregated residential patterns fixed by the private real estate and housing interests. On the con-trary, the federal government adopted as *its* policy the residential segregation pattern applied absolutely by the banks, mortgage companies, building and loan groups, and the real estate organiza-tions. In 1938 the newly formed Federal Housing Administration urged its valuating staff to make certain that the property for which a loan was being considered be protected from "adverse influences."

Such protection from "adverse influences" was defined by the federal agency as including "prevention of the infiltration of business and industrial uses, lower-class occupancy and inharmonious racial groups." And when the agency valuators were considering whether or not to make loans for the purchase of homes in undeveloped or sparsely populated areas, they were told to consider whether ". . . effective restrictive covenants were recorded against the entire tract, since these provide the surest protection against undesirable encroachment and inharmonious use. To be most effective, deed restrictions should be imposed upon all land in the immediate environment of the subject location."

One of the restrictions the government sought to have imposed was "prohibition of the occupancy of properties except by the race for which they are intended." The overall consequences of that federal policy are easily discernible: of all the new housing developed in California from 1950 to 1960 for families with annual incomes of approximately $6,500, only 20 per cent was made available to non-whites. And since most of the Negroes and Mexican-Americans in the state have incomes below that figure, practically no new housing has been available to them.

In Los Angeles alone, for example, new housing construction has been at the rate of almost a billion dollars a year, more than is invested in forty-six other states. But very, very little of the newly built housing is open to Negroes and Mexican-Americans; they must live in the older, deteriorating houses the whites leave behind when they move out.

The active contribution of the federal government to continuing segregated housing can be seen not only in its acquiescence to the discriminatory policies of the private housing industry, but in its granting FHA loan insurance only to those who are eligible to get loans "normally," through any bank. Thus, even though nominally the FHA has now rescinded its support for restrictive covenants, its program is still of little use to the minorities, many of whom don't even know it exists: since all the FHA program does is insure loans made by private banks and lending institutions, low-income Negroes are not financially eligible, while the restrictive policies of these institutions prevent higher-income Negroes from moving to the white suburbs. The federal government not only encourages the continuation and extension of segregated housing, it also helps assure that the segregated housing in which the minority poor live remains wretched.

The data on FHA loans made in Los Angeles are very meager because the agency does not wish to release what it maintains are confidential materials. Normally, FHA loans represent about 20 to 30 per cent of all loans recorded; but a much lower percentage of loans is made to minority families. From the best estimates it appears that FHA is making only about 1,200 loans a year in the Los Angeles minority areas, in a market estimated at about 180,-000 houses!

That tiny percentage of FHA loans demonstrates absolutely the complete falsity of the claim that all Americans have a free choice of where they wish to live in Los Angeles: fewer than a thousand Negroes in Los Angeles live in the vast white suburban areas surrounding the city. Yet 40 per cent of the Negro homeowners living inside the ghettos have said they would move out if there were no prejudice against them.

As a result of the lack of FHA loans and the unwillingness of banks or other lending institutions to make non-FHA loans, a much higher percentage of the homes purchased or sold inside the ghetto are financed by private individuals at very high interest rates and loan costs. And even when savings and loan companies, mostly Negro ones, do make loans to Negroes, the loans are made at a higher rate of interest and for a smaller percentage of the appraised value than elsewhere in the city.

Another result of this policy is that Negroes move from one old house to another old house inside the ghetto, while the whites move outside it: in 1960, 68 per cent of the internal migration of non-whites in the Los Angeles area was from one Negro area to another Negro area; while 70 per cent of the internal white migration was to the suburbs outside the city—a figure which does not even include movement into the San Fernando Valley, an almost totally white suburban area considered part of the city.

The average age of the houses the whites leave behind for the Negroes is far greater than that of houses elsewhere in the city. Between 70 and 94 per cent of the houses in East Los Angeles are old, too; but only 41 per cent of the houses in the whole county, including the Negro and Mexican-American sections, antedate 1939. Between 1950 and 1960 home construction in the Negro sections ranged from only one tenth to one fourth of that in the rest of the county; since 1960 there has been no increase in new construction. And since 1955 not a single new unit of public housing has been built.

As they get more crowded the older and more deteriorated houses in which the minority families must live fall into even greater disrepair, for even if their owners want to fix them, they cannot do so because they are almost always so heavily mortgaged that no bank or individual will make another loan for repairs. And most lenders are very reluctant to make loans in the ghetto in any case, because they are convinced that the area is declining into what will be one of the nation's worst slum areas.

The lenders are correct: ample evidence exists to corroborate their belief that the ghetto is well on its way to becoming a physical slum, as well as the psychic one it is now. In 1950 the city embarked upon a program to enforce the building codes in the area south of the central business district, with special attention being given to the Negro sections. But the Los Angeles City Department of Building and Safety, which is responsible for inspecting older houses to make sure they are safe and habitable, admits that this part of its work is only a "stepson" operation. The department's real priorities are in making certain that the *new* homes being built meet the city's standards, and therefore three of its four bureaus and most of its personnel are concentrated in this work rather than the inspection and "conservation" of older buildings. In fact, although the department itself has been in existence many years, the Conservation Bureau did not exist before 1947, and has never been more than a limited operation.

". . . What happens when you come to budget time," the director of the bureau has stated, "the work load that you are creating yourself is the one place you can cut back, so if you were to plot the original personnel we had in this activity [inspection and conservation] and how it goes along, you will see that it saw-tooths, because when the money gets tight, this is the place you can pull back, and it's logical—well, I don't know that's the right word. You can make an argument for it because the people say, 'Well, this property has been here for sixty years and nobody is excited about it. Why can't it go on for another twenty years?' You see."

It could hardly be otherwise in Los Angeles. Nominally, the billion dollars' worth of new construction is under the jurisdiction of the Building and Safety Commission, which is charged with en-forcing all laws relating to the general areas of public health and safety, exclusive of fire, police, and public works. But the com-mission, which is appointed by the mayor, meets only once a week, and its members receive only a $19 expense reimbursement for the meetings they attend. In fact, of course, the Building and Safety Commission is run by the civil servants in it, most of them tech-nical men with engineering backgrounds, rather than by people concerned with developing major policies.

The department head is a former military officer who runs his organization on rather strict, formal, military rules. Its personnel turnover rate is high, perhaps as a result of its rigid internal rules, with little opportunity for redress of grievances and severe penal-ties meted out for the making of mistakes. As a result staff mem-bers at the lower echelon are very reluctant to make any decisions, except those which are demanded of them and for which clear provisions are made in the codes. If the building code states that a four-foot cement wall should be reinforced, the department says it shall be reinforced. And any attempt by a builder to convince the department that the cement wall doesn't require reinforcement in order to be safe will meet with a rejection, for nobody on the department staff wants to accept personal responsibility or liability for any failures of safety. Instead, the staff refers all such applica-tions to the commission, abdicating any responsibility for making decisions not called for in the codes.

As a result, the commission has no time to work on policy

development even if its members wanted to do so. Almost all of its weekly business is concerned with reviewing applications for variances from building codes or other regulatory provisions which have been disapproved by the department's staff.

Characteristically, commission members are of various backgrounds—real estate, building contractors, architects, and occasionally someone from a university, either an authority on property law or real estate. But obviously such a group of commissioners can have only limited experience with the problems of minority housing. In addition, any commission member from the building industry would have a natural reluctance to oppose any staff decision lest he endanger his own future interests.

With a limited staff faced with overseeing hundreds of millions of dollars in new construction, inspecting schools, and checking for overhead parapets which might be hazardous during one of the area's earthquakes, the "conservation" of the older houses where the minority poor must live obviously gets a low priority. Of the more than 800 men in the department, only a maximum of 170 are assigned to this work; they have very little time to explain to the owners of the deteriorating and dilapidated houses what must be done to bring them into good repair, assuming that the owner could afford to do so. And the department's task is made even more difficult because owners who do have some funds available to them are prone to respond to the advertising pressure for building new kitchens or otherwise "prettying up" their houses rather than making more basic but usually unseen repairs to foundations, roofs, sills, etc. And inspectors do not venture into some areas of the minority ghettos for fear they will be attacked—whether or not their fears are justified matters only a little to the consequences of them: some houses in the city are totally uninspected, and no one, except perhaps the social workers, knows what the living conditions are in those homes today.

The department's role is limited still further by the fact that the commission members are appointed by the mayor and can be removed by him if they take positions openly opposed to what he believes to be his political interests. This situation, too, cuts down on the number of people willing to give as much of their time and energy as is required of a commission member. (Unlike those in some other cities, however, the Los Angeles department is generally free of graft, bribery, or corruption. Its top staff is honest but very rigid and limited in its view.)

Thus, although by 1960, at the end of what the Department of Building and Safety described as a major effort in the Watts area, the over-all percentage of deteriorating or dilapidated homes was 18; by 1965 the percentage of deteriorating and dilapidated homes in the south and south central section had risen to 33. Even more ominously, while in 1960 82 per cent of the homes in the area had been described by the census bureau as "sound," five years later the bureau found only 67 per cent in that category, with the same rate of physical deterioration also taking place in the barrios.

Still, living in the ghettos doesn't necessarily mean living in a slum. Indeed, if slums mean only the overcrowded and dilapidated tenement houses of New York's Harlem and Lower East Side, or Phoenix's shantytowns, where the poorest Mexican-Americans live, then Los Angeles has had very few slums.

Even in Watts, one of the poorer Negro areas, you can drive down streets and see men mowing the lawns in front of their houses or women stopping to gossip before getting into their cars. It's hard to conceive of such a street as being part of a slum, for it looks as if it were any lower-middle-class street in America. But the very next street will look quite different: seedy, run-down, more like the one described by a Negro woman who owns three houses in Watts: "Watts is a pretty bad old neighborhood. It's not a neighborhood where people would love to be too well, because we have too many broken-down bad houses and unkept homes and things of that kind. We do need a better system in Watts than what we have. What I would say would be better than anything else, we need people to go through Watts and take inventory of what is there and how these places are set up and what the people are doing. The people don't have decent homes to stay and a lot of people don't know that. The people who would be able to do something about Watts, they don't come there, they don't know about these things. Now, all around where I am living now the yards and the lawns, which is the same thing, is all very unkept."

And what cannot be seen from a car window is how crowded some of the houses are inside, or how some of the garages and sheds fronting on the back alleys are being used to house people under the most primitive conditions, without heat, running water, or toilets. This jamming of human beings into spaces designed originally for horses and cars began during the wartime housing shortage, when whites as well as Negroes and Mexican-Americans suffered from having to pay high rates for garage accommodations. But when the war ended and the postwar housing shortage eased, the whites were able to move into the thousands of apartments and tract homes that shot up almost overnight all over the city and its suburbs.

Ten times as many people live in the Negro sections of Los Angeles as in the white areas. In the ghetto the lowest density of population in 1960 was 10,419 persons per square mile and the highest 14,348 persons. But in Los Angeles County as a whole, which means the figures for the Negro area are included, the average density was only 1,479 persons per square mile!

"Living at home is lousy," says one young man now going to junior college, "not because my mother treats me badly. She doesn't. But it's so damned crowded, I don't have room to turn around. Like, I'm sleeping in one room with my three brothers, and my two sisters are sleeping in the next room with my mother. I'm on a cot, so I'm lucky. Two of my brothers sleep on a sofa and the other one on a mattress.

"How am I supposed to study or write some paper? I was a hell of a lot better off when I was living in a room by myself. But I haven't got enough bread to make it by myself and still go to college. If I want to live alone, I got to go out and hustle. Then I could help out with my mother, too. But if I want to go to school some more, I got to stay at home, and it's lousy. I don't even take a shit at home if I can help it. I'd rather wait until I get to school if I can hold it in. At least no one's bugging me to get out of the can, like at home with the seven of us trying to use one can."

The human consequences of such overcrowding are known to and dreaded by every perceptive city official. "Cool weather" was the answer given by a New York police official asked what he thinks would do the most to avert racial disturbances in the Negro slums, because he knows that during the hot spells when people jammed into poorly ventilated apartments or houses bake in the heat, their tempers rise. They quarrel more with the others in the house and escape to the streets, which are also like ovens.

"I think when you go and look at the riots in the country, you'll see areas where a house is housing probably three families where there ought to be one," says a Los Angeles real estate expert. "Maybe those places are housing even five or six times more people than they should. Then you get hot, muggy weather and you've got two or three people in a single bedroom. So what do you do if you're living like that? You go out on the streets. You get some relief out there, and you know if you go back to that house, it's going to be noisy and you're going to have all those other people around. You can't even get any rest, so why not stay out on the streets or go over to the park?"

"And you do that two or three nights in a row and you're losing sleep. You're getting irritated. And no one is doing anything to improve the conditions. So, if you get a chance, you riot."

But the people in the cities whose living conditions are worst are not those members of minority groups who own their homes, but those who rent their living quarters from private landlords or from the government in the form of public housing. And the number of renters in the ghettos is far greater than owners; the percentage is also increasing every year as even those who can afford to rent apartments outside the ghetto find it almost impossible to get a landlord to accept them.

"Do you happen to know of any other work I might be able to do after this program is over?" asked the young woman who had been running an anti-poverty program at UCLA for upgrading the educational level of kids from ghetto high schools. "I really need a job because after the first of the year my husband and I are going to be supporting two households."

"Why are you going to have two households?"

"Well, my husband is a physicist, and his company is sending him back East for a year of postgraduate study. So we'll have two apartments to keep up because the kids are staying with me."

"How come you're not going with him if he's going to be gone a whole year?"

Silence for a few moments. Then the woman looked out the window at the bustling campus. Sadly she continued: "My husband works for an aircraft company over in Culver City, and eventually I want to finish my own graduate work at UCLA. So we want to live out here in the Westwood section. But it took us six months and three lawsuits to finally get an apartment in Westwood. We can't give it up and go through that experience again. So we have to keep it and I'll have to work to pay the rent."

The difficulty in renting an apartment experienced by the physicist and his wife is not unique in Los Angeles; it is almost the rule. From the evidence of one recent survey, fewer than one third of the landlords in the city said they would rent apartments to Negroes when asked specifically, and the percentage may be much smaller since it is assumed that at least some of those who answered affirmatively were merely speaking for the record. In the Westwood area, where the couple was living, out of nine apartment managers who said they would be willing to rent to a visiting Viennese professor only two said they would rent to an American Negro professor.

"This area would shoot me dead if I rented to Negroes."

"No, I did it once and the other tenants moved out."

"The individual wouldn't be happy here because there are no Negroes in the neighborhood."

"I won't get involved again. I rented to a Korean engineer and his wife a few years ago, but there was a big protest from all the neighbors."

"No! No Negroes here. When you get one, you don't know what's gonna happen."

"No. I can't. The savings and loan company discourages this sort of thing."

"I'm sorry for them. I recognize the problem. I know this housing thing is a big mess, but I won't rent to them. We have to think of other people. We couldn't take a chance on all the tenants moving."

A young Negro soldier, home in the ghetto on a furlough, stands outside his old high school, reminiscing about the days when he was active in student government and played on the school basketball team: "I liked Jordan High and I think it's a good school. My brother and my two sisters all graduated from Jordan, too, and they were all kind of big shots, too. I used to like living in Watts, too. We lived here all my life and my mother and father were pretty strict with us. He worked for the Navy and she was some kind of clerk, but when we came home from school, there was always someone home, not like it is with some of these kids who got no one to tell them what's right and wrong.

"But I don't think it matters much. My one sister is married to a schoolteacher and he makes pretty good money, but they still have to live in the ghetto, out west. My other sister, she's stuck too. Me, I think I might stay in the Army. At least overseas it's not so bad. The foreign people don't treat you the way the Americans do. Anyway, I sure don't want to come back here and have to live in Watts again."

Yet, most of the minority groups' landlords in Los Angeles are not slumlords who grow rich on tenement properties. Indeed, the number of landlords getting rich from their investments in the ghettos is probably very small: slum properties do not bring in high returns unless they are multifamily units rather than the smaller homes found in the Los Angeles ghettos. Apartment houses, even medium-sized ones, aren't found in any abundance in the older eastern and southern sections, where the Negroes and Mexican-Americans live, nor is it likely that there will be any large-scale investment in such properties.

Instead, the landlords are more likely to live in the area themselves, barely able to keep up the payments on their houses, much less make repairs for the tenants, who in their search for more space or less expensive rentals move in and out much more often than do tenants in the white areas. This kind of musical-chairs routine with houses and apartments is especially characteristic in those parts of the ghettos which have a high percentage of transients, people making their first stop in Los Angeles before moving on to more permanent housing.

One Negro woman who owns three small houses, renting out two, describes her experience as a landlady: "My little house has been vacant, I think, about three or four times. Since I have been there, just that many people have lived in it. I had three or four families there, and those that are there now, they are planning on moving; I don't know, maybe tomorrow or next week. I don't know just what day they will move, because they are finding a place with more space . . . And my houses are very rundown, too, now . . . I managed to decorate one of the houses, where the people are planning on moving out.

"When I had rented it to them, I had cleaned it up very well, painted, and got it straightened out, and so on and so forth. And is isn't because I don't have mercy on children. I do. I am a grandmother. I have mercy on children, I don't want no one to think I don't. But it is only to my financial standing, I am not able to do these things. So they told me they had one baby and another little child not old enough to go to school. But they had four and a dog. The dog died, and the children, they are not too destructive but they are very unkempt. And they have it pretty hard, taking care of those children and keeping them up. And that is the reason there is so much vandalism, too, around in the neighborhood. People don't have their own places and they don't care for others'.

"What I think is the most trouble that we are having in Watts is, well, people would have their own places and not be tenants. And that kind, they are the ones who are giving us the more trouble than anybody else because they are people that will not clean up and they just seem to live it up like what's his name and they won't do no better. You just can't get no one to do right around there. Everywhere you go you find beer cans and garbage and trash around in the yards, and you just can't do it by yourself because you have no other way out. You have nothing else but the people that really don't care. So what can you do?

"My problem is rundown dirty streets and alleys and so forth. That is, my places is on the alley, and money I don't have to fix things like I want to. It seems to be the same way with many others. Although as I tried to say and make it clear, it is people probably that has lived there many years, and maybe their mortgages has been cleared and they don't have the problems I have. And their places are kept well. And I would like for mine to be like that, and all in the neighborhood the same way.

"I feel very sorry for that family—there is a family over there— the mother is in the hospital and there's about four or five children there and the home is rundown terrible. And the children don't have no guardian or nothing over them, but just him, although he seems to be a very good father to his children. But it is the thing that they do need a woman to keep those children and keep them clean or to keep the surroundings better.

"And he is a mechanic, because he got the cars and all like that on the yard—well, that don't look so nice in a residential neighborhood. So you don't like to look at all those things, which I don't. He seems to be making his own job. I don't like to kick on things like that because I tells you I likes to see everybody making a living. And I am not, but I do think he should have some help some way or another or get him a job where he wouldn't have to build cars and work on them in his yard and that grease and all of that stuff around is pretty bad."

Yet the worst slums in the city are found not only among the dilapidated, deteriorated, or unsound privately owned homes. There are terrible psychic slums in Los Angeles, slums of the spirit which are not the responsibility of private landlords or the Building and Safety Commission. These slums are owned and operated by a public landlord, the Housing Authority of the City of Los Angeles.

At a typical bimonthly meeting of the Los Angeles Housing Authority the five commissioners were routinely approving the recommendations of the staff. Then a commissioner asked a question during a discussion of a fairly new Authority policy: it is now leasing housing from landlords in various parts of the city, guaranteeing the rent for a year and subletting to tenants, generally senior citizens.

"A woman I know complained to me," said the commissioner to the staff, "that she had been turned down for leased housing when she applied. I know her income is small enough to entitle her to get into leased housing because she's a widow with three little girls. But she says she was turned down. Can you tell me why?"

"It's probably because she hasn't got a husband," was the answer. "We have a general policy of not allowing women with children but no husbands in leased housing. She should apply to one of the housing projects. Leased housing is a step above the projects, and we feel we have a tremendous responsibility to the landlords and to the homeowners in the neighborhood to allow only the best tenants in leased housing."

"But I think she's a widow, not an unmarried mother," protested the commissioner. "She doesn't want to move into one of the projects. She wants her girls to be brought up in a nice neighborhood, and that's why she wants to move into leased housing. There must be other widows in the neighborhood."

The staff man was firm: "Maybe there are, but we have a general policy and we can't break it for individual cases. Women with children and no husbands don't make the best kind of tenants for leased housing. She should apply to one of the projects."

When that Housing Authority staff member explained to the commissioner that "leased housing is a step above the projects," he was making explicit the contempt in which the tenants of the public housing projects are held today, not just by the community outside the projects, but by those officials responsible for their administration.

Back in the 1930s, when the New Deal liberals pushed through the legislation setting up federally financed public housing, none of them would have dreamed that thirty years later the dwellers in the projects would be suggesting that dynamite be used to blow them up. The tragedy of public housing in Los Angeles is that it began with some elements of social idealism, with some characteristics of a movement, and has become a social distilling apparatus in which every evil associated with ghettos is concentrated, while none of the ghettos' potential strengths are given the opportunity to develop. And what happened in Los Angeles has been duplicated in nearly every city in the country.

The public housing projects of Los Angeles stand as racial and ethnic islands inside the subcultures of segregation and poverty.

On these twenty-one islands live approximately eighty-three hundred families of thirty-seven thousand people, the great majority of them Negroes, most of whom receive their income from some form of public assistance program. Their average monthly rent is $53.08.

The present public housing program in Los Angeles can't be separated from the welfare program, but it was not always so. A former official of the Housing Authority says: "Once public housing in Los Angeles was involved with more than just housing people the way it is now. It had many social aspects in it. We tried to get as many services as we could into the community to serve the people in the projects. We had very good parents' councils to air their frustrations so we could work out their problems with them. They had people from adult education come into the various projects to give homemaking courses to mothers, and there was a sense of pride, of working together with management and the families. However, over the years that has changed."

When Congress passed the Housing Act in 1937, the public welfare program was still comparatively small. Initially, at least, the Act's objective was the provision of "decent, safe, and sanitary dwellings for families of low income and the eradication of slums," but at that time no one assumed that low-income families meant only welfare recipients: vast numbers of middle-class Americans were poor only because of the Depression.

The public housing program was plagued with difficulties from the start. It came into being as a compromise between the social reformers, who saw it as a tool to wipe out the slums, and those who saw it as a vehicle for no more than a much needed infusion of capital into the economy. Even before the Housing Act was passed the government had started helping the private housing industry by stopping foreclosures, encouraging mortgage financing for home construction or repair, and supporting the industry through loans and credits.

Because of the primacy of the private sector, public housing was never designed either to compete with private housing or be a substitute for it. Thus, one provision of the Housing Act—that requiring the destruction of buildings "substantially equal to the

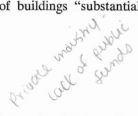

number of newly constructed dwellings in the project"—satisfied both those social reformers who wanted to eliminate slums, which they thought of only in terms of physically dilapidated buildings, and those supporters of private housing who were fearful that an oversupply of housing would drive the price down when the country was once again out of the Depression.

From its start, too, public housing was a joint operation of the federal, state, and local governments. The fear of centralized federal control resulted in the creation of a federal housing authority, whose function was to help state and local governments develop and operate low-rent public housing by providing long-term, low-interest federal loans and annual cash contributions.

The purpose of the federal annual cash contribution was to bring rentals down to a level the temporarily depressed middle-class families could afford. Simultaneously, the concept developed that rents in public housing should be graded by income and family size, so that those with low incomes would pay less for their apartments than those with higher incomes. And a ceiling was put on income, too, so that when a higher income level was reached, the people would have to leave to make room for others who were poorer. And the financial operations of the housing authorities were designed to make the projects self-supporting; current operating expenses were to be met with rents received.

Most importantly, public housing was initially designed for lower-middle- and working-class families caught in temporary financial straits, not as subsidized housing for those without any income or hope of it, the unemployed, the paupers, or those "unworthy poor" who depended upon charity. As Senator Robert F. Wagner, Sr., the author of the bill, said, "There are some people whom we cannot possibly reach; I mean those who have no means to pay the rent . . . this bill cannot provide housing for those who cannot pay the rent minus the subsidy allowed."

The 1937 Act also set limits on the average cost of construction for the housing units. Those limits, together with the emphasis on the urban non-pauper family, meant that the projects were designed with only one- or two-bedroom units. Eventually every one of the provisions had catastrophic effects.

In March of 1938 the California legislature passed a bill authorizing the cities and counties to set up their housing authorities; three months later the Los Angeles City Council established the city's Housing Authority. The first program of slum clearance and construction of new housing began in 1939, but before the operations had really gotten under way, World War II began and the emphasis of the program was shifted. Because thousands of war workers were needed in Los Angeles and no homes were available for them, the housing authority built and operated eight thousand dwelling units for them, including trailers, a three-thousand-bed dormitory, and twelve of the twenty-one projects it now operates.

When the war ended and the returning veterans sought places in which to live, another acute housing shortage hit the city. Many of the veterans were new residents, too. To help meet the great demand for housing from this large group of people, the Authority, with the financial help of the federal and state governments, created 3,000 additional dwelling units by converting military barracks and quonset huts into apartments. By 1948, at the height of the postwar housing shortage, the Authority was running 28 projects, with 13,500 dwelling units in them; but the demand for housing was still so acute that 5,000 applications were always on hand.

"There was a good feeling in the housing projects, then," explains a middle-class social worker who lived in one of them after returning to Los Angeles from the war. "It was fine, it was very nice. We had the happiest time we ever had in our life and we saved more money than we ever did again. Most of the families came from the war. And they were very, very anxious to move ahead and give their kids dancing and all sort of other things. All kinds of activities were going on in the projects, and it wasn't only the people who lived in the projects who were enjoying them. Our friends who lived on the other side of town would come to visit on a Saturday night and we'd have a ball, we had something different, we had a cement floor, we had a band. And we were able to save money because we didn't have to pay light, didn't have to pay water, and we didn't have a high gas bill. So in about eighteen months we bought a duplex and moved out of the project."

Then the veterans of World War II and the war workers for whom the projects had been a temporary haven during the housing shortage began to move out, either by choice or because their income levels had gone over the maximum allowable yearly figure set by the Housing Authority. In their place came the new immigrants to California, the Negroes from the South and the Mexicans moving up from areas close to or across the border. But this new group of tenants with large families were strangers in the city, unused to its ways and not able to adjust easily to the new patterns. Most of the men, without urban skills, were not able to find jobs, and they drifted away, leaving behind the women and children. Thus, the dominant figures in the projects became the women; the men's role was increasingly subordinate, as if they had been relegated to a men's auxiliary.

The new tenants needed help and needed it badly. They needed medical advice and counseling about children; they needed suggestions about budgeting and training for jobs. They needed to be shown how a gas stove worked and what it meant to vote. They needed to be told about PTA groups and tenants' councils, and above all they needed to become part of a community. But their needs went unmet, as the Housing Authority staff orientation shifted away from such activities.

The change in orientation had taken place for a number of reasons. As is inevitable in any agency, the normal bureaucratic institutionalization process had set in, and the top staff had lost touch with the field workers, who in turn had lost contact with the people living in the projects.

"The concept of the housing program changed tremendously during the middle fifties," states a former professional employee of the Authority. "Instead of having some emphasis on the social aspect of the families, the concept developed of just housing people, just providing them with rooms. And so, over the years, many of the sharp people quit the Authority. They liked the original concept of housing. For example, you take a family that came here from Mississippi or somewhere in the South that have never been—never seen a bathroom in their life or a gas stove or a refrigerator, they wouldn't know how to use them. So, originally, they had demonstrations for these newcomers, they would show them how to use the appliances that they had in the homes. But all that stopped.

"During that period, the administration actually swung away from the social aspect; I think that this was perhaps out of fear that there was too much emphasis that had been put on the social aspect of how the families were living. I think that was really one of the policies. I think that the director didn't want to get involved any more. That was the beginnning of the change to just house people. They cut out the parents' councils, and so from then on it began to change."

And the process by which any administration becomes more formal and less inclined to risk-taking was also accelerated, in Los Angeles, by McCarthyism. When Frank Wilkinson, the Authority's public information officer, was cited by the House Un-American Activities Committee he refused to answer the committee's questions, so he was fired; in the wake of the firing other members of the staff quit, and those who remained became even more cautious about doing any social work that might be considered controversial.

So started a spiralling process in which the projects began to be tenanted by those people with the most problems who got the least help in solving them or the worst directions about where they might find some help. The projects began to get the reputation as the homes of welfare recipients; the children who lived in them were scornfully identified at school as "project kids," an appellation that conjured up images of nothing but young hoodlums. There were more and more vacancies as non-welfare families moved out; in order to fill the vacancies, still more and more welfare families were brought in to fill the empty apartments.

The project managers, disturbed by their new clientele and unused to dealing with the sort of problems these tenants brought with them, responded by becoming more paternalistic and restrictive. Always conscious of the need to operate the projects in a "businesslike" manner, they developed a policy of very quickly evicting the families who didn't pay the rent promptly or who were difficult tenants, tenants who didn't understand the need for cleanliness or who let their children run around in the project unattended.

A lack of finances also forced cutbacks in those programs which might have aided the newcomers to adjust to life in the city: those social work programs which had been subsidized by the budgets allocated to the housing projects were cut as public support for public housing declined.

By 1955, when nine more projects had been opened, including the largest, Nickerson Gardens, an all-Negro project at the south end of the Watts area, public housing had lost most of its old support. No new housing projects have been built since then, for public housing no longer has any appeal, even to the liberals who once supported it.

To some extent the current problems of a project like Nickerson Gardens can be traced to the flaws in the Wagner Act. Because the initial laws stipulated limits on building costs, the projects have had to be built of cheaper materials as building costs have increased. Tenants in some of the public housing projects are prohibited from hanging pictures on the apartment walls because the walls are made of cheap concrete blocks: a nail driven into such a wall leaves a jagged hole. Also, because the apartments were built with only one and two bedrooms, an increasing number of vacancies began to develop: such small apartments were useless to the large families that were beginning to make up the bulk of the tenants in the projects. Similarly, the provision that a family had to move out once its income reached a specific level meant that only the poorest families remained, with no other models than other families equally poor.

So even before it was opened Nickerson Gardens was doomed to become what it is today—a cauldron of social diseases. It was designed badly, with too many apartments in too little space. Hacienda Village, one of the city's better projects, is made up of 184 units spread out over 17.6 acres; Nickerson Gardens, which has six times as many units—1,100—is only four times as large, with 68.6 acres. To compound the problem, this large project was built in an area without any adequate transportation, shopping areas, or recreational facilities.

"They've got three play areas for over three thousand kids," says the mother of three of the three thousand children. "There's a sandpile in the back with one swing, they got another sandpile and a thing to crawl through down the street, and they got another one with no swings over here about three blocks that way. That's about it for three thousand kids."

"Well, I know my kids were playing marbles over by the housing office," chimes in another mother, "and they come out of the office and done told the kids to come on to the playground to play and I said, 'For what? Every time they go there the big kids jump on them and take the marbles and everything; they're scared to go over there and play.' "

By now, too, only a few traces remain of the "emphasis on the social aspect of family life" that once marked the atmosphere of project living. In its place there has developed a rigid system of uniform regulations of the petty details of family life. The government feels that it has more rights than a private landlord and that its "subsidized" tenants, especially those who are welfare recipients and therefore doubly "subsidized," have fewer rights than those living in privately owned apartments.

In general, the Authority staff today bears little resemblance to the men and women who worked for it when public housing was a movement. Many of the project managers and administrative staff today have backgrounds in engineering, maintenance work, or administration. Many of them speak of the tenants as "those people" and demonstrate very little empathy with their problems. Their primary concern is with evoking concurrence with the rules, keeping their projects free of "troublesome" tenants, and getting all the apartments rented.

The discretionary power of the project managers is almost total; they operate autonomously within the Housing Authority regulations, and the only appeals tenants can make is to the director or the commissioners, people who are more likely to back up the manager than overrule him. The only staff people in the projects who are likely to have some background in helping people with problems are the tenant relations personnel, who are responsible for explaining the Housing Authority's policies to the tenants. But even though this group places some emphasis on establishing better relationships with the tenants, their power is limited and they are under the direct control of the individual project managers.

Partially, too, the tenants are suffering from a serious internal problem that developed within the Authority itself. In the early 1960s the director of the Authority and his assistant were fired; both had been with the agency since its start. They began a lawsuit to regain their jobs, and after a period of internal turmoil the operation of the agency was taken over by the federal agency, which still exercises supervision over the Authority because the government's original loan to the Authority has not yet been totally repaid. But the staff was demoralized, and that demoralization spread out to the project managers.

"When you move in a project, you must have twenty-five-dollar deposit," explains a tenant. "He must have the amount of rent from you. Well, if it's the first of the month, so then he has a certain amount, and if it's in the middle of the month, well, then he have the rest of the month plus twenty-five dollars. So this is a strain on you because you must have eight dollars more for garbage cans and water hose. So it's eight dollars, twenty-five dollars, and then the rent and lights if you have to have them transferred, or you might never had lights, then you got to do that, too, this in the beginning is a strain, you know. You gotta have all of this stuff before you get in. And they don't take part of it. You have to have it all. Then after you move in, they give you the rules and regulations."

The "rules and regulations" which the Housing Authority attempts to use to control the tenants encompass nearly every detail of daily life. Tenants who do not put trash cans out alongside the house are charged for having it done by the maintenance crews; tenants who don't clean up their own yards are charged for having that done. If a maintenance man decides a lawn needs watering and turns on the hose, the tenant is charged for that; if a stove is broken and it is the property of the Authority, the tenant is charged for the repairs. The tenants may put only those screen doors on the apartments which are supplied and installed by the Authority, and they must pay for both the door and installation at the usual commercial rates. "We must have uniformity in the project so that the apartments all look more or less alike," says the director. His words are echoed by a member of his top staff, explaining why the tenants are not permitted to put up their own screen doors: "We want to keep a standard position instead of having someone put up an oddball type of screen. If all the doors didn't look alike, it would be an unsightly appearance."

"The kids can't climb the trees and they can't even play on the grass in front of the house," bitterly complains a mother. "If the kids get out there and play ball and put a spot out there, the housing, they charge you to put the grass out there. So then if you tell the kids to play ball in front where you can watch them, it's your own risk if someone breaks a window, say, if they bat a ball and break my window, that's seven dollars and sixty cents. So I get worried when I see the kids playing out front, and I holler at them and they holler back and run over to the parking lot to play. That's where they can learn to strip cars—that parking lot. That's an awful position for kids to be in."

The principal of an elementary school a few blocks from a housing project in East Los Angeles explains how one of the teachers brings her cat to school so that little children can see and touch the cat. Wide-eyed, the little boys and girls tentatively stroke the cat as it stirs in the teacher's arms. *"El gato,* look at *el gato,"* they say wonderingly, as other children might speak of a giraffe or tiger at the zoo.

"In the project, no one is allowed to have a pet," explains the principal, "and so these kids come to school without ever having had much contact with pets. Dogs and cats are strange to them."

"Pets cause a mess," states the director of the Housing Authority. "Now, personally, I wouldn't live in an apartment house with a dog around. I have enough trouble now with dogs on my own lawn. Here the cats are under the same rule. I couldn't operate the projects this way even though I am very partial to cats. I like cats, but no one owns a cat. Did you ever try to control cats? You can call the city and try to get them to pick up a stray cat and they won't do it. We don't object to parakeets and canaries, but no dogs, cats, and no pigeons. They can't be controlled."

"Once, years ago, the manager of one project set aside a piece of land near a dump yard on the project," says an old-timer on the administration staff, "and the families had a vegetable garden, a flower garden, and the kids had animals up there. The kids would take turns to go up there and take care of them, they would feed them and this was a good experience for them, but, of course, that got knocked out. A new man came in and he said it was too much trouble and they needed the yard for something else, for maintenance or something."

Still, not all the projects are places in which the description of "suicide" is apt. A few of them never have any vacancies: the smaller ones, with fewer people in them; more centrally located, they are spread out over larger areas, and they have better facilities for children and more sympathetic managers. A few of the larger projects, where the managers attempt to establish some channels of communication with the tenants, are better than the prison camps which most of the projects resemble.

Of all the Housing Authority's rules and regulations, two disturb the tenants more than all the rest. Under the regulations the tenants have very little privacy: members of the project staff have the right to enter the tenants' apartments to make inspections for repairs and check on the general conditions of refrigerators or items of furniture which the tenants may be renting from the Authority. In some projects the tenants are not advised in advance of the forthcoming visit, and in others the tenants are convinced that the staff members interfere far more than they should in their personal lives.

"When we first moved into an apartment here, I had put in a request for something to be fixed," one tenant reports typically, "and I was in my bed sleeping a few days after. It was early in the morning when the man first came in. And I was in the bed. And I got so mad, I couldn't say anything, you know. I told him, excuse me, 'Get the hell out of here until I get up and get me some clothes on.' And he said, 'Well, I'm sorry, lady, but you put in a request and I'm here to do my job.' And I said, 'But that don't give you the right to open my door and come in here to my house when I'm in bed.' But he wasn't sorry, he just kept saying, 'Well, lady, I have a job to do.' And I told him, 'Well, I pay rent. I pay rent here in this apartment and it don't give you the right to use your key and come in. You give me the chance to get up and open the door.' "

Another describes her experience: "A man from the office come and told me to take my ham bone out of the icebox. I had paid nine dollars for a ham and we had trimmed it all down to the bone, and I was saving the bone to cook with some beans. He wanted me to take it out. He came to the house for something, to inspect. They got a key. They walk in when they get good and ready! They don't have to inform you; they come. He walk in when he good and ready and he looks in the icebox—well, the icebox belongs to the house, but the bone don't belong to the house. So he told me that the bone shouldn't been in there because it was dried and this kind of stuff. And I said, 'Who in the hell are you talking to? I paid nine dollars for that ham, and if I want to keep it until next Easter, then I'm going to keep the bone.' So we went round and round about that."

The director of the Authority justifies the need to enter the tenants' apartments in these terms: "We don't like regimentation but at the same time we can't let them live in filth. And as to maintenance, the men are invited in when the tenants make a report, like, they've got a stoppage. If the maintenance man goes up, knocks on the door, and no one is home, he knocks on the door three times distinctly. Then we unlock the door with a master key, stick our head in and holler 'Maintenance man,' and then proceed with the work that's to be done. Now snooping, no. But we do have to look into our own refrigerators because I've seen them iced up where you could hardly get the door shut, and we have to see that kept up."

Another official, however, agrees that the tenants do see the staff as invading their privacy. "There was a big complaint that the managers in the Housing Authority exercised a Gestapo-like approach—they would come in at all hours of the day on these so-called inspections. Some of the managers feel that they are obligated to check to see if there's a man in the home and then relay this information to the welfare department. They do it voluntarily, and they shouldn't—this isn't part of their job. They may also make a needless inspection on a family, maybe to harass them. After all, they're human beings. Maybe these inspections should be cut out. One of the constructive suggestions we've heard is that the family get some reasonable notice, by way of a letter, a two- or three-day notice, that the managers are coming out to inspect the unit. I don't think the managers should just go up there and knock on the door and expect the family to be there and admit them. After all, some people have some pride in their housekeeping and don't want a stranger in the house if the place is a mess."

The sliding scale of rents, based on income and the number of people in the family, is also a source of continual tension between the tenants and the Authority. When the projects were the temporary homes for tenants whose incomes were on the rise, the sliding scale was of no great significance. But as the ceiling on income forced these groups out of the projects and they were replaced by tenants whose incomes were fixed at very low levels, either because they were low-paid unskilled workers or because their income was in the low levels of the public assistance program, the sliding scale began to be seen as a penalty when some slight increase in income occurred or when the size of the family increased.

"Now, if you're on a job, next month you might get a raise. Now when you get a three-cent raise on your job, you get a six-dollar raise on house rent. So then, we're in this place but we have certain things we can't do in our own home while we're paying rent. For instance, you can't come and visit me no more than two weeks. If you stay longer than that, they'll assume that you live there and you have to start paying some rent."

The tenants in the projects reiterate again and again their bitter complaints about the rents, for they see the increase as a penalty for attempting to raise the standard of their living, a handicap to bringing themselves out of the low-income levels to higher ones. If, for example, the teen-age son gets a job delivering newspapers, the amount he earns is added to the family income and the rent increases. And even though the rent increase is only 20 to 25 per cent of the increase in income, it is resented: it represents to the tenants the government's taking away from them something they have earned.

Without doubt, however, the group most strongly resentful of the Housing Authority's rental policies are the great number of people whose sole or major source of income is from the public assistance programs. Their lives are under the double controls of the Authority and the welfare department. They see that the Housing Authority sets a flat rent for them which may be higher than that charged for identical apartments whose tenants are not on public assistance. For example, a family consisting of a mother and three children, with the mother working or getting unemployment insurance, may pay less for rent than a family of the same size whose income is derived from the Aid to Dependent Children Program. In addition, any time welfare increases the family's monthly allowance the rent is increased, too. In some situations it is even possible for a family on public assistance to be charged more rent by the Authority than is allotted it by the welfare department, with the result that money must be taken from the already meager food budget to pay the rent.

"Let me tell what happened," says one of the tenants in a project. "The City Housing Authority and the welfare department sign an agreement that the county would allow so much for rent, and Housing would get it. Now, when I first moved into the project, my rent was forty-one dollars a month. I was working. Then I got a three-cent raise, and my rent went to forty-six dollars a month. Then when I got sick and couldn't work no more, I was placed on the county, and my rent went to fifty-eight dollars per month. Then I got a two-dollar raise on the county check and it went to sixty dollars a month. In most cases, you pay more money for rent if you're on the county. It came about because of an agreement two people signed.

"But this is the point I don't understand. Say, for instance, they come and give you a two-dollar raise on your check, like the cost of living is high. What good is it going to do you? You're still in bad shape. You still can't get the things you want to eat 'cause they, the Housing Authority, got it."

That tenant isn't the only one who can't understand how the

rental policies operate for welfare recipients; very few other people can either, including many government officials. But she is wrong in her belief that the origins of the policy can be traced to an agreement between two people in the City Housing Authority and the county welfare department. Actually, the policy originated at the federal level and is another instance of how the unquestioning acceptance of the values of the market system produces inexorable tensions. And to make the situation even worse, the development of the policy also reveals not only a lack of coordination among different government agencies, but a total ignorance of each others' operations.

The first assumption underlying the increased rents paid by welfare recipients is that public housing *must* support itself from its rentals. Because of this policy either rents for all the tenants must be raised to pay operating costs as those costs increase, or one group of tenants must pay more than another to help balance the varying amounts paid by the poorer group. So, insane as it appears, in public housing welfare recipients are treated as if they were richer than the other tenants, although actually their real income is usually less and certainly no more than that of the non-recipient tenants. Rentals for welfare families are set at flat rates, in proportion not to income but to apartment size, and the flat rates are fixed at what the Housing Authority states to be the actual operating costs of the apartments.

In 1957, because housing projects all over the country were getting increasing numbers of welfare recipients as tenants, the Public Housing Administration of the Housing and Home Finance Agency established a set of regulations to guide local housing authorities in determining the rents recipients should pay. The regulations stated: "Wherever possible Local Authorities negotiate special agreements with relief agencies providing for flat amounts of rent in the family budgets of their clients . . ."

The requirements laid down by the PHA for the local authorities included: "The amount of rent to be charged such families shall not be less than the rent which would be charged if the same amount of income were received entirely from non-relief sources.

In no event may such schedule be less than the established minimum rent."

The PHA then went on to say, "It is not the function of the Public Housing Administration to augment or supplement the funds of local relief agencies by providing housing, for welfare recipients, at a lesser amount than such agencies normally allow for private housing. Therefore, Local Authorities shall not agree to any flat Welfare rents which are less than the average rent the Welfare Agency will allow families for private housing."

The U.S. Department of Health, Education and Welfare dutifully passed on the PHA regulations to the California State Department of Social Welfare, telling it that the reasons for the policy were that the federal housing agency had "advised local authorities that low-cost housing must be financially solvent" and that the agency had also "advised us that the higher the proportion of assistance recipients in low-cost housing developments, the greater the cost of operations becuse of the attendant social services and other costs which result."

The HEW director continued: "Although we recognize that there are some inequities inherent in this policy, we believe there is sufficient latitude in the Federal policy to allow State and local welfare agencies to negotiate with local authorities on the rentals to be charged." The directive ended with the comment that the federal housing agency policy "is so firmly fixed we have doubt we can change it and thus the best prospect for success lies in State and local negotiation."

In all the discussion between bureau chiefs of various agencies, not much seemed to have been said about the possible consequences of the policy for the recipients. As always, it was assumed that since the government was providing the money, the recipients were not entitled to much consideration in how it was to be disposed of, much less a voice in making the decision.

As dutiful as the Department of Health, Education and Welfare, the State Department of Social Welfare passed down the word it had received to the county welfare departments, adding its own suggestion that the counties "give consideration" to determining the rental plan on the size of the unit, rather than the number of people who occupied it. And so eventually the special policy for recipients went into effect in Los Angeles, to the confusion of all the tenants.

More than eight years later representatives of the state welfare department again met with their FHA counterparts to discuss the question of welfare recipients' rents, especially those being paid by the AFDC families. The state officials' report of the discussion points out: "We interpreted to the federal staff something that they were not previously aware of: that is, the AFDC need standard is based upon a combination of items and the grant does not vary with the amount of rent paid. We also explained the difference between total need and maximum participating base in AFDC."

But even after the FHA representatives discovered that California families on AFDC do not necessarily receive what they "need" if the amount needed is above the maximum set by the state legislature, the situation for the tenants remains unchanged. The financial solvency of the projects, rather than the needs of the human beings who live in the projects, remains the basic determinant of the federal agency's policy.

"I don't appreciate this," says one of the women who are the victims of the government's policy. "And every woman that I've talked to, we don't appreciate it. Not only AFDC mothers but this goes for them with husbands in the home also when they get a litttle ahead. We wouldn't be here if we could afford a private home. We're here to try to make it and try to live. But every nickel we get, the office gets, the Housing Authority gets, every nickel."

One fact emerges from all the bureaucratic relationships or lack of them between the government agencies concerned with public housing: no agency feels responsibility for the character of the tenants' or recipients' daily lives. When the government set a flat rent at operating cost for welfare recipients, it gave little or no consideration to the social consequences of its policy for the tenants in the project; when the county welfare department agreed to the policy, it was responding to another set of bureaucratic pressures and never examined the consequences of its actions.

And so the endless downward-spiralling process continues in the projects. To live in public housing in Los Angeles has become a mark of shame, for it means that one has no effective voice in determining the conditions of his own life in one of its most important aspects—the living space that each human being needs. Inside the projects there are some community activities going on that involve some of the tenants; and the overwhelming majority of the tenants are decent people, trying hard to make decent homes for themselves and their children. But they must live in close contact with the antisocial personalities who flourish in such atmospheres. And because the projects are so often isolated, even within the ghettos, they become havens and sanctuaries for the hoodlums and criminals of the area who use the projects as their own base of operations, the parking lots as a place to strip cars, the playground for glue sniffing, the bushes as a cover from which to venture out to snatch a purse and flee to a waiting car.

And unless the mother or the parents are able to battle continuously against almost overwhelming enemies for the minds and souls of their families, the children of the projects grow up in a world in which government is the enemy and society is only a large replica of the jungle the projects have become.

Segregated housing in the cities is the most visible manifestation of the social disease from which America suffers; segregated public housing in the cities shows the disease in its most virulent and noxious form. And the existence of segregated public housing is the fault of the government, just as government must accept a major portion of the blame for the continuation of segregation in private housing.

Health and Medical Care

The long bench was crowded with people waiting for their names to be called by the nurses who popped in and out of the examining-room doors. Many of the people seemed to know each other by sight if not by name; they talked volubly of their current conditions, interrupting each other as they vied in giving the minutiae of their ills and complaints.

Physically it might have been a clinic at the Kaiser Foundation, where I go for treatment of my ailments, instead of at a county general hospital—but there were differences, some obvious, some more subtle. One of the obvious was length of waiting time. At Kaiser you rarely wait more than ten or fifteen minutes if you have an appointment, and perhaps a half hour at the most if you go without an appointment to the drop-in clinic. But at the county hospital, people with appointments waited an hour or an hour and a half before the nurse called them to the examining room, where they might wait an additional fifteen or twenty minutes. Waiting time at the pharmacy, too, is very noticeably different: at Kaiser, I've occasionally had to wait as long as twenty minutes; at the county hospital the pharmacy wait can easily be as long as two hours.

But the contrast between the atmosphere of the two clinics is *what is even more revealing. There is some social distance between the medical professionals and the patients in any clinic situation, but at Kaiser that distance is diminished by the fact that I pay Kaiser $200 a year plus $1 a visit. The doctors, nurses, and administrative staff are my employees, at least in the sense that I can change doctors at will or inquire of the administrative staff about why new procedures are instituted. Kaiser is still far short of what a medical plan ought to be, and it should have some means for patients to influence its procedures, but at least there is a small measure of reserve power in the patient's hands.*

Not at the county hospital. As I sat, waiting for my turn to be examined, I felt as helpless, temporarily, as the woman next to me who was complaining bitterly about the way "they" were treating her. At best any patient has little control over his own fate when he gives over decision-making to the doctor, but in a public clinic the patients are prisoners, for they have no alternatives.

And their prisoner status is recognized by everyone involved in public medical care. It was not until after I had left the clinic and got back into my car that I felt a sense of relief and realized how grateful all of us who don't use public clinics ought to be.

The relationship between a police department and society must, to some degree, always be abrasive. The welfare department, too, will probably always have some abrasive elements in its operations, and perhaps the most that can be hoped for is that it remain neutral in its relations with those who must deal with it.

But the institutions of health and medical care ought not and need not be either abrasive or neutral. They should be supportive because for anyone, rich or poor, sickness is an abnormal condition of the body and soul, a dysfunction with profound consequences: pain begets fright, panic, and the terrifying fear of death. The social health of a society is linked to the physical health of the individuals in it. Rabbi Abraham Joshua Heschel has said: "The patient is a person. A person is not a combination of body and soul but rather the body and soul as one. Health is profoundly related to one's way of thinking, to one's sense of values; physical well-being and the chemistry of the body are not independent of the condition of the inner man."

Two systems of health and medical care prevail in Los Angeles, as they do throughout the country, and one of them, the public system, upon which hundreds of thousands of people depend, does *not* give help and support to those who need it most. Public medicine is not only inadequate but feared—and with good reason.

As yet in America health and medical care have never been considered part of every citizen's birthright. Just as the nation's public welfare laws are derived from and operate in the spirit of the Elizabethan Poor Laws, so the practice of medicine and the care of health have developed within the context of the private fee system for doctors. In America the physicians' hold over the practice of medicine is complete: they set fees, coerce the hospitals, control the medical schools, and maintain a powerful political lobby to make certain that the economics of scarcity dominate their profession.

Thus, despite the increased need for medical care growing from an increase in knowledge about the body and mind, the ratio of doctors trained by medical schools has *declined* since 1900 rather than increased in proportion to the population. In 1900 there were 157 physicians per 100,000 people; in 1960 there were 133 per 100,000; on the basis of present medical school enrollment the ratio will drop still more by 1975, to about 126 per 100,000.

Under ideal circumstances health must be viewed as a dynamic condition, a continuum in which the doctor is part of the citizens' normal lives, seeing them regularly, rather than only when sickness comes. New data indicate the possibilty that even a disease like cancer might be related to a *general* state of health and is therefore more prevalent among the poor; among the non-poor, certainly, the possibility of early detection is far greater. Health education, ideally, is an integral part of the whole educational process, and the entire community is viewed as one integrated health unit whose parts affect each other. And ideally, if a healthy person does sicken, the doctor follows the patient no matter where the treatment takes him. If a patient must be hospitalized, the doctor also goes to the hospital, and the patient's family is included in the hospital experience, for now it is understood that when people are hospitalized, they take their problems with them. If specialists are required for the treatment, the patient's own doctor works with the specialist, and if post-hospital care is needed, that too becomes the doctor's responsibility. Theoretically, the emphasis is on the continuum, on maintaining a continuity of care that brings with it confidence.

All of American medicine today falls far short of this ideal, but however short it may fall even for those who can afford private care, many of the people in the cities *do* have at least adequate medical coverage available to them. The satellite communities have enough neighborhood doctors, medical buildings, and private clinics to serve their population without difficulties. Medical plans maintain neighborhood clinics, and many white Americans have health insurance. Dentists abound, and every city has its drugstores that look like supermarkets.

But even under the most ideal circumstances both the private fee and public systems of medicine deprive the poor of proper health and medical care. In the ghettos the people see a doctor only when they are sick, and then generally only for a hurried, impersonal visit in a very crowded office or outpatient clinic. Treated without dignity in all of their medical care, they are consequently deprived of it. If they must be hospitalized, their families cannot be with them to help ease the burden of the experience, and they often leave without any sense of post-hospital needs. If they are lucky, their disease will have been treated well; but they will surely have been treated badly as human beings.

Among the poor, and especially among the minority poor, health and medical care is a gamble whose odds are stacked heavily against them from birth. In the two large Negro ghettos the ratio of private doctors to the population averages two-thirds *lower* than that in the rest of the county. And most of the doctors who do practice inside the ghetto live outside it, so that the physician is not part of the community in any role other than his white-coated professional one. Again, Los Angeles is no more than a typical instance of what has happened all over America.

But the people in the ghettos suffer from more than a small number of doctors, for few of the private doctors who do serve them have the professional qualifications of those practicing in other parts of the cities. In Los Angeles, only 16 per cent of the 106 doctors in the two Negro ghettos are specialists, as compared with 55 per cent for the rest of the population; and of the 17 specialists in the Negro ghettos, only 5 have been certified as such by the specialty boards. In the central Mexican-American barrio of East Los Angeles there are no pediatric specialists.

"There's only a few of the doctors down here that cares about us," says an old man who has lived most of his life inside the ghetto. "The rest of them jes' wants to get the money. And plenty of times they cheatin' the county, claiming they given you a treatment you ain't never had. And another thing, first chance they get, they move out of here and go live someplace else, so you never can get them except in their offices."

Like the private physicians, the private hospitals in the ghettos are too few in number for the population, and the quality of the service they offer is much lower than non-ghetto hospitals. Eight private hospitals ring the Negro ghetto, but only two have been approved by the Joint Committee on Accreditation of Hospitals. In the others, inspection reports show that mouse droppings were found in a kitchen, drugs are stored with foods, cockroaches scurry around coffee urns, no nurses are on duty at night, the nurse-call signals are broken, no reports are kept on cases (which is illegal), no written manuals exist for maternity nursing procedures, and formulas for infants are not recorded (also illegal).

The conditions listed in some of these private hospitals by California Department of Health inspectors include food stored under sewage lines, baby formulas kept with narcotics, no registered nurses on duty in the newborn nursery or maternity ward, broken disinfecting equipment, pigeon droppings on the kitchen windowsill, infected dressings thrown on the floors, X-ray room not shielded, no health examination for the personnel, unvented gas heaters, leaky roofs, uncovered and unclean garbage cans attracting hordes of flies, no fans in rooms requiring mechanical ventilation, uncovered foods kept in unclean refrigerators, baby formulas not tested for bacteria, etc., etc., etc.

Year after year the same reports are made by the inspection teams, and the hospitals do little or nothing to change the situation. Only in very rare cases is the Department of Health's power to close down a hospital exercised; indeed, the kind of relationship that exists between the private hospitals and the department is best demonstrated by the fact that the department routinely informs the hospitals in advance of the date of the annual inspection.

Meanwhile, the few accredited hospitals near the ghettos had fewer Negro patients: from 1960 to 1965 the number of Negro physicians on the active medical staff of the biggest accredited private hospital near the ghetto dropped because, according to the doctors, their patients couldn't afford the steadily rising hospital costs. Seventy per cent of all Americans pay part of the increasing hospital and medical costs with prepaid health plans, but it is estimated that until Medicare came into existence in 1966 less than 20 per cent of the ghetto citizens had any form of health insurance.

The ghettos also contain a few small private nursing homes, with a total of 305 beds. Such institutions aren't very good at best, and those in or near the ghetto are considered to be well below even the low average quality. "If you want someone to die, you just put them in one of those places," says a woman, "and sure enough, they'll die."

The picture of private medical care always includes the neighborhood druggist, too. But there are only eleven drugstores in the two large Negro ghettos, two of which are reported to overcharge consistently for drugs and supplies.

The lack of private physicians, private clinics, hospitals, medical plans, and druggists is matched by the lack of private dental care. In fact, the number of dentists practicing in the ghettos is even smaller, proportionately, than the number of doctors: there are four and a half times fewer dentists serving the ghetto population than are found in the other areas of Los Angeles. And while some public facilities exist for medical treatment, almost no public dental care is available.

Thus, not just "Blue Cross" is a meaningless phrase to the poor; "See your dentist every six months" has as little significance. The idea of dental visits is so foreign to the children of the poor that when free dental care was provided for those teen-agers bright enough to be selected for the Upward Bound college training projects, some of them stubbornly refused to go to the dentist even when they were faced with the threat of being dropped from the project if they did not accept the care. And what other behavior could be expected of sixteen-year-olds who have never been to a dentist and have only rarely seen a doctor? The Upward Bound teenagers were more accustomed to deprivation of health services than were the small children in Los Angeles' Head Start program, but both groups were in need of routine care. Among the Head Start children, 62 per cent suffered from malnutrition.

And the lack of adequate private health, medical, and dental care is not compensated for in Los Angeles for the minority poor by tax-supported facilities or those offered by voluntary social welfare agencies. When the poor get sick, especially the minority poor whose general health is bad anyway, the already distressing physical illness becomes a bitter social experience, another of the frustrations and traumas that have brought about social revolts.

The inadequate and abrasive qualities that private medicine has for the poor in the cities are equally characteristic of the way in which public health and medical services are made available to them. First, even before they can make use of whatever public services are provided, they must pass (fail would be a more accurate word) a means test; unless they are acutely ill they must prove that because of unemployment, disability, age, or dependency they cannot afford to pay for medical and health care. Once they establish their condition of pauperdom to the program's administrators—the same group of county officials who are concerned, above all, with saving rather than spending tax funds—they are given medical care for their specific illness, but little or nothing is done to prevent them from getting ill again.

Furthermore, the health and medical care available in the United States to those who, for any reason, cannot afford the private fee system is based on a different set of moral standards than those which operate for the rest of society.

In New York City, for example, the ratio of therapeutic abortions ordered by physicians is in direct and startling proportion to the patients' incomes: therapeutic abortions were performed on 3.9 per 1,000 persons able to afford private hospitals, on 2.4 per 1,000 persons in private rooms in voluntary hospitals, and 0.1 per 1,000 poor patients in the municipal hospitals. In Connecticut the now unconstitutional anti-contraception laws were enforced only in the public clinics, thus making certain that the people most in need of birth control information were deprived of it.

One common thread runs through all the services given those directly dependent upon public funds for their health care— the services are fragmentary, discontinuous, inadequate, and tension-creating. And the bitter resistance of organized medicine to any attempt to alleviate these conditions is one of the most characteristic features of American political life. But whatever the overall disturbing consequences of the American Medical Association's policy are for the country at large, in the poverty areas health care has been another source of tension and frustration. These are particularly apparent in Los Angeles, where the control of the public sector of medicine is shared jointly by physicians and the County Supervisors.

There is a natural converging of interests between the two groups. The doctors, private hospital boards, prepaid health insurance companies, and the business groups involved in health services all have a vested interest in keeping medical care a private industry; the County Supervisors share the interest, for they want to keep down the expenditures of public tax funds used for those who cannot afford the price of private free-enterprise medicine.

Physically and in almost every other way the private and public systems of medicine are separated. The Los Angeles County General Hospital, for example, with more than two thousand beds, is used by the poor, while facilities for the poor patients do not exist in private hospitals, except for a few so-called "charity" or clinic beds and a few outpatient clinics. The kind of medical care given the poor, too, in the public sector is hardly the equal of what is available in the private fee system.

In fact, about the only way for the poor to get proper medical care in Los Angeles is to become acutely ill or have a bad accident on a freeway. If that happens, and especially if the wrecked cars are blocking a traffic lane, the victims of the accident will be taken off the freeway in a matter of minutes and rushed to a hospital emergency room. Then, if their injuries are not only critical but are also "interesting" ones from a medical viewpoint, the patients will get conscientious attention from doctors and nurses. But the kind of care given to those having accidents on the freeways is the apex of medical service for the poor in Los Angeles. After that it's all downhill.

The primary source of public medical care for the poor, especially the minority poor, is the county hospital, where under certain conditions they do get better medical care than they might receive from private physicians. But just getting to the hospital from the Negro ghettos in the city's south and southeast sections is difficult and expensive for those without their own cars. Until recently such a bus ride took from an hour to an hour and a half on buses which ran infrequently; it also meant changing from one bus line to another, and paying at least a dollar and usually more in fares for each round trip. Direct bus service from the south to the hospital was begun only after the August 1965 upheaval; but since the schedules were designed to bring people to the hospital clinics which are open only on weekdays, those buses do not run on weekends at all.

There is another large public hospital, Harbor General, closer to the south and southeast ghettos than Los Angeles General, but until 1966 the hospital service area boundaries drawn up by the county kept the people who live in those areas out of Harbor General's district. In extraordinary emergencies treatment could be obtained at Harbor General, but would-be patients were usually referred to Los Angeles General. (One man in the area who refused to take his children to Los Angeles General solved his referral problem by having only enough gas in his car to get him to Harbor General.)

A much smaller facility, the John Wesley Hospital, is at the edge of the ghetto, but its bed space and its facilities for the treatment of acute illness are so limited that it can accommodate only a tiny percentage of the patients who need care. Thus, Los Angeles General is the only "family doctor" known to the poor, the basic medical resource both for outpatient and hospital care. In 1965 more than 19,000 operations were performed there, more than 750,000 outpatient visits were made to its clinics, and 205,305 visits to its emergency rooms. For better or worse, Los Angeles General Hospital has been the *only* doctor, nurse, and hospital for most of the poor in Los Angeles, just as the San Francisco General Hospital has played the same role for the poor of that city, and other similar hospitals have performed similar functions in cities all over the United States.

The majority of the Negro and Mexican-American children born in Los Angeles County were born in Los Angeles General; 40 per cent of all the people hospitalized from the ghettos were bedded down there; 56 per cent of all the pediatric admitting-room visits at Los Angeles General Hospital were made by Negroes, although they represent only 7 per cent of the county's population, while 29.6 per cent of the visits came from Mexican-Americans, although they represent only 8.5 per cent of the population.

In the characteristic pattern of Los Angeles everything about its general hospital is oversize. With twenty-eight hundred beds it is probably the biggest general hospital in the world; its physical plant extends over seventy-six acres, and its main unit comprises two million square feet. Its outpatient clinics serve a larger population than any other hospital in the United States; it even manufactures its own drugs, and it fills more prescriptions than any other pharmacy in the world. One of its top staff comments that he wishes LAGH treated its patients as well as it treats diseases, a view shared by many people in the ghettos.

"The hospital, it's terrible, just terrible," says a woman. "I went in on Friday night at eleven and they took me right away because I had a bad pus tube. It was about two-thirty when I come to on Saturday afternoon. I was on bed rest and I went to about five-thirty before I could get a bedpan, and I didn't get no water at all that evening to wash my face or anything like that. The toilet system was terrible. They were nasty. Most everybody on the ward where I was, they was having—what do you call these things? —hysteramies, and that other thing that go along with it, well, most of them were using some things and they were laying all over the toilet and everywhere, and the toilet didn't get cleaned up in about three days, and then they had to complain.

"You never see a nurse as such unless they have a pill or something. That's all. Sometimes you get your bed made up and sometimes you didn't. And the food was terrible. Most of the time I was on low sodium and they didn't never have enough for a low sodium and you know low sodium ain't suppose to eat no jive, ham and wieners and franks, and that's what I got every time I ate."

At Los Angeles General bad patient care begins at the front steps. To get into the front entrance of the Los Angeles General Hospital, patients walk across a concrete pavement and then climb a flight of wide stone steps leading up to the hospital. A nearby elevator, rising only one story, is unused, and the sick people drag themselves up by the steps, stopping every few feet to catch their breath. After they have climbed the steps they get to the entrance of the main unit. From there they have to walk more than a quarter of a mile to reach the clinic building.

When the Los Angeles General Hospital was designed, front steps were obviously of no importance, in human terms, to either the architects or the hospital authorities. The notion that climbing stairs might be difficult for the sick people who were to use the hospital probably never occurred to them. While today, because of routes and schedules, some buses bringing the patients to the hospital are able to discharge their passengers at the entrance to the clinic building, where there are no steps, the old design of LAGH requires hundreds of other bus riders to use the front entrance.

Hospitals are never pleasant places to be under any circumstances, but the physical facilities of the Los Angeles General Hospital are an example of the real contempt in which the poor are held in America. With the exception of one five hundred-bed medical and surgical unit and its pediatric and psychiatric facilities, the hospital has hardly been able to improve its plant since 1932, although it is serving three times as many people. Los Angeles General Hospital is prevented from being far worse than it is only by its often dedicated but overworked and underpaid interns, resident physicians, nurses, and its permanent staff.

In some of the hospital wards ten beds are being used, separated from each other only by hanging canvas curtains, in a space designed to crowd four or at most six patients. Even getting to the wards is an agonizing process, for there are too few elevators carrying too many people. In the wards the beds are old and creaky. The rooms are dark and dirty, the floors unswept. All have a single toilet and a single shower to serve each complex of thirty to forty patients. In some of the wings beds are jammed together in the halls; in the electrocardiogram room a weary doctor goes though a fat mass of EKGs, giving each as much study as he can in the limited time available to him. "It's mass production reading," he says, with a grim smile, acutely conscious of the fact that despite a very high rate of myocardial infarctions, it is impossible for a heart patient to get proper care at the Los Angeles General. After all, how can complete quiet and bed rest be given ten patients crowded into four hundred square feet?

The pediatric facilities are much better than those available for adults. Children up to the age of fourteen are hospitalized in a separate and much newer building with much less crowding in the wards and a larger staff, proportionately, than is found in the general hospital itself. But even the pediatric facilities are bare, without sufficient bedside furniture to soften the chilling hospital atmosphere.

From an intern's viewpoint Los Angeles General is an ideal learning situation. Few other hospitals in the world offer so wide a range of cases, and few other institutions provide better or more dedicated teachers; for Los Angeles General is a teaching hospital, operated jointly by the Department of Charities, the University of Southern California Medical School, and the California College of Medicine of the University of California.

The hospital offers something else to those interns concerned with the problems of community medicine: most of its permanent staff are examples of the best tradition of medicine, men and women who have given up far more lucrative careers in private practice to devote their best years to the care of the poor. The staff knows how inadequate the hospital facilities are, knows that many of their patients are discharged before they should be because of the bed shortage, and knows how much more should be done to give proper medical care; in medicine only the best is good enough, and less than the best may mean death. Not so much can be said for the thousands of private physcans of Los Angeles; two thousand of them voluntarily spend from four to eight hours a week at the hospital in teaching and patient services, but many thousands more resist any increase in public hospital facilities.

A young woman who lives in a housing project speaks: "I would like to say that the conditions at the county hospital are bad. What we need are more county hospitals because the county hospital is not able to take care of all the people. Say, for instance, suppose everybody that lives here in the project used the county hospital. There are eleven hundred units in this project, and what we need are more hospitals. And what the hospitals need to do is hire more help because like it is now, they really can't."

It *is* extremely difficult for the hospital to recruit employees for kitchen, laundry, or orderly work, to cite a few examples, since the wage levels set by the county administration are so low.

"We have had people who worked for the county for years and years in the most difficult hard labor possible getting three hundred dollars a month," stated one county supervisor in May 1965, when he wanted to increase the pay of hospital workers by thirty dollars a month. "But," he continued, "every year on the board it is a struggle to pay the minimum wage; every year we have resentment by the chief administrative officer, but I think there is some responsibility to a living wage, and I think there is some responsibility for paying a human being a decent salary."

The supervisor's efforts to raise the pay by $30 a month failed; instead, the salaries of the custodians, porters, laundry workers, and seamstresses were increased by only $19, still keeping them below the poverty lines set by the federal government.

The result of the help shortage in the county hospital shows up most clearly in the handling of routine cases. "It takes a long time for them to wait on you," says a mother, describing what happened when she gave birth at the hospital, "and, like, usually you're in a ward. Now when I had my oldest child—that was about eight years ago—I was in a ward with about twenty other people, you know, because that night people were having babies.

After the delivery they treated the baby good because they forgot me. They gave the baby all their attention but they forgot all about me."

In all probability the nurses and orderlies did not forget all about that woman; but since the amount of nursing care given to a patient at Los Angeles General averages only three hours per day as compared with four or five hours at private hospitals, obviously only the sickest patients are going to get the kind of nursing care they need. Indeed, since the three hours represents an average, some patients get an hour or even less of nursing care, despite the fact that anyone admitted to the hospital must need to be there. And the inability to serve patients properly disturbs many nurses, enough to cause them to resign.

The hospital's lack of coordinated ambulance facilities is another of the agonizing experiences faced by the poor.

"My mother was visiting me," says one woman who lives far south of Los Angeles General, "and she has diabetes. Well, she had an insulin reaction one night—you know, when you go into a coma and you can die. We called for an ambulance from General Hospital but they sent one from the Central Receiving Hospital downtown. The ambulance came and my mother was very sick and we were very scared, and they went upstairs and they told us my mother was having an insulin reaction but they couldn't take her to the hospital. They couldn't take her to Central Receiving because it wouldn't be anything they could do there."

"You see, at Central Receiving, if you get hit by a car, that's an emergency and they can work with you. But the ambulance man told me that at Central Receiving it was nothing they could do for her. You see, she was sick and she would have to be hospitalized for a long time, whereas when they take you to the Receiving Hospital—if you are hit by a car or something, they'll take you to the Receiving Hospital—they'll give you first aid and they'll transfer you. But she didn't need any first aid or anything like that, and the ambulance man said, 'Well, she's having an insulin reaction but there's nothing we can do. We can't take her as far as General.' So I called my sister and she came over, and we took her in the car to the hospital."

"They don't carry doctors on the ambulances like they do on General Hospital on TV," adds a man. "On TV the doctor, he rides with the ambulance. They get a call and the ambulance takes off and the doctor's sitting right up there on TV, but they don't do that in real life."

Another woman tells of her experience when her child was hit by a car while playing in the street outside the house: "My daughter got hit by a car and some ambulance picked her up and took her to one hospital, and then after she got there called another ambulance; she didn't go to the same ambulance. Didn't go to the same, they called another one. It came from General and he had a whole lot of people, you know they stack them in, some on the top and others on the bottom. She must have got hit about one-thirty and they must have picked us up at Morningside about three, and it was eleven before they had it fixed, before her leg was put into traction."

The descriptions are accurate: ambulances from Los Angeles General are not allowed to operate on a routine emergency basis in the area, while the Central Receiving Hospital handles only emergency first-aid cases, and the private ambulance companies require either payment in cash for their services or prior authorization by an LAGH admitting physician which allows the county to pay the bill.

Patients who do get to Los Angeles General get there later and more critically ill than those who can afford to use the private hospitals. And the results of these conditions are clearly visible in the higher percentages of acutely ill patients at Los Angeles General than at the private hospitals.

A revealing illustration of how indigent citizens are normally treated was provided from May 27 to June 3, 1965, when a group of angry interns and residents at the Los Angeles County General Hospital began a "heal-in" at the hospital as a protest against the failure of the County Board of Supervisors to grant them the wage increase they had been promised more than a year earlier.

The technique of the "heal-in" was simple: the doctors refused to discharge from the hospital those patients who were *legitimately* entitled to remain there by reason of their illness. Normally, as the doctors pointed out, it is necessary for patients at Los Angeles General to be discharged *before* they are sufficiently healed, in order to accommodate new patients. And if the premature discharges were not made, threatened the doctors, the hospital would be so jammed within twenty-four hours that no new patients could be admitted.

The "heal-in" was very successful. The Board of Supervisors, under the pressure of a jammed hospital, did find funds to meet the increased monthly salaries of the group. The doctors immediately went back to the normal practices of turning out their indigent patients before they were medically ready for discharge.

The contrast between the kind of health and medical care available to those who can pay and those who can not is shown most clearly in that normal and usually joyful part of family life—having a baby.

When a woman living in the white sections of the cities becomes pregnant, her family doctor usually refers her to an obstetrician, who then sees her regularly. When the time for delivery comes, the obstetrician, now thoroughly familiar with the details of her condition, is with her in the hospital to deliver the baby. Once the baby is born she is under care of the same kind, and a pediatrician joins the obstetrician in seeing mother and child on a regular basis; as the child grows a dentist also becomes part of its life. And if the mother ever feels that the doctor is not treating the child properly or keeps them waiting too long, she is free to choose another physician.

But if a woman living in the poor Mexican-American or Negro ghettos of Los Angeles becomes pregnant and is unable to pay for private medical care, pregnancy becomes a frightening and dangerous illness. When she discovers her pregnancy, she goes to one of the weekly prenatal clinics operated in the ghettos by the County Health Department, if she knows the clinics exist. Until the August 1965 events she could only register but not see a doctor on her first clinic visit; now she gets to see a doctor during the first visit, rather than several weeks later. Three weeks later she returns to the clinic, this time for an interview with a county social worker to determine whether or not she really is eligible for medical care at the clinic. And since the waiting time during clinic visits can take up the entire day, she has to make all sorts of complicated arrangements for leaving her other children with neighbors as well as get someone to drive her to the clinic and then come back to get her hours later.

"They give everybody an eight-o'clock appointment in that clinic," says one mother bitterly. "Eight A.M. in the morning, everybody have eight A.M. in the morning. And so you get there at eight and you get out at six. And on the date you're due, the date before you're due, on your last visit to the clinic, they give you a paper to take into the hospital and it has all your records on it and everything. But it don't seem to matter much if you take the paper with you or not."

"Now when I went into the General to have my baby," says another mother, "I didn't go in by myself, but they put me on a table because I was, you know, ready to have it but I wasn't in pain. And after they examined me they put me on a stretcher with a red blanket. Now, this is supposed to be an *emergency*. After they examined me, well, true, my pains did start, you know. And my baby was overdue and he was coming. And they're—I'm still layin' on the cart and calling somebody to come help me, and they're walking around like I wasn't even there. So when they came in, they finally took me around to X-ray. They took me to X-ray and brought me back. I laid on the table and then they found out the baby was breech and they had to turn the baby around. But see, all this *time* elapsed in between. I'm waiting here for them to turn the baby around—waiting for X-rays. I'm still hurtin', you know, and the baby's still comin'. 'Oh, the baby's not comin', you're not ready,' but I *know,* I know when the baby's coming. But they tell you what you don't feel, like they're laying there having the baby, you know, like they're feeling the pain.

"So, when they got—when they turned the baby around, the pains really started coming. The baby was almost here, halfway here, and I keep telling them—they didn't give me anything, they just turned the baby around, and that is hell, you know, that is hell. And they had strapped me down. And I laid there until the baby was born in the bed. I kept telling them the baby was coming.

And they kept saying the baby wasn't coming, but the baby was there, laying right there. So that's General. But after that I swore off—I wouldn't go. I didn't care what kind of emergency I had. I would borrow, beg, or steal the money before I'd go over to the big General. And I have been going to the General ever since my mother was takin' us. And I remember sittin' up in that long hall with all those beds with all the people, just sittin', sittin', sittin'. And I said—but when I had to go with my oldest child, that's because I *had* to go—other than that, I am not going. If I have to beg, borrow, or steal the money."

The best indicator of the contrast in medical care given pregnant women is that the maternal death rate in the predominantly Negro south health district is two and a half times that of the county as a whole; the rate of premature babies born in the district nearly twice that of the county; fetal deaths average nearly 50 per cent higher; infant mortality, the single most reliable indicator of general health conditions, is 40 per cent higher in the ghetto than outside it. And these figures do not mirror even the statistical realities, for if the rates in the Negro and Mexican ghettos were excluded from the county averages, the contrast in the rates of mothers and children surviving at birth between the minority poor and the rest of the city would be even sharper.

In fact, the people living in the poor southern section of wealthy Los Angeles have about the same amount of health care available to them as do the people who live in poor areas of Greece. The difference is, of course, that no organization takes ads in the *New Yorker* to plead for help for the children of the Watts area as they do for the poor children of Athens. For example, the poor children of Los Angeles get only a very limited amount of routine pediatric care made available at the Well Baby clinics held in the districts. Normally, there is a six-week waiting period before a new baby is admitted to the clinics; only babies under one year are admitted to them, and they are able to go only until their second birthdays.

The clinic routine consists of an initial interview with a public health nurse, a weighing of the baby, and then an examination with immunization shots by a doctor. The first visit with the doctor takes ten minutes; five minutes are given to each subsequent visit.

Most of the doctors who serve the clinics are general practitioners, taking time out from their private practices. And to get that five-minute session with a doctor, the mothers and their babies must often wait hours and hours in the clinic. "I get there at twelve-thirty and I leave at four," says one mother. "The clinic is one day a week for the whole neighborhood, and sometimes they have only one doctor. And in this particular project you got eleven hundred and ten families and you got about three thousand and ninety kids from the ages of one week old up." But despite the long waits they know they will have, despite the difficulties of getting transportation to the clinics, and despite the totally inadequate examination time given to their little babies, between 45 and 50 per cent of the newborn babies in the south and southeast area are taken to a Well Baby clinic at least once in the first year of their lives.

Typically, too, a mother will take her child to the Well Baby clinic for immunization only to be told that the baby is running a fever and cannot be injected. But to get treatment for the baby's fever, the mother must take her child to a hospital outpatient clinic where only sick babies are treated. After the baby is well again, she can return to the Well Baby clinic for the immunization. And if she has more than one child, getting each of them immunized under such conditions is so difficult, time-consuming, and expensive in bus fares that of all the children given emergency pediatric treatment at Los Angeles General only 60 per cent had been adequately immunized against diphtheria, whooping cough, and tetanus; only 50 per cent were protected against smallpox; only 57 per cent had received the proper doses of polio vaccine, and only 6 per cent had been vaccinated against measles.

Once the children have reached age two, there are no public facilities available for pediatric examinations until they reach school age.

When the children reach school age, they may get only a brief examination by the school nurse on entering school, if the school has a nurse, and three times more before they graduate, if they do. They may also get a dental examination, a test for tuberculosis, and certain immunizations. Like the sick infants who cannot be treated at the Well Baby clinic, the sick older children must be taken to still another facility. Where? In an emergency, the primary source of medical help for the poor children of Los Angeles is the Pediatric Emergency Room of the Los Angeles General Hospital. Such treatment destroys any possibility of the continuous, normal relationship with a doctor that is so important in providing a long-term view of a child's growth and development.

Hundreds of children are brought to the Los Angeles General Hospital every day by their parents, the overwhelming majority of whom are Negroes and Mexican-Americans. Many of the Mexican-American parents don't speak English, and a good number of them are illiterate in both Spanish and English. More than 50 per cent of the white and Negro parents get some form of welfare benefits; more than 40 per cent of the Mexican-Americans are also dependent upon public support. Unemployment is high among the parents, with the percentage highest among Negro fathers. When either parent is working, it is almost certain to be on a low-paid, unskilled job.

On the average only half of the children brought into the emergency room have ever been seen by a private doctor; a very high percentage were born either at Los Angeles General or at some other public facility, and their primary source of health information since then has been the public health centers. They are younger, too, than the kids who go to private doctors, and they are brought to the hospital only after lengthy discussions by their parents with other members of the family, neighbors, the druggist. For many of the children the trip to the hospital is long and exhausting, involving an uncomfortable bus ride and even changing buses. And the parents' lack of previous health education as well as lack of contact with physicians is attested to by the fact that a quarter of them are brought in for treatment of chronic rather than acute diseases.

Characteristically, too, most of the children are brought to the hospital emergency room for minor rather than serious complaints. But in the absence of any kind of medical care, the parents obviously must choose the kind of disjointed, fragmented attention their children get in the hospital emergency room, where the frightened children are seen by the overworked interns and residents.

Most of the children or adults from the ghettos who require follow-up medical attention go to the outpatient clinics of the Los Angeles General. The main clinics are all located in a 180,000-square-foot modern building a few hundred yards away from the hospital building. Just as the hospital itself is the one used most by the minority poor of Los Angeles, its outpatient clinics are the primary source of continuous medical care for the same people: in 1965 they treated more than 700,000 patients.

American hospital outpatient clinics have been described as "the Siberia of the hospital" by J. J. Vorsimer, a physician in New York. In 1965, 85.5 million outpatient visits were made in the U.S., and, according to the New York physician, the medical care received by the millions of people who use such clinics is "totally inadequate." He charges that this inadequacy exists because of the failure of physicians, hospital boards, and the prepayment planners to develop a program that will provide medically acceptable patient care; because physicians who work in the clinics are more concerned with the disease than with the patient; because the physicians' only interest in doing clinic work is as a means of getting a hospital staff appointment and admitting privileges; and because medical school education, as well as university and professional training for hospital administration, is oriented toward teaching and research with little concern for service. And it could be added that, to date, medical schools have produced no education in community medicine, although the University of Southern California has recently created a department of community medicine in conjunction with its role in establishing a community clinic in the Watts area.

(In recent years not much public attention has been given to the manner in which many medical schools operate, to the detriment of society. Discriminatory racial and religious admission patterns still exist in far too many schools, and the general orientation given the students breeds contempt for the poor.)

And although the clinics at Los Angeles General are not "Siberias," and while the clinic facilities are much better than those at the hospital itself, the experience of being treated there is at best difficult and at worst traumatic.

The great distances to be traveled and the inadequate public transportation facilities of Los Angels are a fierce handicap to getting to the clinics for the hundreds of thousands who visit them. It is so difficult, so time-consuming, and so expensive for some people to make the trip from the ghettos that an inevitable tendency develops to avoid going except when the medical problem is so bad that it can no longer be neglected.

Then comes the wait at the clinic itself, which can last from an hour to two or three, although such a long interval before treatment is getting to be less common.

"I have an appointment to the clinic in the morning," says one patient. "I have to be there at eight. So I have to leave home about six-thirty in the morning to get there in time for my appointment. Mind you, now, I have to be there at about eight, but I will not get waited on until maybe ten or later. And I'm not going to get out of that hospital to get back home until after twelve. And if I got to get medicine, I'll be lucky if I get out of there at two."

Tiredly, another regular clinic patient speaks: "They give everybody appointments for eight. Then you have to stand in line for so many hours—well, not so many hours—but after you stand there for half an hour, you feel like you been standing all day. Then they're going to pull your chart and sit you down, and you have to wait. All right, they have so many doctors there, they got so many rooms; they will call you and have you sitting in there, waiting in a room, and the doctors ain't going to come nowhere near you. Then he gonna come in there; if you're laying on a table, he going to look up you and say, 'Okay, go on home,' or maybe he'll give you some kind of medicine, and half the time he don't even know what he's giving it to you for.

"Then you got to go downstairs and sit there and wait, and I sit down there for over two hours for the medicine. And I had told the man that I had been there for over two hours, waitin' on my medicine. He said, 'Well, go home and come back tomorrow.' I told him, 'Look here, where do you think I'm going to get the damn money from? Am I supposed to make it or steal it?' " (In fact, that woman could have received her bus fare, after an interview, from a medical social worker stationed at the hospital. The social worker's function is to determine whether the county or the people using the clinic must pay for their care. Nothing is free at the clinic, even to the very poor, although if they have no money, they will still be taken care of; an attempt will be made later to collect what is owed.)

When the patients are ultimately seen by a doctor, the examination is likely to be a hurried one, for the clinics must serve more patients than its staff and facilities can handle adequately.

The permanent hospital staff is very much aware of the patients' problems at the clinics. "We know we keep the people waiting too long," states one administrator, "and we know that they shouldn't be scheduled for their appointments in lumps the way they are now. But there's very little we can do about it. We're understaffed in the clinics and besides that, it's hard to buck the general attitude that the people who come to the clinic don't have anything better to do with their time than wait, while the doctors' time is very valuable."

The permanent medical and administrative staffs of the clinic try, in other ways and within the limit of the budget allotted them, to make the institution as pleasant as possible for those who use it. There are nurseries to take care of kids while the mothers are waiting for treatment; the hallways and waiting rooms are painted in bright colors, kept clean, and supplied with reasonably comfortable benches.

"When we were holding clinic in the hospital building, before this one was built, conditions were terrible," reports a member of the clinic staff. "All we could do was separate patients being examined from each other with sheets; the rooms were jammed and the whole place was filthy. No one seemed to care, either, and the patients would throw orange peels or cigarette butts all over the floor and any place they happened to be. But since we're in this facility, which can be kept clean a lot more easily, we haven't had that kind of difficulty. The patients put their trash in the cans we provide, and seem to understand why we want the clinic to look like a decent place. What's more, since we've opened up here, we no longer have nearly as many missed or canceled appointments as we did when we were over in the hospital itself."

Another equally characteristic failure of the public hospitals is the lack of proper health education for the patients. The patient's disease is treated when he is sick, but little or no attempt is made either to relate the disease to the general conditions of his life or to equip him with some knowledge of what is required for good health, especially under the difficult physical conditions in which he is so often forced to live. Only the pediatric services at Los Angeles General provide the parents with any education, about chronic childrens' diseases.

There are reasons aside from limited budgets why this education role has not been adopted by the hospitals and physicians. Modern medicine seems to have little understanding of or patience with the special medical problems of the poor, especially the minority poor. It does not take into account the different ways in which different ethnic groups may view concepts of sickness and health, nor does it understand that in the priority system of the poor, health may be put at a different level than is true of the middle-class. And too often, when resistance is encountered among the poor to concepts that have developed as part of the American Way of private fee medicine, the poor are simply dismissed from any further consideration with, "Well, that's all you can expect from them, anyway."

In fact, the physicians, hospitals, and clinics that care for the poor in the cities have had little real connection with the communities they allegedly serve. Until very recently organized medicine in the U.S. was very reluctant to recognize that medical and health knowledge is *not* the exclusive province of the physician, but that many poor people, with only limited educations are capable of understanding in these areas. Now, however, cracks have appeared in the hitherto undivided public stance adopted by the medical establishment in its relationship to the public. The County Medical Associations, once the undisputed single voice of the doctors, no longer have quite the same amount of prestige, and a small but growing number of physicians, medical school leaders, and hospital administrators are beginning to make their voices heard.

The character of most of the medical institutions' leadership is one of the inherent obstacles to making the institutions more responsive to total community needs. On the whole, the men who actively seek to become the leaders of such organizations as the American Medical Association are the older doctors who come to their positions with already fixed ideas about the supremacy of the private fee system of medicine, based on their own success as *practicing* physicians. But once in the leadership role, a good many of them modify their views: the job educates them and they begin to understand the need for developing concepts of community medicine. Unfortunately, just at the point at which they have become aware that society has new needs or that the older needs must be met with new instruments, their terms of office expire and they are replaced. Thus, they are no longer in a position to have much effect upon the policy of their organizations. As a result, those considered by the medical establishment to be medical radicals almost always operate without much support from their organizations.

The power and prestige of the medical establishment extends to its relationship with the institutions of government as well. The California Department of Public Health, for example, is not likely to take a position of active opposition to the County Medical Society, although this is not the only reason the department has failed to play any significant role in protecting the health of ghetto dwellers. The department's primary mission seems to be focused on all kinds of technical matters: problems of smog control, replacement of antiquated X-ray equipment, and safeguarding the water supply, rather than dealing with problems of social policy. The Department of Health gives the narrowest interpretation to its functioning in the field of environmental effects upon health; it takes environment to mean primarily the physical conditions in which the society exists, and it excludes the social ones as being outside its province or mandate.

The presence of the Department of Health in the ghettos is hardly discernible. Department inspectors do check the hospitals and nursing homes once a year, but without much effect upon conditions.

What is true of the California Department of Public Health is even more so of the United States Department of Public Health: the only contact a ghetto inhabitant might have with a U.S. Public Health official would be if a Negro baggage porter at L.A. International Airport brushed by the doctors checking the inoculation records of people arriving from abroad. So even the meager health education and preventive medicine offered is assumed to be the sole jurisdiction of the County Public Health Department, which the Board of Supervisors forces to operate on an extremely small budget.

Except for the general hospital clinics, very few public health services are available in Los Angeles. The County Health Department does operate venereal disease and tuberculosis clinics in the ghetto areas which serve a good many people, but a large number of VD and tuberculosis cases still remain either undiagnosed or untreated.

Very little health service is offered by the Los Angeles school system, either. Except for the routine examinations made four times during the twelve school years, the children's health is assumed to be a family responsibility. Two health centers operated by the Los Angeles PTA do operate in the ghetto areas, with a group of part-time doctors offering the equivalent of about three and a half full-time doctors. But these two centers, plus the skimpy dental and mental health services available, touch the lives of only a tiny portion of the children in need of eyeglasses, dental care, and emotional assistance.

The County Health Department offers one other service to all the poor: a small group of sanitarians inspect the food establishments and houses in the depressed neighborhoods of Los Angeles. But even though conditions in both restaurants and houses are very often utterly deplorable, little can be done to correct the situation, at least in the homes, for many of them are occupied by tenants who move about a good deal and are owned by absentee landlords. And just as in the case of the general hospital staff, the dedication of the sanitarian staff cannot make up for its inadequate size in relation to the number of problems it faces. The basic bureaucratic fear of forcing new programs to open which might offend the Board of Supervisors inhibits the development of any imaginative but possibly more expensive programs for solving the health problems of the area.

The same lack of services in the face of a great demand for them is found in the mental health needs of the poor. It is true that frequently the poor are admitted to state mental institutions with conditions for which middle- and upper-class persons are treated at home or in private hospitals. But the sense of being trapped in any ghetto brings with it the sense of frustration and anger that causes an increase in mental illness. And the mental health statistics of Los Angeles bear out this conclusion, for even taking into account that poor Negroes and Mexican-Americans are sent to state institutions more often than other groups, the admission rates to these institutions from the ghettos are still very much higher than those from other areas in the city.

There are very few other public facilities to which the mentally ill can go for help. Since the PTA School Clinic in the area has available to it the services of less than one full-time psychiatrist, even those few parents who know about the clinic must wait months to get their disturbed children to the doctor. The County Mental Health Department operates a larger clinic, with two full-time psychiatrists and two psychiatric social workers, but the ninety patients a month it admits, almost always on referrals, are only a fraction of the people who need help.

A few months prior to the August 1965 outbreak the county opened a service center near the area with three full-time Negro psychiatrists. Most of the patients were referred by the welfare department, and in its early period the center worked more in consulting with other agencies than in direct therapy.

In all of the public health services offered to a community the essential personnel are the public health nurses. In an area like the Los Angeles ghettos one public health nurse to each 2,000 people would be a reasonable ratio; the actual ratio is one nurse per 5,230 people. The result of this disproportion is that the overworked nurses must spend most of their time in the clinics, leaving them with virtually no opportunity to make home calls or follow up on broken appointments in the VD or tuberculosis clinics.

And behaving in its usual niggardly fashion where the interests of the poor are concerned, the County Board of Supervisors not only refused to give the Health Department enough funds for hiring an additional two hundred nurses in 1965-1966, but acted in such a fashion that fifteen then existing nurse positions were cut out of the budget; salaries, however, were improved as of October 1, 1966.

Before the advent of Medicare, a limited amount of medical care was also available to those persons whose major source of income was the public welfare program. Persons on the Old Age Security, Aid to Families with Dependent Children, Aid to the Blind, Aid to the Totally and Permanently Disabled, and the Medically Indigent Aged programs can be helped with special medical grants, usually administered by county agencies, although most of the funds come from federal and state sources. The state administers a joint federal-state program to help employable disabled people, but such a tiny number of persons in the ghettos have been assisted by this program that it has had hardly any effect.

In most of these programs services rendered are within the private enterprise fee system of medicine; thus, the doctors, dentists, or drugstores are reimbursed by the county for whatever services they give their patients. As a result, even though a great deal of public funds are spent on such health care, it is often spent inefficiently and for low-quality service. A very high proportion of all the medical costs of the Los Angeles welfare programs is spent in the two Negro ghettos; and where the quality of the medical services given is so poor, substandard medical practices are found regularly by the physicians who review medical bills for the county. And even those doctors who are the equal of the physicians practicing outside the ghetto face great time pressures, inadequate laboratory facilities, and the lack of professional consultation with specialists, or contact with medical school faculties, which keep up with the rapid changes in information and technology.

The publicly supported medical welfare program also concentrates on the very young and the aged, two groups to whom society feels at least some moral responsibility. But teen-agers, and young and middle-aged men and women, who may become unemployed because of bad health, get no care of any kind. For example, if a man's teeth hurt so much that he cannot go to work, he will lose his job and become caught in a whirlpool of unemployment and its consequences, which will suck him down into abject poverty. Yet at no time will he be able to save himself by getting proper dental care, although it was the lack of such care that made him unemployed in the first place.

The lack of contact with a physician of any kind also deprives those who live in the depressed areas of even the services offered by the voluntary health groups. A visiting nurse, for example, whose services can be given free of charge, cannot make a house call unless it has been authorized by a doctor; but since so many of those in the area are too poor to afford a doctor, their very poverty thus acts as a barrier to their getting free nursing help in the home. As a result, only sixteen nursing visits per thousand were made in a year inside the Negro ghettos, where such visits are needed most, in comparison with twenty-three per thousand in other sections of the county, where the visiting nurses are needed less.

Every other important voluntary agency in Los Angeles follows the same pattern: the Tuberculosis and Health Association has none of its four branch offices in the depressed areas; the Los Angeles County Heart Association carries on only a very minimal program in those sections; the American Cancer Society can offer its services only to people not eligible for government help, which means that it does almost nothing in the area; the American Red Cross has done nothing more than offer one course in training home aides, and the Family Service Agency never had an office in the ghetto, nor did it help its inhabitants.

Yet in Los Angeles organized medicine, the prepaid health insurance planners, hospital boards, public officials, and community leaders still persist in attempting to block any attempts to solve these grave social problems in any way except through the system of private medicine.

Take hospitals as an example: as far back as 1933 the need for more medical care was known, but attempts to meet that need were consistently resisted by the physicians. In 1958, when plans were developed to ease the burden on the already overcrowded Los Angeles General Hospital by building five satellite hospitals throughout Los Angeles, the program had to be abandoned because of determined opposition from the Committee on Hospitals of the County Medical Society.

Eight years later, after the August events, the need for enlarged hospital facilities finally became obvious. The McCone Commission recommended that a special committee be established to explore how best to establish a hospital in the Watts-Willowbrook area. The State Advisory Hospital Council, the agency responsible for recommending the allocation of federal and state hospital subsidies, gave the task of setting up the committee to the Hospital Planning Association of Southern California, a typical urban agency in America: it is a *voluntary* planning agency, trying on an areawide basis to "Assist local commuities in the development of hospital and related health care facilities to meet individual community needs without costly duplication of services and personnel or waste of construction money." And while it may be successful in its preventive functions, it has been unsuccessful in creating a positive program to meet the community's health needs.

It is unsuccessful because it could not be otherwise. The Hospital Planning Association is financed and controlled by the very business groups and individuals in the Los Angeles area whose interests are focused primarily on creating what it describes as "a strong, voluntary, community-oriented hospital and related health care facility planning program." The HPA gets its financial support from those groups in the health planning field who are opposed, on principle, to the extension of publicly operated facilities, despite the fact that some of the financing for the county's "voluntary" facilities comes from public funds.

The organizations dominating the HPA are groups like the medical societies, health insurance companies, and large corporations which share a common interest in resisting the social insurance birthright concept of health care. The individuals who dominate the board of directors represent that mode of thought, and the board has no members from the areas of the community which are always neglected.

The clearest indication of which group the HPA, this community agency, considers to be its important constituency came in its response to the report of the committee which the State Advisory Hospital Council had asked it to establish to investigate the need for a hospital in Watts. That special committee was not typical of the HPA's usual subcommittees; it was not drawn from its own board of directors or its constituent organizations. Instead, acting on the McCone Commission's recommendation, the HPA set up a special committee, which included the deans of the University of Southern California and UCLA medical schools, the head of the City Health Department, a few Negro physicians and a number of residents from the southeast area. The special committee met and worked hard for months at preparing the report. Early in 1966 the report was submitted directly to the State Advisory Hospital Council; it recommended that a publicly financed hospital be established in the area.

The Hospital Planning Association board of directors promptly and quietly disavowed the special committee's report, publicly evaded support of it, and ordered the dissolution of the committee. Yet there was nothing revolutionary in the report, except from the viewpoint of these conservative business and professional people and organizations who get a visceral reaction to anything smacking of socialized medicine.

And later in 1966 the Board of Supervisors refused to face *its* responsibilities in the same situation: instead of allocating funds for such a hospital, which it had the right to do, it avoided getting into a dispute with the medical profession by making the building of the hospital a ballot decision in the June primary election.

Only 60 per cent of the citizens of Los Angeles voted for a bond issue to finance the new hospital; since the issue needed a two-thirds majority, it lost. It is now up in the state legislature.

Most of the doctors in Los Angeles, supported by the boards of private hospitals, the prepaid medical plan administrators, and the community leaders still maintain that the medical needs of the poor in the city are being adequately met by the private physicians and hospitals in the area. Even the Negro physicians, themselves the object of discrimination from their white colleagues, objected to a plan for establishing a community clinic financed with federal funds in the Watts-Willowbrook area. Their organization, the Charles Drew Medical Society, set up fifteen conditions it demanded be met by the University of Southern California, which will operate the clinic. Fundamentally, what the Drew Society wanted was to make certain that its members controlled the operation of the clinic, even though most of them live outside the area.

The same kind of indictment must be leveled against the religious organizations which operate hospitals. When the need for more hospitals was pointed up by the August events, one county supervisor contacted every religious group in the area in the hope that one of them would be willing to accept the responsibility of opening a hospital. All of them had some excuse to offer for being unable to meet the request: their money was tied up, they had to allocate more funds for missionary work, they had prior commitments, etc., etc. Yet only a day or two after one of these religious organizations had turned down the supervisor, it contacted someone in the hospital planning field to find out whether any hospitals were for sale outside the depressed areas.

Mayor Yorty was also willing to use the lack of medical facilities in Los Angeles for his political advantage even if it meant sacrificing the needs of the people in the area. When the University of Southern California was attempting delicate negotiations with Washington for the funding of the community clinic, Mayor Yorty, then seeking the Democratic gubernatorial nomination, issued a statement claiming credit for getting the clinic established, even though one of his spokesmen admitted that the premature statement would consolidate the opposition to the clinic and perhaps hold back its funding five or six months. But as the mayor's emissary said, "I'm sorry we have to do this, but we need votes."

The capitalizing of politicians, white and Negro physicians, and hospital boards on health needs in order to further their own special positions is an institutionalized feature of American city life. The "community leaders" concerned with health in the cities, like those who preceded them, still arrogate to themselves the right to make the decisions about the health of others and effectively deny them the right to participate in those decisions.

If they do survive being born, the citizens of the ghettos will be sick more often and die sooner than those who live outside. Active tuberculosis, truly a social disease, is four times more prevalent in the depressed areas than outside. And every other sickness spread by infection and proliferating in filth is found in far greater proportion in the ghettos than in the city surrounding them.

Ultimately, the combination of disease, bad physical environment, and low standards of health education and medical care take their expected toll: the overall death rate in the ghetto areas is more than 22 per cent higher than that of the remainder of the city. Beginning with their birth, the poor minority ghetto dwellers of the cities are the victims not only of an increased number of diseases, but also of the miserable conditions under which those diseases are treated. Like the other institutions of the city, organized medicine has not only failed in its stated purposes, but is itself a source of tension and frustration.

The Schools

Recently I was giving a lecture at a distinguished university. A friend of mine, there, a high school teacher, afterward asked if I would speak to the seniors at her school while I was in the city. I agreed, and she applied to the school administration for permission, explaining that no fee was involved. The school administrators balked at first, saying that the seniors had already been scheduled to have one speaker that week, and two would disrupt their schedule. When my friend asked who the other speaker was, she was told that a representative from a breakfast cereal company was coming to address the students on Americanism. She insisted that I ought to be invited anyway, since I was going to be in the city for only a few days. Finally she received permission for my appearance.

The next day the two local newspapers, in an article about my lecture at the university, headlined the fact that I had made "radical proposals" to the university students. The news reports of what I said were accurate—so accurate they threw the school administrators into a fright. My friend was called in and told that she would now have to get permission from higher authorities "downtown" before I could speak.

Patiently, she began working her way up the downtown admin-

istrative ladder. No one was willing to accept responsibility for allowing me to speak and everyone seemed frightened, although no one was certain of what.

But the school administrators need not have worried about the possible dangerous effects I was going to have on the high school seniors: almost all of them listened to me apathetically, without any real interest, obviously much more concerned with the dating bureau, which, it was announced, had been set up to provide dates for those who had no one to take to the senior prom. "Downtown" had triumphed.

The school system in every large American city has its own "downtown." And in every American city "downtown" has succeeded in wiping out schoolchildren's natural curiosity, substituting trivia for education. The school official who came to hear what I was telling the students had wasted his time, for one essential to education, the notion of dialogue, was completely missing from the seniors' consciousness: they wanted only to be told, not to question. And probably very few of them even remembered anything I had said by the next day.

She has been an elementary school principal since 1939. Her school, in the heart of the Negro ghetto, has fifteen hundred kids in it, almost all of them Negro, and fifty teachers, nearly 60 per cent of whom are Negro. She describes her pupils: "They don't come with a rich background. I knew how to read when I was in the first grade and there was a time sense in my home that isn't here. They don't have as many clocks, you know, as we do. I probably have a clock in every room of the house, but if they've got one clock, they're lucky. They don't care about time—time doesn't mean anything to them." Then she adds, her voice becoming patronizing, "So we come in carelessly, we have to learn about that, we have to learn to be punctual, we have to learn to finish a thing we start, and all of those other things that are so important."

She walks through the hallways of her very new and modern school. She spots a piece of paper on the corridor floor and calls out, "You there, little boy, pick up that paper from the floor!" As the child reaches down she says with pursed lips, in his hearing, "That's one of our problems. We just drop whatever is in our hand whenever we want to because we don't learn about neatness at home. So we must learn it here."

On the second floor she looks out over a wall toward the school-yard where some of the children are eating lunch and others are playing; three children are sitting on the edge of a concrete box in which a tree is planted. "Those boys don't belong there," she says angrily, trying to catch the eye of a teen-age teacher's aide supervising the children eating at the tables in the yard. But he does not see her and she turns away, repeating "Those children shouldn't be sitting there," just as a whistle sounds and the playing children are shepherded into lines, ready to be marched back to their classes.

She walks through the corridors again, stopping occasionally to knock at one of the locked classroom doors. Inside the classrooms the teachers are nervous at her entrance, the pupils unaware of who she is or hostile. In one room the children are seated around a Negro teacher, frozen—hands clasped in front of them, backs stiff—as he makes them repeat, over and over, the lesson he is trying to teach them.

"I think he's probably just a little too strict with the children," she says after leaving the classroom, "but you see, he's worked up to being a teacher from a custodian's job. But I do think he's probably too strict.

"We have school trips and we have a very lovely library, an A-1 library," she explains in her office. "We teach the children to take books from here, out from the library; in the summer, they take them home and we have an enriched program. For example, we have a garden with animals to bring up the language and environment; all the time it's enrichment, because, you see, they have to have a rich environment to make up for what they have missed.

"Last year, we had two groups who went to the art museum on scholarships, studied art with the other children and were praised by the artists out there, who said, 'Where did you find such fine children?' Oh, that did so much for them. Now we have a sculpturing class going out, so we give them all this environment to get out where they see things wherever possible.

"And now when we take some students, if they have a good IQ to start with and have had some help and have gone through our schools, they'll measure up all right. They need a lot of extra help. By that, they need to know they can go into a library and be accepted, they have to have this barrier down; so we're working continuously at that, and our teachers are all the time, so they will know: you are important, finish your job, this is the thing to do. So I think if they have the ability at all, they'll measure up all right."

Thirty miles away another principal walks through a corridor. This elementary school in the Mexican-American barrio is also new; it has 1,350 pupils, mostly Mexican-Americans. Its teaching staff has four Mexican-Americans, including one who had been a student of the principal when he was a teacher in another school in the barrio, forty-one whites, and twelve Negroes. As the principal steps out into the schoolyard, he spots a piece of paper on the floor. He reaches down to get it, but before he has even straightened up a little boy darts up to him, grabs the scrap from his hand, and walks off with a grin as the principal calls out, "Thank you, Tiger, you're a real sport."

In this schoolyard, too, the children are playing and eating. As the principal strolls around, the children run up to him, shouting his name, grabbing at him; when the whistle blows to send them back into the classes, they simply walk back inside by themselves. And when he walks into the unlocked classrooms, the kids pay very little attention to him, except to acknowledge his presence—it is obvious that he is a familiar figure, one of whom they have no fear. The teachers also seem happy to see him and joke with him when he teases them about how they look. It is clear, too, both from their attitude toward him and the willingness with which they work from early morning to late afternoon, that they are committed to him as much as to teaching.

When they come to his school for a job interview, he asks them, "Can you talk 'nigger'?" In their shocked silence he continues with, "We get two kinds of kids in this school, those that speak Spanish and those that talk 'nigger,' and if you want to teach here, you'll have to learn one of these languages. And you'll have to learn not to be shocked by the common language of the streets. If you're not acquainted with those words, or if you're going to be shocked by them, you'd better start saying them over and over again, because we've got some awfully smart kids here in social adjustment class and they've shocked every little old lady teacher, male and female, they've run into. The teachers send them in to me and I say to those kids, 'What did you say to the teacher?' So the kid looks at me and he says, 'Well, I told her, "Go fuck yourself, you bitch,"' and he's waiting for me to drop dead. So I say, 'Well, what else did you say?' And you see then the kid begins to back off because he sees he can't shake this cat. Then after a while they quit talking that way because you begin to ask them, 'Well, do you really know what you said?'

"If he doesn't have the language, what you've got to do is get him to talk, bring up something ten thousand times and talk with him about it; and you don't have to make a big issue out of it by saying to the kid, 'Compare, listen to how I say it.' The kid's going to listen and get it by osmosis. He doesn't have the experience, and if you tell him that he's wrong, he'll be mute.

"In this school, the basic philosophy is 'Give these kids all they can take.' But if they can't take it, ask yourself why they aren't getting it. Don't tell the kid he's stupid. Find out why you're not getting to him.

"Now, if you still want to teach here, let's try it out."

These two principals represent the polar points of the educational system in the cities; neither is typical, although the one has been and the other ought to be, and between them are more than a thousand other principals and vice-principals in the six hundred schools that make up the Los Angeles School District. Most of these are probably more like the principal of another elementary school in the Negro area who stood uneasily watching a group of children in a prekindergarten class take water out of a big pot with measuring cups and pour the water into another pot—inevitably, some of the water slopped onto the floor. The teacher was explaining that for the first time these children were learning something about measuring volume, but her words were lost on the principal who kept watching the kids. Finally, no longer able to stand the sight of water spilling on the classroom floor, she took the pot and put it into the classroom sink, above the heads of the little children. They stood there then, eyes wide open, a little scared of the strange lady who took away their game because the floor had been getting wet. And if they didn't learn much more about the concept of measurement, they had learned how they were expected to behave. The teacher too had learned a lesson: she knew how she was expected to behave in that principal's school.

The principal's influence over a school's character is enormous, for the principal represents almost total authority over the entire school—pupils, teachers, clerks, and custodial personnel alike. The principal can substantively affect the teacher's future promotions, especially if the teachers want to become principals themselves. The principals can make the teachers' daily work life either a joy or a hell. A weak principal can weaken an entire school; a strong one can dominate it completely: the principal sets the style, establishes the mood, and creates a tone for the school.

Even more, the principals exercise real power over the school system through their own organization, one which few people want to antagonize. And naturally enough through their organization the principals protect what they see as their own interests.

Unfortunately, the environment of most cities' school systems was far more hospitable in the past to the kind of principal who believes that "they" are children who "don't care about time" than it was to the one who is convinced that the basic philosophy ought to be to "give the kids all they can take." And for the same reason the American school systems have fewer teachers of the kind who say of their principal, like the one in the Mexican-American school, "He's a maverick principal, and that's why I enjoy working for him," and more who believe incorrectly in the importance of "uniformity" in teaching methods—"The people who have written the books have worked on these techniques for years and years, and they have come up with most of the methods. And the teachers will find, after trying these methods, that one of them is going to work best for her."

These methods may have worked best for the teachers but they certainly haven't for the pupils: the American school system has failed its students, failed miserably. As the first agency of government with which children come into contact, it has been a negative rather than positive force in helping build the community. And while that charge can be leveled in varying degrees against the ways in which the school system has treated all its constituents, it has failed even more in its responsibilities toward the minority students. These are the truly tragic victims of a school system which accurately reflects what one school administrator describes as society's "twisted priorities."

The facts demonstrating the schools' inadequacies are so well known and undisputed that they need be stated only in their barest form:

1. The cities' school systems are, by and large, segregated.

2. A great many of the poor minority students who enter the schools unprepared by environment for coping with the schools' teaching practices immediately begin dropping behind the middle-class children for whom the schools are basically geared and receive little help of the proper kind in catching up.

3. As a result, the dropout rate among the poor minority children in Los Angeles, for example, is double that of all sixteen-year-olds in the city.

These facts are not in dispute because the evidence of their truth is overwhelming: for Negroes, de facto school segregation is virtually complete in Los Angeles. At the elementary school level, where almost all the children go to schools in their own neighborhoods, segregation is almost total, reflecting the pattern of residential segregation. Of the Negro children attending junior high school, 60 per cent do so at schools whose populations are more than 90 per cent Negro; 13 per cent more go to schools that are between 58 and 80 per cent Negro. In high school almost half the Negroes go to schools with more than 90 per cent Negro students, and another 30 per cent attend schools whose populations are between 54 and 76 per cent Negro.

The segregation pattern for Mexican-American students is not as rigid at any school level. Still, nearly 25 per cent of the Mexican-American junior high students go to schools where 90 per cent of the students come from Spanish-speaking homes, and 12 per cent more go to schools where between 70 and 78 per cent of the students are Mexican-Americans; at the high school level nearly half of the Mexican-American teen-agers go to schools whose population is from 73 to 90 per cent Mexican-American. And the future for both groups appears to be one of increasing segregation as all the schools reflect neighborhood changes. The

Negro and Mexican-American schools, in fact, are sometimes more segregated than the neighborhoods, for there are areas in which whites make up a larger proportion of the residents than is reflected in the school population. This disparity exists because white parents take their children out of the schools as the minority population increases or because white families leave the area, to be replaced by other whites without children.

Yet physically there are not very many obvious differences between the schools which process the middle-class white children and those whose raw materials have black or brown skins. It is true that many of the schools in the Negro and Mexican-American sections of the city are older than many of those in the white areas, but this only reflects the fact that the whites live in the newer parts of the city. Except for the absence of a bike rack, new schools built in the Negro or Mexican-American sections *look* just like those in the white area—from the outside; significant differences can be seen only from the inside. From there the pattern of minority children's failures in the schools is clear: the reading vocabulary and comprehension of an average fifth-grade Negro student, attending an average elementary school in Watts or in the Avalon area, is roughly only 20 per cent of the national fifth-grade average; that of the average Mexican-American kid in an average school in Boyle Heights or Los Angeles is even lower. And by the eighth grade both Negro and Mexican-American students have dropped still further behind.

After the kids have entered the ninth grade their day of release comes, for most of them are sixteen by then and legally free to drop out of school. Of all the sixteen-year-olds in Los Angeles 30 per cent leave high school before graduation, a figure that demonstrates how useless school seems to many students; but in the three high schools in the south central Negro ghetto, *two-thirds* of the students who enter drop out before graduation day!

The disparity between the minority students and the whites exists at the teaching and administrative level of the school system, too: there is not a single Negro, Mexican-American, or Oriental among the sixteen top administrators of the school system; and although Negroes make up 20 per cent of all the pupils in the schools and junior colleges, they constitute only 12.7 per cent of the teachers and 5.2 per cent of the administrators, exclusive of the very high percentage of Negro "administrators" in child care centers. The Spanish-speaking pupil population is 18.5 per cent of the total, but the percentage of Mexican-American teachers is only 2.6 and of the administrators 1.5. There is a better balance among the Orientals, who are 3.6 per cent of the pupils and 3.5 per cent of the teachers; but they are less than 1 per cent of the administrators. The number of non-white principals, vice-principals, and top administrators is even smaller, and non-whites can be found in any sizable number only among the clerks, janitors, gardeners, secretaries, and typists—almost 35 per cent of the total.

There also exists a body of beliefs inside the school system:

1. Especially at the secondary level, a higher percentage of teachers and school administrators in the predominantly Negro and Mexican-American schools than in the predominantly white schools believe that their pupils are lazy or unmotivated.

2. A higher percentage of teachers and administrators in the Negro and Mexican-American schools believe that the parents, especially those of the Mexican-American children, are uninterested in the schools.

3. A higher percentage of teachers in the Negro and Mexican-American schools believe that their school administrators are not as good as teachers in the white schools say their administrators are; the administrators in the minority schools are equally uneasy about their teachers.

4. Most parents of white children in Los Angeles believe that their children's education will suffer if they attend a school with more than a very small percentage of minority children in it.

Is there real evidence for these beliefs of teachers, administrators, and parents? Have they become self-fulfilling prophecies?

In every American city, vast numbers of people think they know enough about education to exercise some control over it, either through elections to the Board of Education or by determining allocation and spending of funds. Everybody has gone to school, at least for a few years. And because everybody quite legitimately wants his child to get the best education possible, the school gets more attention from more people than any other government activity.

Yet in few other areas of government is there so much confusion and contradiction. In Los Angeles, as in America, the function of education has never been defined; instead it has simply been responsive to the direct pressures from interest groups. In Los Angeles, as in America, education has never been thought of as an active instrument to help change the nature of the society; instead it has been viewed as glorifying the status quo and as a vehicle for achieving financial success. In Los Angeles, as in America, education is authoritarian rather than democratic, for neither teachers, students, nor parents are allowed the opportunity to have an effective voice in school policy; instead nominal control of the schools is given to an elected Board of Education while real control of the schools is in the hands of the administrators, most of them white middle-class professionals whose houses have a clock in every room.

Even worse has been the failure of the cities' school systems to deal openly and honestly with the acute crisis of race relations in America. Until 1962 the Los Angeles schools pretended that the question didn't even exist, but then, in response to pressure from militant Negro groups, the Board of Education appointed a special committee to consider the problem of school segregation. Defending the board's past actions, the committee report stated that it "has followed a policy directed toward the goal of equality in that the pupil-teacher ratio, basic curriculum, books per student and transportation rules are equally applied throughout the District. It is conceded, however, that this formula falls far short of providing true equality for thousands of children who enter out schools from educationally disadvantaged environments. They are in no way able to compete equally with children living under more favorable circumstances."

But, the committee said, "There are no easy answers and no speedy solutions to these problems, which include de facto segregation in our schools; the present segregated housing patterns of the community; the high incidence of low economic status among minority people, who for years have been 'last hired, first fired';

and the lack of hope or motivation among some of these families which leads them into negative attitudes toward education and the demands the schools make on their children.

"These social patterns which have been developed over two hundred years," the report continued, "cannot be changed by unilateral action on the part of the schools." Instead, the committee insisted, all sectors of the community must be enlisted to work to create a new climate, adding that "the school should not be the single target or bear the sole responsibility for achieving this objective."

And on the specific issue of ending the de facto segregation through the use of such devices as the Princeton Plan, or paired schools, the committee said, "We are not disposed to urge that free citizens of any race be forced into educational environments not of their own choice even though some may feel it is for their own good." The committee did propose, however, that school doors be "opened wider for students and teachers to move into different schools and sections of our school district. These open doors, we hope, will encourage greater integration and we believe many will walk voluntarily through them."

The committee's hope was in vain: the schools continued to be segregated. And only very recently has the school system engaged in any self-examination to discover whether its practices and personnel are capable of dealing with the real world of segregation in which it operates.

Yet blame for these failures must be shared by the state and federal government as well; and insofar as government is a reflection of public sentiment, American society at large must bear the ultimate blame for the miserable conditions of education, especially the education of minority children. The country has not attempted in any substantive way to create a national educational policy; much less has it determined how it can help resolve the dilemma faced by those engaged in the education of minority children: how and what shall these children, who begin school already the victims of prejudice, be taught so that they can live in a society which rejects them in basic ways, even though they may conform to all its standards? What model should the educators present to minority children, whose sense of identity is truncated and distorted by the prejudiced society in which they grow up?

To such questions the Los Angeles School District has no answers—on the contrary, it has behaved as if the questions didn't even exist. Yet the Los Angeles School District is the second largest educational enterprise in the country. It has nearly 60,000 employees and 800,000 students attending 587 schools, ranging in size from the Solano Street Elementary School, with 188 pupils and 8 teachers, to Los Angeles City College, with 18,708 students and 700 teachers. The school district covered by the Board of Education covers more than 710 square miles; it administers an 881.45-square-mile junior college district. And the system must continually expand to accommodate the 25,000 children who enter it annually.

The school system's day-to-day operations are vast. Its chief operating officer, the Superintendent of Schools, receives $45,000 per year, even more than the mayor and as much as the Governor. More than 32,000 teachers go into classrooms each day, supervised by more than 1,000 administrators; the backup and housekeeping staffs number more than 13,000, divided into 676 separate classifications; 10,000 additional Board of Education employees are in such unclassified groups as professional experts, student aides, and youth services.

Actually, however, these official figures are deceptive: the true ratio of administrators to teachers is more like one to seven than one to thirty-two, since for every four full-time certified teachers, the equivalent of one full-time certified teacher is engaged in non-teaching activity—that is, not only are the officially designated administrators doing work outside of classrooms, but non-classroom work is also being done by people listed nominally as teachers, mostly on half-days.

The administrative headquarters for this huge government is "The Hill"—an area in downtown Los Angeles near the City Hall and other public buildings—from which a river of paper flows out to the system's district offices, each constituting a sub-headquarters with its own staff of supervisors, consultants, and administrators. It is also the base of operations for the board members, each with his own office, each office with a desk stacked with papers demanding to be read before the semi-weekly board meetings and the innumerable meetings of the committees which must do most of the board's work.

To be elected to the Board of Education costs a minimum of $250,000; in exchange the board members receive a maximum annual salary of $7,800, if they attend every Board meeting. Yet despite the high cost and low salary, the election fights for Board posts have been some of the most bitter political struggles in Los Angeles, for everyone feels strongly about the kind of education his children should be receiving.

But very little of what happens downtown on "The Hill" seems to have a direct connection with the teacher in the schoolroom. The system is so big that it has lost any direct contact with those who play subordinate roles in it, and the board members and high administrative officials thus remain remote figures to the teachers and even to the principals and vice-principals.

And this huge government, whose annual payroll is more than $300 million, operates independently of any other city agency. Fifty-six per cent of its operating funds are raised through its own tax assessments; the state legislature provides 33 per cent, and the remainder comes from the board's surplus funds plus federal assistance. The state's "gift" is not without strings, however. In exchange for the money it provides, the legislature, in the American tradition of everybody knowing something about education, attempts to exercise control over curriculum, teacher certification, special programs for gifted and poor children, and a wide variety of other school matters, from requiring a salute to the flag to the giving of polio vaccinations. In response to pressures from a variety of special interest groups the legislature's control of curriculum has insisted, for example, that all secondary schools simultaneously teach the importance of wine in the state's economy and the dangers of alcohol. At a time when elementary schoolteachers are in short supply the legislature has raised the requirements for elementary school teaching from four years of college to five, without raising the pay offered, thus effectively cutting off the supply. In one recent session of the legislature almost 20 per cent of *all* bills introduced dealt with education, and more than half of these passed.

The school administration sees itself as paying a high price for the financing it receives from the state. Legislative shifts and changes must be complied with, often at the cost of disrupting existing programs. And since the legislature passes education programs for the state as a whole, a city like Los Angeles often sees itself as forced to embark on a program which may have little or no application to its own problems. Because there are very few trained educators in the legislature, the professionals in the school system feel their work to be at the mercy of amateurs who can act without having to accept responsibility for carrying out their demands.

Without the state's one-third contribution, the city would be even more helpless than it is to conduct its educational operations. Since 1955, the overall cost of education has risen sharply in Los Angeles; the number of pupils has increased with the population, as has the cost per pupil. In 1955 the average daily attendance in the schools was 436,671 and the cost per pupil was $343.09, an annual total of nearly $150 million. Ten years later the average daily attendance was 658,164 and the cost per pupil had risen to $522.30, a staggering total of $343,808,426 for the year. While the cost of education has been increasing, its sources of income have been shifting: where once the state contributed 50 per cent of the educational costs to the local communities, the legislature has cut that to the present one-third; and although the federal government now puts some funds into education, the major share of educational financing in Los Angeles is still from local taxes.

All over the country local taxpayers have been resisting increases in their share of the school bill. School bond issues, once almost assured of passage, are being rejected by the voters, with the result that teaching staffs must be cut down, transportation boundaries must be pushed beyond reasonable limits, and curricula must become more limited, with such subjects as art and music the first victims of the tighter budgets. School officials have been forced to spend more and more of their time acting like fund raisers, persuading the public to vote the money necessary to operate the educational system. Inside the system increasing status accrues to the "money men," the people most familiar with financial problems and most capable of solving them by voter persuasion or budgetary control.

There is precisely the same pattern in every city—and in the competition for the tax dollar the school system has gradually become the loser. The lack of adequate financing is advanced by a high official in the school administration as a key element in the system's failures: "We've never really said to the public schools in the United States, 'Okay, let's quit arguing about money and get the job done.' No one has been willing to say, 'Let's pull out the plug, let's do the job, because what we really know is that the kids in the year 2000 are going to have so many more fantastic problems than we can imagine.'

"We don't even begin to know how to cope with our own social problems; we don't even begin to know how to communicate these problems, much less understand them. We have all the sophisticated computer technology, we can project figures ad infinitum, but we're so data conscious now we're forgetting the thing that happens when two people come together in a classroom—the magic of teaching. If you took all the teachers who cared and if you could get them left alone to do the job and if you could continually provide them with support and services, part of our problem would be dealt with.

"But we're out of money. We're up against it. The society is making its judgments about the schools only on the basis of money. It's a matter of priorities, and ours are kind of twisted."

The annual need for somehow getting larger amounts of money from the taxpayers has had serious effects on the school administrators: there is a great hesitancy to introduce even modest changes in the school policy because they fear that it will endanger the school system's financial support if programs are pushed which might antagonize the dominant white community. As a high official of the school system observed: "The superintendent has been so deeply concerned to pass the bond issues and the tax issues that he hasn't wanted to do anything daring which would upset the applecart. So he's been very conservative about picking up or implementing any very new programs, either to serve the minority schools or to integrate the schools, either way."

Still, no one believes that the investment of even large sums of money alone will solve the school crisis, and although primary responsibility for that failure must be placed at the city level, the state government has also been at fault. The State Board of Education, for example, prints all the textbooks used in all the schools, buying the plates from the textbook publishers. As a result the first-graders in the 112th Street School in Watts, with its 1,046 Negro and no white or Mexican-American students, and the little children in the Brooklyn Avenue School in Boyle Heights, with its 998 Mexican-American, 13 white, and 7 Negro pupils, use the same textbooks as the 603 white children attending the Cowan Avenue School on the west side of Los Angeles, where there is one Mexican-American child and no Negroes. And the textbooks, unfortunately, were written with only the little white kids in mind as an audience.

The State Board of Education is also responsible for accrediting all the teachers in the state who have met its requirements; the local school board may impose additional standards of its own, as the Los Angeles board does, but the city cannot hire as a teacher anyone not certified by the state. The state board also operates a statewide pension plan, makes available manuals and other teaching aids, and conducts educational research. But the State Board of Education is far removed from the lives of the minority groups. Its view of the schools starts with the teachers.

"It's the teachers," says one group of parents. "The teachers are so oriented toward middle-class white children they can't understand or cope with minority children."

Typical of that viewpoint is the Negro parent who says, "The school system is not geared for the minority groups because the theories of teaching are broadly covered for the whole city, where in a minority group, in the Negro ghettos primarily, they need a different type of education.

"Number one, the teachers that come in the minority groups, the colored and white teachers both, they come with attitudes of 'We're going to teach these poor undeveloped kids,' and they have a tendency to look down on the neighborhood, the community, and the parents, and they don't really know the need and very few look for the needs and they come with the attitude that 'these people are beneath me,' that 'there isn't too much you can do for their child.'

"And that goes all through the school system, elementary through high school. For instance, when our children graduate from high school, it's a very small percentage of them that can go on to college, academically, because they just don't know, they haven't been taught."

But for every minority parent who blames the teachers for the failures of the school system, there are those who say the fault lies with the minority parents themselves, that, as one Negro mother says, "We have not got the parents that get behind the schools like we should. Those white women get behind the teachers and principals and everybody else to see that they bring the children up to par. The white parents—maybe I shouldn't say this but then I feel like it's the truth—they do get behind, they demand more for their children than we do. When we go to the Los Angeles City School Board, they don't really hear what we have to say and we give up, we have a feeling that there's nothing to do anyway because they'll say what they want to say anyway."

Many minority parents believe, too, that it isn't possible for them to influence the schools in the traditional ways of the white parents: "There isn't much you can do to change the system. Because you can make a lot of vocal protests and go to higher places and have it written up, and then they will drag the chain and nothing happens.

"Out in Beverly Hills and in the San Fernando Valley the PTA is strong because the mothers and fathers are rich. The mothers have the time, the ones that are interested to go to PTA meetings. And the child needs—if they needs a Christmas tree at Christmastime with all the trimmings and all the gifts, no matter what the expenses are, they have the money and give it. And the principal can't fight them too well because if they have a strong PTA, they have all the money and the interest and the backing, and they run the school."

"We had a good PTA at our school," says another PTA activist, "but we had to have an overturnance of principals. We went and asked him could we start a PTA, and he told us that we couldn't have one because there wasn't anybody in that whole community that he felt had the leadership or the capability of being, of running the PTA. And he had over eight or nine hundred kids in that school . . . And we asked him twice, we asked him again please, you know, because we wanted, we wanted some representation in the school because it was an elementary school. And I told him, I said, 'I feel that as a new mother in the neighborhood and my kids just started school, I want to follow them, I don't want to let them get away. They've been used to home and me, and I want to follow them to school but I don't want to just walk into the school; I'd rather belong to an organization that represented the parents and the school.'

"But this is what he told us, and I called and asked him did he, had he changed his mind and can I have another appointment for the next day. He said yes. I went over and showed him all kinds of points, and he said as long as he was principal we would not have a PTA there. I said, well, if that's what you feel about it, the first thing to do is to get rid of you as principal. And then we'll have a PTA, I said, because I really intend to have one."

Many minority pupils, too, believe their color and ethnic background to be a handicap in the schools. "The white kids have a big advantage of the colored ones," says a high school senior. "The colored kids and the Mexicans, too, they don't have that much money and their parents are not puttin' in much effort, you know, to help out the school. See over there, near the white neighborhoods, you know, these parents make a little bit more money and they interested in their kids and their education, so they help them more and they drive, you know, send 'em to college and things. In the Negro neighborhoods, they don't, say, like a lot of the parents don't care that much."

"That's not true," retorts another student. "The white people do have a little more than we have, but it's not that the Negro parents don't care. It's just that they have too much on their mind and they don't have that much money to do the things white people do."

"The teachers, they like the Buddhaheads in our school," says a Mexican-American student in a mixed Mexican-American and Oriental school. "The Buddhaheads are picked for everything—it's because they're smarter than us or lighter than us, and they do just what the teachers tell them. The Buddhaheads take anything off anybody."

"One teacher told me this," says another minority student: 'I come to school to teach. If you learn, you learn. If you don't, forget about it.' So I feel that the teachers come to school to get their pay. They earn their living. I feel they should have some obligation to the students."

Another corroborates the same kind of experience: "You see, some teachers, they don't care that much, as long as they're getting their money. Because I heard a couple of teachers say that myself. I heard him say, 'I let 'em cut up. I'm sittin' on my tail, you know, and I get paid for it. So why shouldn't I let 'em cut up. They act like they don't want to learn. And I don't blame 'em too much— I'm sittin' on my ass, too."

One typical student's reaction is: "I was over to a white school and I was just looking to see what I could see. I think those people out in Beverly Hills, they got all the money and, you know, this Congressman that's representin' them are—these people got big money and they got power. And so when they start demanding something, I think they'll pay more attention to them. Because they have to. But they won't pay any attention to us unless we get out there and demonstrate or do somethin'.

"And it seems like the work they have to do in those schools is much harder or of a higher class than sometimes a lot of the work that we have to do. Like one of my teachers showed me this big—it was about a ten-page thing—saying it was a book report that you had to do at some high school out there. And at my school, a book report I mean, you know, you just write a two-page summary of the book."

Another high school student adds, "They have an international relations course we don't have. I think that the, well, at least I think the college prep courses are a little more advanced. The courses for kids who don't intend to go to college, I think it's the same for them. But I think because of the big demand for the better college prep courses which they have in other schools, they don't have them at our schools."

No one knows precisely how many of the minority students in the cities believe that their teachers and principals are prejudiced against them, for the school systems have made no effort to make such a determination. But there is certainly a good deal of evidence that a great many of the Negro and Spanish-speaking pupils do believe that the general prejudice against minority groups extends throughout the school systems. And whether or not this is true, they believe it to be so and act on their beliefs.

The task of overcoming this barrier between the students and the school system is made infinitely more difficult by the authoritarian methods aimed at all students. American high school seniors are treated at least as strictly as first-graders. Tension is created between students and faculty by the school system's rules on how the students dress, by the demands that they carry a hall pass in the corridors, through the policy of locking the outside doors of the school. In the Negro schools the tensions are exacerbated, for there the haircut in question might be a "process," utterly foreign to the middle-class white and Negro faculty and administrators but very important to a student's sense of identity.

So, too, the stressing of the paramilitary model is often a continuous source of tension. From the time the little children in elementary school are told to "line up" in the schoolyard until as teen-agers they are given ROTC training, order and efficiency are the values. "Lining them up is the easiest way to move groups of children," explains a school administrator, defending the practice at a PTA meeting; he may very well be right that it is the "easiest" way, but it may be the worst as well.

It is also not accidental that many of the principals in the school system used to come from the fields of physical education and mathematics, fields in which order and efficiency are very important. This is not to suggest that every former physical education or mathematics instructor who is now a principal behaves like a military robot—some of the best principals have that background—but such training generally produces men and women whose values are skewed toward the maintenance of formal order.

The school systems' refusal to permit student participation in any but the trivial aspects of school life is also very revealing. The view of the student as being incapable of making any serious decisions is apparent in the refusal of many junior and senior high school principal to allow discussion in the schools of such "controversial" questions as the racial problem. The principals' distaste for such discussions is shared by a good many teachers who may feel unequipped to direct or participate in such discussions. They are right to feel uneasy about their abilities to cope with such problems: very little in the background or training of most American teachers would equip them to deal with their own prejudices or their students' feelings, for most come from middle-class backgrounds and are trained so badly in colleges and universities that they come to the schools utterly unprepared for dealing with the real problems of education. Until very recently the primary emphasis in teacher training has been on techniques, on methods, rather than on equipping teachers to recognize and meet the special problems of poor minority children. Only lately has there been a grudging recognition of the need to shift from method to substance.

Proper in-service training about these questions is also a fairly new practice in the school systems, and inevitably it has met with resistance from the older and more traditionally oriented administrators. Maverick principals, like the one in the barrio school, were regarded as "showboats" and contemptuously described as "book-burners" because they refused to follow the rules and use the school system-provided books which until recently had practically no connection with the daily lives of their audience. One member of the Board of Education points out: "Our textbooks are all written for the white middle-class image. In the first-grade textbook the father comes home with a briefcase, the children are playing on the lawn with a white dog, and they all go in the house where the pretty mother has supper all ready for them, laid out on a white tablecloth. And maybe the next episode is a visit to grandmother on the farm. Well, a lot of people in the slum areas have just gotten off a farm, have no desire to go back, and simply don't care about Dick and Jane's grandmother and her farm." (Since a lot of people outside the slum areas "simply don't care about Dick and Jane's grandmother" either, such textbooks are not of much use anywhere in the school system.)

In Los Angeles the board has made an effort to improve the primary textbooks used by minority children by printing some books in which minority group models are portrayed. But unfortunately, there is as little connection between the models' lives and those of the minority children as there is with Dick and Jane's grandma: in one such book, for example, Los Angeles Negroes held up to be emulated are a slave who became a wealthy landowner, a boy who took a job at no pay in order to become an architect, a Boy Scout who became a judge, and a tomboy who became a policewoman and who, according to the book, believes that Los Angeles has the "best big city police force in the nation." (!)

Such textbooks can do very little more to help the teachers than the ones they replace, especially since the teachers are so inadequately prepared for their task. Los Angeles schoolteachers are among the best paid in the nation, but their salaries are still low, especially at the elementary school level. Traditionally in America elementary school is taught by women; more than 85 per cent of the Los Angeles elementary teachers are women, a proportion which drops sharply to 44 per cent in the secondary schools and 31 per cent in the junior colleges. This disproportion creates a greater turnover among elementary than secondary schoolteachers because of marriage, and it makes the elementary schools places where timidity and traditionalism are more likely to flourish. This commitment to the status quo becomes especially strong when the salary schedules of the teachers and administrators are examined: the starting salary of a Los Angeles elementary schoolteacher is $6,220 a year, while the initial salary for a principal is nearly twice that. Thus, it is perfectly understandable that a teacher will be ambitious to rise in the school system, and is not likely to challenge the authority of the superiors in the system, especially since it is those superiors who will judge, in a very competitive oral examination, whether or not the teacher shall be promoted into the august ranks of the principals.

But even the most dedicated teachers using the most modern methods need enormous psychic resources to teach in ghetto and barrio schools. It is true that poor minority children come to school less prepared than do the middle-class white children for whom the school experience has been a natural part of life almost since they could talk; it is true that their vocabulary and word concepts are far more limited than those of the middle-class white children. A reading teacher in the East Los Angeles elementary school explains: "The Negro children and the Mexican-American kids don't get the experiences the other children have. They don't get the attention at home; they have large families and the mother often works or the father is out of the home so they don't have the experience of being held on a lap and being read to. They don't get that. There's too many children in the family, there's too many things to be done. There isn't time for this kind of thing. They don't get the discussions, like, some children will sit at the table, even at breakfast or at dinner-time and the parents will be talking. Well, the children, even though they're not comprehending everything that is going on, are still being exposed to all this vocabulary, the advanced ideas and so forth. But not these children.

"So, for instance, say I'm teaching a sound, the S sound. I present a box of objects and then I have each child take out something from the object box and I have them tell me what it is. And then I have all the children repeat what it is. Now, in some cases, they will not know. For instance, I had a fig, an artificial fig in my phonics box, and they held it up and nobody knew what it was. And so I told them what it was, and the next day to develop this concept further I brought in a jar of figs and some dried figs and we discussed what they were. We even had a science lesson on evaporation and why the figs were so big in the jar and why the dried figs were so small. But normally they're not familiar with things like that."

Unfortunately, too, even if a Negro or Spanish-speaking child is lucky enough to be one of the few thousand who get a chance to learn from teachers like this, the learning process may not be sustained: poor children move from school to school far more often than do middle-class ones as their familes seek work or cheaper quarters, or as they get shifted from relative to relative. And even if they do stay in one school for a sustained period of time, the next one may not maintain such high standards; all the good work done in an elementary school can be and often is wiped out in junior high school.

It is also true that there are more serious discipline problems among the poor and especially the minority poor. In some cities, some of these problems develop from language difficulties, for there are Mexican-American or Puerto Rican children who come to school speaking only Spanish. But since speaking Spanish is discouraged, the children begin to drop behind their classmates, and grow less interested and more hostile. The development of the hostility brings the discipline problem, so the children may end up in a "social adjustment" class and eventually even in a "social adjustment" school, where all the children are in serious difficulties.

Characteristically, the system makes the less dedicated teachers give in quickly and conform to the pressures upon them, fearful that if they don't teach the children to read at the pace the books set as normal, their reputations as teachers will suffer. And so they pass the children on, untaught, to the next teacher, who in turn passes them on until they graduate from elementary school, still not really able to read, still with a tiny vocabulary, still expressing themselves in only one tense.

In junior high the discouraging process continues, until finally the teen-agers are old enough to drop out. Some dropouts are very bright and turn to hustling, dealing in narcotics or gambling to survive; the rest will drift into the American netherworld, swelling the numbers of unemployed, underemployed, and welfare dependents.

"These dropouts are some of the best kids," says a non-dropout high school senior with very good grades. "They know a whole bunch more than those that didn't drop out but they just didn't like school because it wasn't interesting to them. And now they have nowhere to turn."

Eventually, too, the system will beat even the most dedicated teachers, those willing to innovate and run risks. After years of trying to work with children who have been ruined by the time they get into the rigid, formal, and highly bureaucratic school system, their spirits begin to flag. They, too, then seek to get out of these schools and into those where the students are more responsive to them as teachers.

"The satisfaction you have as an instructor comes from, at least in part, the fact that the kids appreciate what you're doing and partly from the fact that when you teach, someone seems to be getting what you're doing," is a typical teacher reaction. "And if what you're doing day after day is just repeating something and nobody seems to be understanding it, nobody cares, nobody seems the least bit interested in what you're doing, the community doesn't care, the students don't care, the administration doesn't care, then you've had it.

"So you move to a school where the difficult problems are practically non-existent, you move to a school where you can teach something and the kids seem to be enjoying what you're doing. Parents come in when there's a PTA meeting; instead of one parent coming, you have thirty or forty standing around to tell you how much their kids enjoy the class, and there's a difference. The administration comes by to commend you on something—maybe one of your kids has won a prize or a National Science Foundation scholarship. But the kids at the Negro schools and the Mexican schools don't win prizes or get science scholarships; if they do get a scholarship, you know it's not because of their ability, but because they're Negroes. There's a difference."

"The minority kids come to high school inadequately prepared," says a white junior college instructor who has been in the school system for many years. "I taught at a high school which was almost all Mexican, poor Chinese, poor Japanese. There were no Negroes, but a few whites, a few Anglos. I used to give an assignment—I was teaching English—and if I had two kids that would come in with their homework, it would be something. The attitude of the kids towards the ones who brought in the homework was 'Why, you foul ball, you fuckup you.'

"Then I got transferred to an all-white school, and I went there completely unprepared. So when I walked into the class, I figured the best thing to do was discuss current events. Well, here were kids who've all had *Time* and *Life* and *Look* and *Harper's* and *Atlantic* in their own homes, and who listen to dinner-table conversation about what's been read in the magazines or the morning newspapers—these kids were up-to-date and we could have a discussion. Then I assigned them something to prepare for the next day, and the one or two kids who came in without the assignment, the others looked at them and said, 'How could you dare come in without homework?' "

Because this teacher's experience is not unique, the desire for maintaining separate schools is found not only among those "reactionary" Americans who have always been deeply prejudiced against Negroes and other minorities, but also among many of the communities' "liberals," who are fearful that mixed schools will lower the quality of education given *their* children. They do not object to having their children go to school with children of other ethnic or racial backgrounds—they even prefer it—but, and a very big but it is, they want those children to be as similar to their own as possible. This group of whites is convinced, sadly perhaps, that the home and cultural backgrounds of Negro and other minority children render them incapable of absorbing the kind of education their children are capable of receiving.

For these parents the ideal American school would have children of all races, ethnic backgrounds, and religions happily engaged in studying about the world and each other, singing folk songs in different languages, and being able to identify quickly Chanukah, Cinco de Mayo, Booker T. Washington, and haiku. This school's PTA president would be a Negro woman doctor, the vice-president a Jewish philanthropist, the secretary a Japanese accountant, the treasurer a Spanish-speaking policeman, and the chairman of the education committee a Protestant housewife who had graduated from UCLA.

But when the parents look out of their car windows and see a gang of Negro teen-agers strutting down the street in loud clothes, their heads covered with "do-rags" to protect their "processes," they grow fearful. They don't know that the model for those teen-agers is a singer named James Brown, who earns extraordinary sums of money and whose own "process" is a trademark. They have never heard of James Brown, or if they have happened to see him on one of his infrequent TV appearances, they have looked at him gyrating and shouting his "funky" songs as if he lived in another world. He does. And if the white parents encounter a group of "chicanos," they are just as apprehensive. In the graffiti scrawled on East Los Angeles buildings the Anglos see only the names of Mexican-American youth gangs; they do not perceive that the lettering is an authentic art form, the record of a group striving to find its own identity, seeking to connect itself, even in the way it writes, with a past in which one could be proud to be a Mexican.

So because these physical signs of difference are perceived as a threat to their children, the white parents begin their retreat, moving from the neighborhood, sending their children to school further away or to a private school. Slowly at first and then with increasing speed, the school population becomes more Negro or Negro and Spanish-speaking, or Negro and Spanish-speaking and Oriental. And then the teachers grow discontented, first reminiscing about the good old days when their pupils were easy to reach and eager to learn and when they had no difficult discipline problems. As the discontent grows in direct proportion to the increased number of minority students, the school's status within the school system starts to drop; fewer teachers seek to be assigned into it, more seek to be transferred out. The school finally has nothing but minority children in it, and the entire process has come full circle: another segregated school has come into existence with inferior status attached.

That inferior status is identifiable to everybody in the school system, pupils, teachers, and administrators alike. "They low-rate schools like this one," says a Negro teen-ager standing in the corridor of a Negro high school. "They're always trying to low-rate the schools 'cause half the kids at those schools drop out."

The white vice-principal of a Negro elementary school describes the reactions of her friends to her post: "When I tell my friends where I am now, they are usually rather surprised that I'm here. On the whole, many people who are not educators feel that it's easier to teach in a situation of a higher level."

The counseling program carried on in the American schools also has been of little or no use in helping alleviate these problems. First, counseling begins comparatively late in the student's lives—at the secondary rather than at the elementary levels—and although the minority schools have received far more counseling time in recent years than have those in other parts of the cities, the time given is often worthless.

Inside the school system counseling has little status, although a teacher who works as a counselor does get extra pay. "High school counseling is horrible, absolutely horrible," says an ex-high school counselor. "Most of the people doing it have never had a job except teaching. Their knowledge of other jobs comes from their friends, but their friends are mostly professionals like themselves, and they think in terms of these professional jobs, doctors, lawyers, other teachers. They don't even really know what's involved in being a clerk in the school. Most of their work is just making up programs for the kids.

"Here's how I got to be a counselor. I attended a course at the University of Southern California at which there were two hundred other people and the professor read from his textbook. At the end of the semester you had to take a test. And when I heard him lecturing from his textbook, I didn't come for the rest of the semester, but I read his book. And I took the final, got a B in the course, and so I'm a counselor.

"The counselor hardly ever sees the student. What he does is, he knows that this person has marked down on a sheet of paper, 'I'm a liberal arts major and I intend to go to UCLA.' So the counselor looks over the courses this kid has taken, and the kid knows or is supposed to know what to take to go to UCLA. The counselor checks to see that the kid has taken enough math, enough science, and so on. If there isn't enough science, he'll call the kid down and say, 'How come you haven't taken physical science yet?' 'Well, I'm going to take it next semester.' 'Okay.' 'Thank you.' That's the end of the interview on counseling."

Perhaps this teacher's bitter picture of the perfunctory nature of counseling is exaggerated, but it contains the essence of the truth. Not many minority students seem to have much regard for counseling in high school, and while this is also true among the more privileged students, it is not as important, for in a home where the discussion of vocation, occupation, and the choice of college begins early in life, the student generally has some sense of what he will be doing after high school graduation. But the poor, and especially the minority poor, have no such opportunities at home, and the school is a very inadequate substitute.

The teachers and the principals face another serious source of tension in their work—the pressure exerted upon them from the outside by militant groups of parents not connected with the PTA movement. Despite the common belief that minority parents don't care about their children's education, they do care just as much as the middle-class parents—but they don't know how to express their concern, for nothing in their life experience has provided them with the background to do this in an organized way. They think: "The educational system is like any other charitable system around, they treat you like, you know, okay, you don't deserve too much because you don't show too much. So, you know, take what I give you or just leave it there, you know. And mothers that have children that's attending school, unless they can, I tell you it's a funny thing about persons who have been poor. I mean poor, poor, poor all their life. It's a funny thing, you don't just say, 'Come on in, I want you to help.' They don't move like that. They have to *see* something in order to feel something that's really needed. They have not in the past had an opportunity to come out and really help or show their faith. They have not been *needed*. So now here all of a sudden, 'I want you. Come on and help.' They resent this because it's just like everything else—the Bureau of Public Assistance, when they say to you, you're not what it takes to be in the society, you get over there with your group of people and you stay there."

And so because these parents do not believe that the school system is concerned with their problems, they present their grievances outside the "normal" channels. The Los Angeles Board of Education, like that in every city in America, has had to face the anger of frustrated minority parents, lashing out in fury at a system they believe is cheating them. Yet when the Board of Education established an office of urban affairs to help ease such tensions, it characteristically held fast to the view that the problem was basically one of communication: the work of the office was defined as representing the board's viewpoint to the community groups, but not the reverse. The urban affairs constituency is thus defined as the board rather than the community; it must defend the board to the community. But it is the reverse process that needs the most attention. For years the American school systems have made no attempt to discover in any organized and scientific way what the cities' minority people want.

Should there be integrated schools? "I'd rather go to an all-mixed school than the all-colored one I go to now," says a Negro high school girl, "because I think it's better, you know, to be around somebody who—instead of being, like, most time, like, if I stayed in this neighborhood, you don't be around different people too much. You be around your own race, you know. When you go to another school, like, you go to school like that, I think it's better because then you're associating with many different people."

Is that viewpoint more characteristic than this one? "I would feel this way if I would go to an all-white school and I would be the only colored boy there because I think this way: if I go there, they might think, 'Well, he's the only nigger here, you know, we don't want him here.' And they might think that I was—well, you know, you ain't gonna go to an all-white school and meet people that's not prejudiced toward Negroes. So I say, I think this way: if I'm the only colored boy there, why shouldn't they accept me as a black or white or Japanese or Mexican or something like that, you know. Otherwise, most of the time, if you would go to a white school, you'd see 'em dressed up different from you and you know they eat things better than you and all that. But most of—well, I see it this way, I don't have—no, I'm not prejudiced towards 'em but I say if I was probably walking down the street, okay, and I'm the only colored boy on the street, they'd maybe fight with me to make me go home and somethin' like that, you know."

No one in the school system ever attempted to find out which of these views is more common, for no one thought it important enough to worry about what the minority groups wanted. Nor did anyone think it important enough to discover whether or not teachers, parents, and students thought it was possible to have a segregated school that was good, or at least better than those in the ghettos and barrios.

More than anything else, the admitted failures of the American school system grow out of and demonstrate the failures of the society. What is lacking in the school system is lacking in the society: voices to challenge the fundamental premises of our present educational establishment.

The myth that all children in the cities have an equal opportunity for education is credible to society only because very few people in the school systems, from the members of the Board of Education through the administration to the teachers, are willing to be the voices calling for values in keeping with the city's present needs.

In the new school plants built in the cities a central monitoring system enables principals to stay in their offices to speak to and hear from the teachers and students in the classrooms. The technology is remarkable and the principals who use this device can hear and be heard quite distinctly—but the words they listen to and those they utter can communicate very little.

And because there is so little real communication and so little real education in America's schools, far too many children, and especially poor minority children, view the schools as just one more government agency which has very little to do with their lives. And now the schools, too, are becoming racial battlefields.

The McCone Commission

"What do you think is the most important bar to minority employment that could be eliminated quickly?" the McCone Commission staff member asked me. *We were sitting in the commission offices in downtown Los Angeles, and it was about the midpoint of the three-month investigation which was held before I began this book. Some members of the commission staff were friends of mine, and I had met with them and others on the staff a number of times to discuss some of their general problems. But now I was being questioned as an expert on employment.*

"The handicap that would be the easiest to wipe out is the arrest record," I answered. *"If arrest records weren't held against people, you could probably change the employment situation overnight and put a hell of a lot of people to work."*

The staff man looked at me, almost indignantly, and said, "I don't think a man who's got an arrest record should be employed in most businesses. I wouldn't hire anybody who had an arrest record for my family's business."

I sat there stunned. "What were you doing before you came to work for the commission?" I asked.

"I was a prosecuting attorney," he answered. "That's why I feel so strongly about people with arrest records."

At that moment I was convinced that the commission was going to fail. If a member of the commission staff had so little understanding of minority life, the investigation was doomed.

Months later I sat with McCone in his business office, talking with him for a long time about the commission's work. He was so sure of himself, so confident of his own correctness, that he never bothered to evade my questions or give me obscure answers as had some other people involved with the commission. He is the prototype of the American business and government success; on a table in the reception room of his financial empire is a large scrapbook with clippings attesting to his success as the head of the CIA. And he also is the prototype of the influential American who has failed to deal with the world in which we live.

Today, men exactly like him can be found on every commission appointed by governors and the President to investigate the wars in the cities. And those commissions will probably be of as little use in helping to end the wars as was the McCone Commission.

Perhaps Governor Edmund Brown might have made a worse choice than John A. McCone to serve as chairman of the governor's "Commission on the Los Angeles Riots." Perhaps. But in all of California it would be hard to find a man less qualified by training and attitude to investigate a social phemomenon like the one that shook Los Angeles in August 1965.

Yet the initial selection of McCone, the manner in which the other members of the commission were picked, the character of its staff, its methods of investigation, and the report it issued were all perfectly in character. The failure of government was a major cause of the terrible outbreak; it was almost inevitable, then, that in its investigation of the events government should also fail. And it did.

That failure was ordained from the moment the idea of an investigating commission was discussed in Los Angeles by Governor Brown and his staff, including two of his closest political advisors, Hale Champion and Warren Christopher, a Los Angeles attorney, who is now Deputy Attorney General of the United States. The governor, who was vacationing in Greece when the social volcano erupted, had hurried back to California as soon as Champion telephoned the awful dimensions of the event to him. Christopher, on a holiday with his wife in the Bahamas when the first newspaper reports began to appear, had also cut short his holiday to rush back to Los Angeles.

The staff, shaken badly by what had been and still was happening, met in the governor's hotel suite in Los Angeles on Sunday, the day after his return to California. The city was growing quiet again and it seemed as if the worst was over; now it was time to assess what had occurred, find the causes, and make recommendations to avert any further outbreaks. The idea of the investigating commission was discussed, but neither the governor nor his associates had any clear idea of how such a commission would function. They did talk vaguely about patterning it after a British Royal Commission. As it turned out, no such comparisons can be made.

The initial failure of the commission was in the very limited conception the governor and his associates had of its function, a concept which led them inevitably to the choice of McCone as its head. "The governor was anxious to make a sound approach to the problem," states Christopher, "and he wanted to make a deep inquiry. But at the same time, he didn't want to do anything precipitous.

"He believed that what we needed to try and do was to move the total community to support the disadvantaged areas, and so he was instinctively drawn to a man with an impeccable reputation in the business community who would yet have enough experience with this kind of problem so that he could take a broad view of it."

In fact, neither the governor nor anyone on his staff understood what had happened in Los Angeles. Politically and psychologically they were unprepared to face the reality of the social cancer destroying the heart of the city and country. At a time when the city's future life depended upon making the most accurate diagnosis of its ills and perhaps prescribing drastic steps to help it survive, the liberal governor and his liberal staff still didn't want "to do anything precipitous."

Not only did they not want to do anything precipitous but in addition they sought a diagnosis of the city's sickness which would be acceptable to the very groups in the city which bore a heavy responsibility for creating the cancerous environment. Threatened by a real possibility of political defeat from the right, they gave the initiative to the right.

"The governor's basic purpose was to get a consideration of what had happened by some machinery that would be likely to have some persuasive effect with the establishment community down there," states Winslow Christian, then the governor's executive assistant. "The theory was that the Negroes themselves, living in those areas, perhaps had fairly realistic ideas of what was going on, and the liberal community likewise had ideas that from our point of view were fairly realistic . . . What we needed was to rub the noses of the establishment in some unpleasant facts in order to get their acquiescence in and understanding of the changes that were needed to deal realistically with the problems. And the notion was that McCone was personally a rather conservative sort of man, and we accepted that."

Certainly, McCone is the archetype conservative with "an impeccable reputation in the business community." A slender, rather short, wiry man with piercing eyes, McCone is a native Californian, a graduate in engineering from the University of California at Berkeley, and a very successful and wealthy businessman. During World War II he had operated engineering and shipyard enterprises engaged in overseas construction work and aircraft modification. He owns shipping companies that operate on a world scale and is on the boards of such corporations as Pacific Mutual Life Insurance Company, Western Banking, the First Western Bank, TWA, and Standard Oil. He is also a director of the Stanford Research Institute, a Trustee of the California Institute of Technology, a Regent of Loyola University in Los Angeles, and a founder of the Los Angeles World Affairs Council.

McCone's first experience with national government began in 1947, when President Truman appointed him to the President's Air Policy Committee. In 1948 he became a special deputy to Defense Secretary James Forrestal; in 1950 he was appointed Undersecretary of the Air Force, and served in that post until October 1951. Three years later he was appointed to the Dulles Public Committee on Personnel, which studied the personnel problems of the State Department. In July 1958 he became a member of the Atomic Energy Commission, moving into its chairmanship shortly afterwards; he remained on the AEC until January 1961.

Within the AEC, McCone was an advocate of the "Big Bomb" group, opposing those in the agency who favored developing limited nuclear weapons, test moratoriums, and controlled use of weapons. In 1956, when the issue of a moratorium on testing nuclear weapons became an issue in the Presidential campaign, McCone severely castigated ten Caltech professors who publicly supported Adlai Stevenson's position in favor of a moratorium. But he did more than attack them, according to Senator Eugene McCarthy, who claimed that McCone had attempted to get the ten scientists fired, a charge denied by McCone. At Caltech, however, many faculty members were convinced that McCone had called in the scientists and threatened them for their position.

In January 1962 John F. Kennedy, the liberal Democrat, appointed McCone as head of the CIA, a position he held until 1965. As the CIA chief McCone was also the chairman of the U.S. Intelligence Board, which coordinates the activities of all government intelligence agencies. Always a man supremely confident of the correctness of his views, McCone ran the CIA as if it were one of his business enterprises.

McCone's experience in the CIA was considered to be one of his potential assets as chairman of the commission, according to Christopher, who says, "His reputation in the CIA was a very good one. He went in at a time when it was easy to criticize him as a replacement for Allen Dulles, and I think the people in the CIA were initially quite skeptical about him. At least this is the story I'd heard and we discussed at the time. But over a couple of years he gained the complete confidence of most of the people in the CIA who were of an intellectual or academic type.

"And he demonstrated an open-mindedness to not dissimilar problems. The problems of developing countries, many of the intelligence problems have analogies here. How do you deal with minority groups in developing countries? I don't pretend to suggest any close parallels and I think the emphasis was more on his open-mindedness and his willingness to study an issue and to take a hard look at it.

"There was beyond that the very favorable things that were said about him by people who had obvious qualifications in this field, Bob Kennedy, for example. I think Bob McNamara thought very highly of him, too."

McCone was in New York attending a business meeting when he was called by the governor and asked to head the commission. He was somewhat reluctant to do so because he had only recently returned to California and was in the process of getting resettled both in his home and business life. But he didn't refuse the governor completely. "I told the governor I would give it thought," says McCone, "and see what my own commitments were, both with my business and with several government commissions on which I was working."

After this first conversation Brown called the White House, asking that President Johnson urge McCone to take the assignment. Johnson did contact McCone. "The President urged me to do it, if I possibly could," says McCone. "So on the basis of that and the conclusion that I could spare the time, I agreed that I would serve as chairman with the understanding that the governor and I would confer on the appointments to the commission, which we did." (McCone's conversation with Johnson was the first of a series of discussions between McCone and the White House about the commission, discussions which continued through the entire investigation and writing of the report.)

Like Brown and the members of his staff, McCone initially had no clear conception of the commission's mission. But he soon developed one, and it was his view of that mission, rather than the governor's, which became decisive. "There wasn't any model," he says, "and when I talked with the governor and his people on the telephone from New York and Washington over a period of two days, when we talked two or three times, I didn't really have a conception. Coming home on the plane, I gave it a good deal of thought and jotted down a few ideas, and then after I got here the first thing I had to give thought to was the frames of reference for the commission that the governor had to address to us. So Warren

Christopher and I sat down and drafted a memorandum, a sort of frame of references, and this memorandum was transmitted and became, with such modifications as the governor's staff added, the directive to the commission from the governor."

Within the next few days proposed names for other members of the commission were discussed by Brown and McCone. Christopher was suggested immediately by the governor and was accepted by McCone along with the Very Rev. Charles S. Cassasa, President of Loyola University in Los Angeles. McCone then raised the question of putting Negroes on the commission, and Judge Earl S. Broady, a conservative Republican, was selected. Later another Negro, Rev. James Jones, a member of the Los Angeles City Board of Education, was added. Jones had been touring the Los Angeles area with Martin Luther King immediately after the upheaval and was at a meeting with King and the governor in the governor's hotel suite when Brown asked him if he would be willing to serve on the commission. Jones accepted and was approved by McCone.

"We wanted somebody that was in the field of medicine and health and also in the educational system," says McCone, "and the governor first raised the name of Chancellor Murphy at UCLA who was unable to serve because of other commitments. But he proposed Dr. Sherman Mellinkoff, who was not known to me at that time, but after one or two phone calls it was obvious that he would be an excellent man. There were two or three names that were brought up that the governor and I couldn't agree on, and so we dropped them." The seventh member of the group was Asa Call, like McCone a wealthy and conservative businessman, who had been president of a large insurance company for many years.

After the seven men had been chosen, McCone realized no woman was on the commission. "I believe I raised the question of putting a woman on the commission," recalls McCone, "and the governor brought up the name of Mrs. Neumann. She had been President of the League of Women Voters, and of course she was known to me, as was her husband. She was perfectly acceptable."

Only two of the eight commission members had any prior experience in the field of race relations. Father Cassasa had participated in such activities as teacher-training projects sponsored by groups like the American Jewish Committee, and Reverend Jones had been active in supporting Martin Luther King. The rest of the commission members had no special qualifications in this field: they were selected to give the impression of a broad community spectrum of the kind associated with community chest drives or anti-polio campaigns.

And so began the rapid transition from what had been called the "Governor's Commission" to what became known as the "McCone Commission." At the time McCone was appointed, some people believed that the governor and his staff had been looking primarily for a "good" name to head the commission, but that its actual work would be done by Christopher. If this version has any truth in it, McCone soon disabused everyone of the notion that he would play a purely passive role: not only had he insisted on veto power over the other members of the commission and, in addition, outlined the dimensions of its mission, but he also exercised a decisive voice on the appointment of key staff members, ran the commission with the same kind of discipline he had used in his CIA operations, dominated the commission hearings, and eventually made his personal stereotypes into the basic theme of the commission's report. Indeed, the commission was so much McCone's creature that its official secretary was Terence Lee, his longtime private secretary.

McCone settled another extremely important question: the short three-month period allocated to conduct the investigation and issue a report. Members of the governor's staff say that the reason for the three-month deadline was that the governor wanted some immediate remedial proposals to take to the state legislature; McCone says that he had his own considerations for setting the deadline: "I set it for several reasons. In the first place, I thought it was important to get the study done and get the recommendations in and get something on the rails to improve conditions. And secondly, this is a subject you can study forever and these were busy men; every one of them, including myself, had a full-time job, and we couldn't be expected to set aside a year of our life. And they worked very hard, day and night, seven days a week, to get the study done and the report out and I think it's just as good as if it took a year."

Evidently, no one gave serious consideration to such alternatives as issuing an interim report, at the end of the three-month period, with some recommendations for immediate action and following this up with a deeper analysis of the problems.

In his "charge" to the commission, which grew from the memorandum prepared by McCone with Christopher's assistance, Governor Brown told the commission at its first meeting on August 24, 1965: ". . . I feel it may be useful if I set out some of the areas in which I hope the commission will make inquiries and recommendations. In a sense, this is my charge as governor to the commission:

"First, I believe that the commission should prepare an accurate chronology and description of the riots and attempt to draw any lessons which may be learned from a retrospective study of these events. The purpose of this would not be to fix blame or find scapegoats, but rather to develop a comprehensive and detailed chronology and description of the disorders. This should include, by way of example, a study of the following subjects:

"A. The circumstances surrounding the arrest which touched off the riots.

"B. Why the riots continued and spread, including whether there was any organization, leadership, or outside stimulation of the rioters.

"C. The efforts of law enforcement officials to control the riots.

"D. The action taken by private individuals, both white and Negro, as well as the leadership in organizations . . . within or without the troubled area . . . in attempting to control the riots.

"E. Events surrounding the ordering in of the National Guard.

"F. The action taken jointly by law enforcement officers and the National Guard to bring the riots under control.

"G. The circumstances surrounding the deaths which took place, and a consideration of the personal injuries caused.

"H. The damage done to property by fires, force, and looting.

"I. The weapons used and how they were obtained.

"J. The disturbances of a similar nature in other Southern California areas at approximately the same time.

"K. The arrests, arraignments, and trials of the persons apprehended during the riots.

"Second, I believe that the commission should probe deeply the immediate and underlying causes of the riots. In this connection the commission will want to consider the following:

"A. The physical and sociological condition in the area of the riots at the time they commenced.

"B. The opportunities for Negroes in employment, education, and recreation in the troubled area; and the attitude and awareness of the Negro community regarding those opportunities.

"C. The public and private welfare programs available and not available in the area, and the extent to which they were utilized.

"D. Pertinent facts regarding the persons involved in the riots, including their age, education, job status, habits, family situation, and associations.

"E. The attitudes of the rioters toward the community and law enforcement officials in the community and whether these attitudes are supported by fact and reason.

"F. The significance of looting in stimulating and prolonging the riots.

"Third, the commission should develop recommendations for action designed to prevent a recurrence of these tragic disorders. The commission should consider what additional can be done at any level of government or by any agency of the government to prevent a recurrence. Of equal importance, the commission should consider whether there are steps which private citizens may take, individually or jointly, to prevent a repetition of the bloodshed."

But the governor's request that the "commission should probe deeply the immediate and underlying causes of the riots" was much less important to McCone than the more limited objective of ascertaining the facts about what had happened during the days of the rioting. So, too, McCone had, from the start, a very limited view of the kind of recommendations the commission should make in its final report.

"I felt," he says, "that those broad pronouncements so common in the writings of political sociologists would, if accepted by a commission such as ours, raise hopes, raise anticipations resulting in more frustrations, more anger, and finally more rage. Therefore, we decided early on that we were going to be as pragmatic as possible about this and make recommendations that were defendable on the one hand and feasible on the other, and if followed would relieve a situation that concerned us. At the time I was reading deeply and intensively in the writings of a great many sociologists who had written on the whole question of the Negro and his place in our society, and while you can't disagree with what they say about a broad, humanitarian view, an official investigative body putting out such ideas in the form of recommendations was just impractical because the ideal of the goal of the complete extinguishing of any racial prejudice, to say nothing of barriers, is something that is going to go on for a long time. And therefore we as a commission felt that was not our responsibility nor our role. We weren't out to try to alter humanity by the printing of a little book but we were out to make some specific recommendations that would improve conditions in our community."

Christopher says he shared McCone's limited view of the commission's mission: "We felt that our mission or our role was to draw together the facts of the riots themselves and see if anything could be learned from the circumstances, the cops-and-robbers part of it. And then to look at what we thought were perhaps not the deepest underlying causes, but the ones that were susceptible of some immediate remedial efforts, some immediate improvements."

The commission began to function very quickly, although very chaotically, in offices provided in the State Office Building in downtown Los Angeles. An executive committee was appointed to make all the important decisions about the hiring of staff and the conduct of the investigation: the committee consisted of McCone, Asa Call, and Warren Christopher, and this small group made decisions on a day-to-day basis, generally without consulting the other commission members.

Very early, too, McCone established the role of his commission as the *sole* official governmental agency investigating the Los Angeles events. A White House task force, headed by Ramsey Clark, now the Attorney General of the United States, had come to Los Angeles to investigate the situation and make a report on it. But McCone, who states matter of factly, "Of course, I have a close relationship with the White House at every level," was able to head off any publication of the task force report.

He suggested to the White House that "it might be appropriate to wait until we came out with a report and recommendations before any White House pronouncement was made on what should be done in our city, and that was respected. And so, to the extent that there was a report, it was never published."

The three-man executive committee made the key decisions about the character of the commission's staff. The first person hired by the committee was the general counsel and executive director, Thomas Sheridan. The choice of Sheridan, and in turn the people he hired as members of his staff, very accurately reflected McCone's view of the commission's primary task and was another decisive element in determining the faulty character of the commission's investigation and ultimate report.

Sheridan, a fairly young man, was a former Assistant United States Attorney in Los Angeles, a member of the Robert Kennedy staff in the Justice Department, whose entire legal career had been as a prosecuting attorney. He had recently gone into private practice with a group of other men who had also been either with the Department of Justice or the FBI. None of the committee members knew him personally, although he was known, at least by reputation, to Christopher. Before hiring Sheridan, McCone discussed him with Nicholas de B. Katzenbach, who had succeeded Robert Kennedy as Attorney General. Katzenbach gave a favorable appraisal of Sheridan.

According to Sheridan, "I understand the basis for the recommendation from Nick to McCone was along the line that I had handled complicated, involved, fact-situation type things. He was going back to such cases as I was prosecutor for the Mickey Cohen case; I prosecuted the Sinatra kidnapping case. This sort of stuff."

The prosecutor of Mickey Cohen and the Sinatra kidnappers was interviewed initially by Christopher and then by McCone and Call. After his appointment had been agreed upon by those three, he began hiring his staff, primarily from among the prosecuting attorneys and investigators with whom he had worked in the past. A few days later Christopher called Sheridan and asked him if he knew Professor Harold Horowitz of the UCLA Law School, telling Sheridan that the commission was thinking of hiring Horowitz as Sheridan's assistant. Horowitz's background was in teaching law plus a few years in Washington with the Department of Health, Education and Welfare. He had also served on a number of state commissions and written on cases involving civil liberties.

Sheridan states that the choice of Horowitz was to balance the top staff: "Hal was coming from the academic community . . . and my legal career being on the prosecution side, dealing with investigators, etc., etc., . . . well, then I think the balance comes in this way—that if you'd try to characterize Sheridan, you'd probably end up characterizing him as pro law enforcement, which is a bad way to characterize anybody, I guess; and Hal, you'd characterize as the liberal academician. And then maybe the two will balance . . . Well, I don't know if we ever balanced or not . . ."

As it turned out the "balance" was precarious at best and in the long run the "pro law enforcement" man, the prosecutor, won out easily over the "liberal academician." And Horowitz's dilemma during the life of the commission was the classic one faced by every other "liberal academician" in such situations: they see their choice only as either quietly quitting the commission or remaining on the staff in the hope of being able to influence the results. Most eventually concede that their hopes have been vain and their influence upon the results minimal, except perhaps in an isolated case or two.

(Two people did quit the commission staff: Bryant Cushing and Carol Ratner, neither of whom were attorneys or investigators. Cushing was a management consultant with an interest in race relations who had done some work with employers in the South; Miss Ratner had some university background in social science.

Both had worked on the study of the conflict between the Free Speech Movement and the administration of the University of California at Berkeley. Authorized by the Board of Regents, that study had resulted in a serious, in-depth analysis of the basic issues confronting the American universities today and had been hailed as a real contribution to the field. On the basis of that experience they had accepted an invitation to work on the McCone Commission, believing that a similar kind of report would be made at the conclusion of its investigation.)

To Sheridan the entire investigation was focused on gathering "hard facts," and in his view "hard facts" included the "underlying" causes of the riots. "Take a look at the governor's charge," he says. "Circumstances around the arrests; the riots; why did it spread; what did law enforcement do; what did private individuals do to control the riots; ordering up the National Guard; action taken by law enforcement and the National Guard to control the riots; circumstances surrounding the deaths which took place; personal injuries; damages done by fire; weapons used; how they got them; disturbances of a similar nature in other parts of the nation; arraignments; trials of persons apprehended during the riots. That's all just pure fact investigation.

"Then secondly, the physical and sociological conditions of the area, the way it's phrased, are really fact questions. At least the physical one—what's the physical area look like; what's involved; opportunities for Negroes in employment; public and private welfare programs available. Pertinent facts to be gotten on the persons involved in the riots, their background—which is again a straight fact thing; attitude of the rioters toward the community.

"Before we could get to the underlying causes, our whole feeling was 'underlying cause of what?' Underlying cause of the riots? Who was arrested? Let's first get those facts; when you've got the facts, present it to the sociologists, psychiatrists, and so on across the board . . ."

Sam Williams, the third member of the staff to be hired, epitomized a role as clearly as Sheridan and Horowitz. Williams was the prototype of the young Negro who from the white viewpoint is becoming integrated properly into the society. A good-looking, husky young man, Williams was a former football hero at the University of California who went on to an outstanding career at law school. After law school he went to work for the State Attorney General and then became the first Negro attorney to be hired by a large "downtown" law firm in Los Angeles. From the moment the governor had announced the appointment of the commission Williams had been very anxious to work with it; his interest had become known to Christopher, and he was hired after the usual interviewing process had been completed. But he was never able to play more than a secondary role, for he was not a narrow "facts" man; his emphasis was on looking at social conditions.

By this time the pace of activity had become feverish in the commission's offices. Dozens of people were volunteering for work, the phones were ringing continually, administrative procedures were unknown or uncertain, and no one even knew exactly how much money was available for the commission's work. The governor had allocated $100,000 from his own emergency funds, but it seemed certain that more money would be needed, and so contact was made with the Ford Foundation for additional help in financing the operation. The foundation sent its representatives to California a number of times, and fairly quickly allocated $150,-000 to the commission.

The first task Sheridan and Horowitz faced was putting together a staff. Sheridan assumed the responsibility for hiring the attorneys and investigators, who were going to get "the facts," while Horowitz was assigned the task of employing consultants to whom "the facts" were to be presented. But as was obvious fairly early, far more importance was given to gathering the "facts" than to their interpretation.

Of the eleven attorneys hired by the commission, three were from the U.S. Attorney's office; one came from the State Attorney General and one from a background as a court clerk; the others came from specialized backgrounds. Only two had done any work in race relations, and only one had any prior experience with welfare problems. Four of the ten investigators were former FBI men, two were former agents of the Federal Narcotics Bureau, one had been a deputy sheriff, and the three others were private detectives. Indeed, the full-time staff did not include a single professional working in the field of social sciences.

One explanation for this lack of social scientists on the full-time staff was that it was difficult to get such people away from their assignments at the universities where most of them worked. As a substitute, therefore, the decision was made to hire them as consultants. But the social scientist consultants were always downgraded by McCone and Sheridan, who viewed them as dreamers and visionaries.

By instinct, training, and professional activity men like McCone and Sheridan distrust or feel uncomfortable with social science and theory. McCone prides himself on being a pragmatist, a man who gets things done. Sheridan was a prosecuting attorney, whose professional life had necessarily been concerned with getting convictions. And since McCone was chairman of the commission and Sheridan its chief counsel, it was inevitable that their views would dominate the commission and its staff. As a result serious tensions developed among the staff as they divided themselves into two rough groupings: the one whose primary emphasis was on gathering facts and making limited recommendations, and the one which sought to probe below the surface and explore a wider range of possible solutions.

That conflict came to a head quickly. As a staff meeting held shortly after the commission began operating, the subject of housing was being discussed. Cushing spoke up: "We are working with a pretty big problem here. I feel that housing is one of the central aspects of the whole problem. And it would be very helpful to us if we can gain from the commission some view as to what range of recommendations you're willing to consider. Not necessarily make, but are willing to consider."

A silence followed and then McCone asked, "Well, tell us what you mean by that."

"Here's the possible range," replied Cushing. "At one end of the spectrum your report can suggest that the way to solve this problem is to encourage little groups not to get into block-busting. At the other end, you can recommend that the President exercise his executive powers in tying non-discrimination in housing into every bank and savings and loan account guarantee in the United States. Now that's the range and there are a lot of things in between. Where does the commission want to fall?"

Once again, silence. Then the meeting adjourned. The next day McCone and Christopher appeared before the staff and gave them a short lecture, the gist of it being that the commission was only interested in "hard facts," not staff thinking on social problems. "We are not here to revolutionize society," they said. "We are not going to recommend any major social changes. We want to come up with some things that can be done right now."

The following day the same point was stressed again when Sheridan responded to a comment by Cushing that the commission had a great opportunity in carrying out its task.

"Mr. McCone and those in charge of the commission have declined that opportunity," answered Sheridan.

Another early source of disagreement in the staff was whether or not the commission should hold open hearings. McCone, supported by Christopher and Call plus a few other members of the commission, was completely opposed to such open hearings—a position shared vehemently by Sheridan. Horowitz, Williams, Cushing, and Ratner wanted open hearings, but their position was given little or no weight.

"We decided not to have any open hearings," states McCone, "for the simple reason that emotions were running high, and open hearings would have produced nothing but a forum for extremes on either side, or let's say all four sides, to come and use the commission as a platform. There had been open hearings held by various organizations, the City Council had had some hearings and I believe the Board of Supervisors, and we were cognizant of the extent to which they had been abused and used. We felt it would be unproductive."

Christopher is more uncertain today than McCone or Sheridan about the decision not to hold open hearings. "We thought that the situation might be aggravated. You have to put yourself back into that period of the fall, when there were still a couple of fires a day down in that area. The amount of press attention when our people went out of the hearings and some of the things that were said just outside the hearings in the press conferences rather led us to feel that open hearings might have incendiary effects on the area and also might not lead to maximum candor and assistance to the commission.

"But it's a very close question, and I don't feel completely comfortable about the lack of open hearings. I think we can argue that both ways."

Like McCone, Sheridan was opposed to the idea of open hearings, which, he believed, "couldn't accomplish as much" as closed ones. "As soon as you go to open hearings, how many people will try and use the commission for posturing, to take public positions, and then just use the commission to make a lot of noise?"

Sheridan's model in preparing for the closed sessions seemed to have been the Kefauver Hearings or those conducted by the McClellan Committee, in which a large staff of investigators gathered information to be used by the committee's counsel in questioning witnesses. But in the actual conduct of the sessions McCone played the dominant role, allowing Sheridan very little opportunity for questioning witnesses.

As a substitute for open hearings the commission members did have some meetings, in the two offices which had been set up in the Negro section, at which people in the community were invited to appear. But this operation was never more than half-hearted; when the commission members did appear, one at a time, most of the people to whom they talked had already been screened by the staff. And the general impression in the community was that going to the office was just a waste of time. The fact that on a few occasions Asa Call arrived at the Watts office in his limousine with a white chauffeur who parked outside the office didn't do much to mitigate the Negroes' feeling that talking to such white people was useless.

Implicit, too, in the character of the closed hearings was the commission's, or at least McCone and Sheridan's, view of whom it was important to listen to. The list of witnesses who appeared before the commission is very revealing: primarily the heads of government agencies who came to defend themselves and their roles either in the rioting or in the events that preceded it. And many of the Negroes who testified fitted the white society's notion of what constitutes Negro leadership; they were not the people who play the real leadership roles in the Negro quarters.

As one white staff member put it, "McCone sees as the Negro leaders the few people who are visible to the whites. He doesn't understand that maybe they're just the tip of a pyramid, and because he doesn't understand that, he doesn't even realize the pyramid exists."

A Negro staff member says, "McCone's whole concept of leadership disturbs me. I think he, like the majority community, think they help build Negro leaders. And to the extent that they do, their Negro leaders are going to have certain built-in defects; because in order for a Negro to be acceptable as a leader to people like McCone, you have to meet certain standards of the white community, you have to make sure you stay in your place and do all the other things which have always been characteristic of the 'Uncle Tom.' And once you build this kind of person, one who can communicate with the white power structure, he can't communicate with his own people because he's out of touch with their real problems. And so it's just a fantastic vicious circle; and then when you end up, as McCone did, blaming those people for what happened, it's like blaming a creation of your own for not being able to control the masses. It's ridiculous.

"I started out having a lot of respect for McCone, but I lost it very rapidly. He did one thing that really threw me: one day he came into the office and told us that he sees things just a little more clearly now. Why did he see things a little more clearly? Because, he said, he'd gone and received an interpretation of these problems from his maid! She'd told him something that had convinced him he was on the right track. And he didn't understand that this maid is dependent upon him for a livelihood; in all probability she likes him because he's probably a good employer, and how could he think she's going to stand up and tell him anything that would in any way disturb him?"

McCone seems to have been disturbed neither by anything his maid told him nor by what was presented in testimony at the sixty-four hearings the commission held in the auditorium of the State Office Building under strict security conditions. In general, the hearings were defensive of the existing agencies of government, and sought to balance any criticism of them with evidence supporting their activities.

While the hearings were going on, attended regularly by most of the commission members, tensions among the staff were growing worse. Administratively, the commission operated like an hourglass, a military operation with the commission members, the officers, on the top, and the staff, the enlisted personnel, below them. Between the two groups, at the center of the hourglass, was Sheridan, the top sergeant.

"We worked out a chain of command right from the beginning," says Sheridan. "Because we had to deal with normal kinds of problems, not serious ones. I drew a little diagram at one of the early commission meetings, and I said, 'This is the commission up here, all the commissioners; this is all the staff, down here; this is me, in the middle. If the people on the commission have anything they want the staff to do, any communications, correspondence, or anything like that with the staff, it's got to go through me. And I'm instructing the staff that if they've got anything for the commission, it goes through me, not because I'm important or anything else, but because if we don't have this kind of a thing, then I'll never know what the hell is going on and neither will the commission.' The commission agreed with this kind of approach, so that after a while McCone and myself had any number of meetings, any number of sessions."

The pressure on the commission members was great, for they were attending the hearings plus the occasional commission meetings called by the chairman. And because they all had to cram their normal week's work into a day or two at the most so that they could spent time on commission activities, most of them were willing to allow McCone, Call, and Christopher, together with Sheridan, to continue making all the daily decisions. Indeed, McCone, a very energetic man, was spending almost all of his time on commission business, flying to Washington frequently to meet with government officials, conferring with people from the Warren

Commission about their experiences, and talking to his friends in the Washington scene. Even when McCone was in California, he kept in constant touch with the White House, discussing the progress of the investigation with Joseph Califano, a top Presidential advisor. Liaison with state officials was maintained through Christopher, who was always regarded as the governor's voice on the commission.

But the abdication of responsibility by the other commission members resulted not only from their crowded schedules and Mc-Cone's willingness to put in hundreds of hours on commission work; other factors were involved, too.

John McCone is not only a strong personality but a powerful one as well, a member of that group in America who exert much influence on the nation's life. Because he combines prestige in business, one of the highest forms of status in the country, with influence in government, he is not a man to be lightly challenged. And few of the other commission members were in a position to do so, even if they had wanted to fight him. The only one who did, and then only at the end and not very seriously, was Reverend Jones.

The original division of staff work had been that Sheridan was to assume primary responsibility for the investigations and hearings, Horowitz for the work being done by the consultants, and Williams for the operations of the field offices. But Sheridan was the overall director of all the staff activities, and this created stress between him and Horowitz, for according to some of the staff, he believed Horowitz was breaking the chain of command by going directly to McCone and some of the commissioners, discussing with them the work of the consultants.

This stopped when Horowitz was relieved of his responsibility for dealing with the consultants and replaced by Cushing, who was in turn replaced by Sheridan himself. And while all this internal tension was growing, time was getting shorter, the offices more and more chaotic, and the staff more and more disorganized and depressed. Memos were written and ignored, plans outlined and forgotten, consultants called in and never seen again. Perhaps the only consistent daily action was the nightly emptying of all the wastepaper baskets and the destruction of their contents by a waste disposal company brought in by Sheridan.

In desperation, for the deadline was growing closer and closer, members of the staff were assigned areas of responsibility without any relationship to their experience or expertise in the field. The result was more chaos, of course, with an enormous amount of effort wasted in writing memos eventually discarded and conducting useless interviews.

" 'Give us a memo,' they'd say," reports one staff member, "so I'd prepare a memo. Then they'd tell me, 'No, that's not what we want. It's too long.' So I'd write another and they'd come back with, 'No, that's no good either; what we want is just an outline.' And once I wrote a very long memorandum, but when I got it back it was just a précis and a lousy one at that of what I'd said. That was when I began to understand that the report wasn't going to have a lot in it."

In addition, the prior attitudes and training of the staff necessarily skewed their views of the problems. The investigators were busy looking for signs of a plot behind the riots and writing reports of their "interrogations" of "subjects," while the attorneys tended to see the areas to which they'd been assigned primarily in legal terms. And the consultants, too, necessarily had to write their reports on the basis of their already established views, for there was neither the time nor the opportunity for them to do any further research in their special areas. The only exception was Dr. Kenneth Martyn, the consultant on education, who received funds to complete his research work.

One of the few consultants actively involved with the commission was Paul Bullock, an economist on the staff of the Institute of Industrial Relations at UCLA. Bullock had been one of the men chiefly responsible for making a detailed report on the Negro and Mexican-American community of Los Angeles commissioned by the Area Redevelopment Administration in 1963. That report had covered, in great detail, employment, housing, consumer practices, transportation, and a variety of other problems in the south and south central gehttos. Bullock's own special interest was employment, and he was considered to be the most knowledgeable person in all of Los Angeles on the situation in the Negro areas.

Bullock was contacted by Horowitz soon after the commission was created and asked to report on such questions as the impact on the area of various training programs, the kinds of jobs that had been developed, where the jobs had been located and what the transportation problems were in getting to them. Since so little time was available to do any new research, Bullock was forced to use whatever data he had already gathered in connection with his ARA report and his continuing interest in the situation.

Fortunately, he had quite a lot of data, and so he prepared a preliminary report and then added a supplemental report to it, following this up with an appearance before the commission members to summarize his reports. By this time it was November and the situation at the commission was one of terrible anxiety, since the deadline for the report was only a few weeks away.

The notion McCone and Sheridan had of the relationship between the staff and the commission members extended over their attitude toward the consultants. "Facts" not opinions were what was demanded of the staff, and "facts" not opinions were all that was wanted from the consultants, too.

As Sheridan says of the consultants, "A lot of material, a lot of information that was coming in at that stage wasn't in the practical world. And when we wanted hard facts, some of the consultants couldn't give you hard facts. So, what they wanted to give you was their opinions. And of course their opinions weren't important. They're important but they're not important. It's the commissioners' opinion that became important . . ."

In the meantime, too, Horowitz had been removed from liaison with consultants such as Bullock and had been replaced by Cushing. But then Cushing and Miss Ratner both quit, convinced that they and the others who shared their viewpoint had lost the battle. Believing that the commission's report was going to be useless, they wanted no connection with it. Unfortunately, however, they left without explaining their position, thus leaving themselves open to all sorts of rumors about their reasons for resigning.

Sheridan then took over the liaison role with the consultants at the time when the staff was beginning work on writing the report.

Members of the commission were also designated to accept responsibility for making certain that specific sections of the report were written. In the case of the employment section, for example, one of the men formerly with the U.S. Attorney's staff, an ex-FBI agent, and commission member Asa Call had been designated as the staff members responsible.

As the deadline came closer and closer, the atmosphere of the commission's offices grew more frantic and tense. As Sheridan describes it, "At this stage we had no end product in mind. We didn't know what we were working toward; we didn't know when we were working toward it. We didn't know the exact date; are we going to turn out a book, are we going to turn out a forty-page report, or are we going to do the same thing as the Welfare Commission did—put out its report, its recommendations, and a separate volume with the consultants' reports attached to it? And all of these suggestions, of course, were discussed with the commissioners. . . . So we drew up several drafts, formats, this kind of thing, for the commissioners to decide what it wanted . . ."

"We had assembled a mass of data," recalls McCone. "We had a great number of witnesses; we had our offices; we had consultants' reports, and we had reports from investigators. And we had a study on education, a study on employment, and we had assembled a lot of information from studies that had gone before us . . .

"So, then we sat around and we took the various areas of importance—employment, education, housing, transportation, various sections of the report—and we concluded among ourselves just what our general recommendations would be. And those were written maybe on one piece of paper. And in fact I dictated most of them and then brought them down and tried them on for size, and we modified them or added to them to meet the will of the commission.

"We found we were in quite general agreement and then we set out to write the report. Now, I wanted a report that would be an interesting, readable document, so I asked a friend of mine to come out and assist in writing the report. And he did. Unfortunately, he was taken violently ill the day after he arrived, and as a consequence the writing of the report fell pretty much on the shoulders of Warren Christopher and myself. And then I insisted that we take the draft that was produced by whoever produced it and that we go over it line by line and word by word by the commission. Now, this was very tedious for them but having had some experience in getting out national estimates for the United States Intelligence Board, I know how to do that. And so we went over it line by line and while we were together, we changed it and agreed to it, and if some wording had to be changed to make a special point or emphasize or de-emphasize something the writer had emphasized, we did that. When all of that was done, then the thing was put to bed."

McCone's calm recital represents one view of the process by which the report was written. From the consultants' viewpoint, the process looked quite different.

Many of them who undertook their responsibilities very seriously believe that they were used by the commission primarily because their names would lend an aura of intellectual respectability to the report. In fact, with one notable exception, the report of the consultant on education, the commission's final report does not contain very much of either what some staff members produced for it or of the lengthy reports submitted to it by the consultants referred to in the final document. In the overwhelming majority of cases, the consultants' work was either ignored or contradicted in the commission's final document.

The experience of Paul Bullock was typical: "In late November," he says, "I got several near-frantic calls from the commission staff working on the report. They wanted me to help out with it. So in the last week of November, I went down, and between us we drafted some preliminary statements that we thought should go into the report. And on the day before Thanksgiving, I got a call, a frantic call, 'We've got to get this thing done over the weekend.' I refused to come down on Thanksgiving Day, but I did go down the next day and spent the whole day working with the staff.

"And I went down again on Saturday morning, the last Saturday in November. We went into an office, we sat down at a table, and we were working on some thoughts for the section. And McCone dashed into the office—this must have been about eleven A.M.

because I'd gotten down there at about eight-thirty—and threw several sheets of paper on the table. Then he said something like, 'You know, I got up early this morning; I got up at about three or three-thirty, and I sat down and I drafted what I think are the things that should be in this employment section. And when I got here, I showed them to Asa and Asa thought they were fine. So this is the employment section.'

"McCone dashed out to another office and we took a quick look at what he'd written. On the first page there was a statement that California provides welfare payments on a generous scale. There were other statements in the report that reflected on the moral stature and the very character of Negroes. But these were mixed in with some very acceptable statements and some that were constructive and accurate. It wasn't all bad. I thought it was the kind of free association of a man who has implicit faith in his own judgment in each of these areas and has picked up from personal ideas and experiences a number of very fixed feelings, some of them right and some wrong.

"Anyway, we remonstrated with McCone. And McCone told us in response to our comments, that he wasn't really interested in what we had to say, that he just wanted us to look at the report and to clear up anything that was vague in the wording and correct any overt factual inaccuracies we could find. But in essence this section was what he wanted in the employment section."

By this time Bullock was almost convinced he ought to have nothing more to do with the report. He corrected a few of the worst factual errors and left the office, refusing to come back the next day, Sunday, to work on it any further. But he did return on Monday, when the report was scheduled to go to the full commission, in the hope that he could disassociate himself from it and even, if necessary, appear before the commission to argue about what McCone had written.

"When I arrived there on Monday morning," continues Bullock, "McCone had obviously had second thoughts about the section. I didn't see him but he had left word for me to go over the section with a man who'd been brought in by McCone to rewrite the report. So we went in and sat down. He had gotten the draft from

McCone and he told us he didn't know anything about the subject.

"So he asked if we would sit down with him and help him redraft it. And this is what we did: we spent that whole Monday on it and then the full commission was to consider it sometime that same afternoon. We went through it; we cut out what we regarded as the most offensive of the statements, though when you read the report you can still see some of the implications left in there in final form. And we put in some references ourselves; for example, the reference to do something about police arrest records was put in by me. The statement about police records doesn't say too much, but at least it raises the issue."

While the men were working on the draft, McCone came into the room a few times to check on their progress. On his first visit he complained to them that a statement issued by the state FEPC committee had been too harsh on business, and that in view of the FEPC attitude he was opposed to the draft report's recommendation that the strength of the FEPC be reinforced. But he didn't ask the group to delete that suggestion.

"The second time he came in, he was livid," reports Bullock. "He was absolutely furious. He came in and said, in effect, what were we doing? After all, we had his draft already, the commission was waiting for the report, and it wasn't necessary to spend this much time on the redrafting. So I spoke up and I said, in effect, that the draft contained some very serious misstatements and that since this report was going to be reviewed by a lot of people, we felt it was our responsiblity to go over it carefully and at least make sure that no serious inaccuracies and distortions or misstatements were included. He calmed down and semi-apologized for his attitude but said he wanted something as quickly as possible. Then we finished off the draft, which included four recommendations prepared by Asa Call and McCone, including the one to strengthen the FEPC. But when the report emerged in its final form, the recommendation for strengthening the FEPC was missing. It did have a relatively innocuous and even meaningless request for legislation to give FEPC the power of making surveys but only for employers of more than 250 employees. And, of course, some of the worst discrimination of employers in this state comes from the smaller and medium-sized categories of employers."

Although there were no other substantial last-moment changes made in the report's employment section, the recommendations for action fall far short of the proposals suggested by Bullock. His analysis of the final report is openly pessimistic. He has written that the report only "mentions Governor Brown's proposal for a national effort to finance useful jobs for the unemployed and underemployed, costing about $2.5 billion annually on a national scale and $250 million in California, which would provide 50,000 new jobs throughout the state. Viewing the Brown proposal with mixed sympathy and skepticism, the McCone report finally dismisses it as impractical in the light of the fiscal demands of Vietnam escalation and fears of inflation . . .

"The report makes reference to police arrest records as an additional barrier to employment for many persons (in a statement added by staff members and consultants to the original draft) and urges employers to review their hiring policies in an effort to increase employment opportunities for persons in this category. Unfortunately, this is not made a part of the report's formal recommendations, and is only hortatory in nature . . .

"The Employment section ends with a repetition of what the Commission regards as the major recommendations:

"(1) A job training and placement center through the combined efforts of Negroes, employers, labor unions, and government;

"(2) Assurances by federal and state governments, through new facilities and better communication, that maximum advantage is taken of the various training programs and employment opportunities;

"(3) The recommended legislation requiring reports from employers and labor unions to the FEPC, relative to the ethnic composition of the work force and membership.

"These recommendations, in my judgment, range from innocuous (#2) to useful and affirmative (#1) in principle, but by no stretch of the imagination can any of them be labeled 'bold.' The role assigned to government is a relatively limited one, reflecting the Chairman's own predilections in this regard. Throughout the report, there are several references to the need for evidence of initiative from and within the Negro community itself, with the implication (it seems to me) that the community has resisted its responsibilities in the past. The principle that the minority communties should assume a more meaningful role in the planning and administration of antipoverty programs is a legitimate one, widely accepted within the Negro community itself and, indeed, the very basis for a community demand that the poor be given more effective representation in the management of existing programs. When, however, the advocacy of this principle is linked with an implication that Negroes currently are unwilling and unprepared to accept such responsibility, and that this explains much of their plight in American society, the result is merely to bolster some of the more vicious sterotypes of prejudiced whites, antagonize many Negroes, and thereby discredit an otherwise sound proposal. In this respect, then, the report manages to strike the worst possible balance."

But while in the case of the employment section the final report only leaves out most of the proposals and recommendations of the commission's consultant, in the case of the welfare section it directly contradicts much of what the expert in the field reported to the commission. The welfare consultant to the commission was Dr. Frances Feldman of the University of Southern California. Her report to the commission is a detailed and lengthy analysis of the welfare system. Like Bullock, she was given only a very short period of time to prepare her report—three weeks. The data in her report were derived, she writes, "not only from reports, ordinances, and laws but also from interviews with individuals and groups who were or had been public assistance recipients or applicants; with present and former employees at various hierarchial levels and in various classifications in county and state agencies primarily concerned with the administration and extension of public assistance programs; with state referees who hear appeals from county decisions; and with representatives of other organizations, agencies and departments whose work brought them into contact either with recipients or staff of the public welfare agencies."

Like Bullock, Dr. Feldman also believes that the final report does have some positive contributions "sprinkled" through it. But the main thrust of the commission's conclusions about the welfare situation were obviously unaffected by what it heard from Dr. Feldman. In one section the commission's report flatly contradicts the facts she presented. The report states: "We have no intention of opposing the humanitarian purposes of the welfare program. Nevertheless, we are profoundly disturbed by the accelerating trend of expenditure . . . A portion of the rapid increase may be explained by the fact that the Negro and Mexican-American population in Los Angeles is estimated to have increased approximately 40 per cent in the last five years, compared with the general population increase of 13 per cent in the same period. Moreover, the high unemployment in this area . . . no doubt has contributed to the increase. However, the increase in AFDC (Aid to Families with Dependent Children) expenditures coupled with increase in population raises a question in the minds of some whether the generosity of the California welfare program compared with those in the southern and southwestern states is not one of the factors causing the heavy immigration of disadvantaged people to Los Angeles."

Yet the data given the commission by Dr. Feldman point to exactly the opposite kind of conclusion. As she has observed, the commissioners "had these facts before them: (1) The growth of the population on assistance has been slower than the growth of population in the county as a whole. (2) Residence requirements for eligibility preclude the granting of AFDC to non-residents or of general relief to non-residents who are ineligible for federally aided assistance and who are not willing to return to the state in which they have legal settlement. (3) The proportion of native Californians among the recipients was similar to the proportion among the commissioners. (4) Statutory limits on the amount of individual AFDC grants are unrelated either to the minimum standards established by the State Department of Social Welfare as essential for adequate care or to the steadily rising costs of living. (5) A substantial part of the increased caseload has resulted from reduced work opportunities for those who are unskilled, untrained, uneducated, or without work experience—particularly minority group members, and from action by Congress and by the California State Legislature broadening the definitions of need in connection with the several federally aided assistance categories; and (6), while the average monthly payment per family has risen a little faster since 1960 than the cost-of-living index, the payment per person has actually declined—so that the AFDC recipient, in the riot month, typically was receiving a smaller proportion of what he needed than if he had been receiving aid five years earlier (and, generally, he had *not*)."

The fact is, as Dr. Feldman states, "The commissioners remained remarkably true to the stereotypes they had held when they were appointed . . ." She goes on to say, "My meetings with the members of the commission staff and with the commission itself offered ample indication of the direction of commission thinking and the difficulties entailed in persuading some of the staff as well as most of the commissioners to examine the evidence objectively and not through the haze of preconceived notions about who accepts assistance and why. It is undoubtedly true that not even the police phase of the McCone inquiry was invested with more of the personalized feelings of the commissioners than was the welfare phase."

And it is true that McCone's stereotyped views remained unchanged by either the Feldman report or the testimony presented to the commission by such experts as Paul Ward, the governor's cabinet member responsible for all the welfare programs in the state.

"I know," says McCone, "that the professional view of the politicians and the sociologists is that these welfare payments do not attract people. But we had just enough statements made by people in the area to lead us to the conclusion that it does attract people . . . We have a very considerable amount of evidence that, averages to the contrary, there are many people that did come here attracted by this and that; they found ways to get around even the one-year waiting period. And so much so that we had to warn that that was going on . . .

"Now I realize that this is a controversial point. I know Mrs. Feldman didn't agree with it; Governor Brown didn't agree with it; Mr. Ward didn't agree with it. But they're defenders, you see. And finally Jones dissented . . ."

What is the "evidence" to which McCone referred? "Statements," is his answer, "and investigating reports, some testimony." From whom? Dr. Feldman describes the people who presented testimony as "persons whose positions were indicative of their competence to render judgments—ministers, landlords, an assorted group of taxpayers and 'social workers' in the employ of state and county welfare departments, the county's probation department and some voluntary agencies. They *knew* that the high standards of relief attracted transients to California; they *knew* of husbandless women who deliberately increased the size of the family in order to increase the amount of the assistance grant. These social workers had several things in common: none when asked for details could provide them; none had either professional education for the jobs they held or other educational or experiential backgrounds that might have contributed to their knowledge about social welfare programs or human behavior."

Added to all this "evidence" were rumors about "parking lots where people meet to exchange children so they can get on the welfare rolls." But the physical location of the lots always remained elusive.

Christopher, too, seems to believe that Southern Negroes plan their moves to California not because their families are there or because they think they can find jobs in the state, but because they make a comparative analysis of welfare benefits in the various states. He says: "Just put yourself in the place of the fellow in Mississippi or Alabama, where they have virtually no welfare programs at all. It's a national disgrace. He looks at California and one of the packages of things that he sees about California is, California has a prosperous economy. There are lots of opportunities out here and also there are better schools, better welfare benefits, right across the board."

In the end, too, like Bullock again, Feldman gives a metaphorical sigh of relief that "the contents of the report reflected some modification—at least to the extent that they were omitted—of ideas of staff and commissioners that I unhappily had expected they would not relinquish."

The dissent of Reverend Jones from the welfare section of the report is one of the only two public instances of opposition developing within the commission itself, both coming from the Negro minister. But his dissent was not labeled as such; instead it was offered in the report as his "comments." Commenting, then, Reverend Jones wrote about the welfare section that he had been unable to find statistics to justify the statement that California welfare programs encourage heavy immigration to Los Angeles, "and violently disagree with this unjustifiable projection . . ."

However, neither Jones nor any other commissioner objected publicly to the commission's report on law enforcement, despite the fact that there are statements in it which were in direct contradiction to evidence introduced at the hearings by many people, including even a high official in the police department.

Over the years bitter attacks on the Los Angeles Police Department had been made by Negroes and other minority groups for its internal discriminatory practices and its external behavior toward members of minority groups. The United States Civil Rights Commission had castigated the department in the report it issued in 1963; Chief William Parker had been the object of mounting criticisms for the department's behavior during the riots and for his statements about Negroes. The entire matter of whether or not the police were themselves a factor in creating racial tension was one of the most important questions the commission could and should have examined.

Yet neither the commission's investigations, its hearings, nor its final report seemed to have had any other objective than that of defending, as much as possible, the past activities of the police and their role during the riots. And this was clear from the start of the commission's work.

According to Sheridan, "The commission felt, as a commission, that there was a delicate balancing here, that the commission was not set up to investigate the police department. What caused the commission to come into existence? The riots. Not the police department. The commission was set up to look at the riots, not to go into the police . . ."

Since the commission did not see any need to investigate the police, no attempt was made to bring in an outside consultant on police problems. Sheridan's view about employing such a consultant was that it was unnecessary to do so because he and his staff were the best people to serve in that role. He points out that he "didn't know anyone better to get than Logan Lane," his chief investigator, who was a former FBI agent. On the staff, according to Sheridan, there were "at least six of us with any number of years as criminal prosecutors dealing with law enforcement. I personally have dealt a lot with Parker, with Pat Brown, with the sheriff's office, with all the investigative agencies: so, frankly, if I was going to hire just a consultant on law enforcement, I'd probably hire myself."

No attempt was made, either, to gather any evidence about the charges of police brutality. When some members of the staff raised the question of outlining a plan for investigating alleged cases of police brutality, Sheridan opposed it, stating that such an investigation wasn't necessary because "the commission is already convinced there is police brutality, and therefore there was no need to take evidence of it." And so no testimony about specific instances of police brutality was given in the hearings, although at least three witnesses offered to provide the commission with such cases. Instead, the commission merely forwarded the files it was offered to what it described as "the appropriate and responsible agencies."

Perhaps Sheridan believed that the commission was "convinced there is police brutality," but there is no indication of this in either McCone's or Christopher's statements. McCone says about police brutality: "There's lots of evidence that it's a two-way street, that there's a kind of planned aggravation of the police by the Negroes. Many, many, but I wouldn't say all by any means, of the so-called incidents of police brutality were aggravated."

At one of the hearings McCone made a very explicit statement about alleged cases of police brutality while questioning a representative of the American Civil Liberties Union who had charged the LAPD with brutality. "We have received a report from the Department of Justice that in 1964 there were seven riots in various parts of the United States. They were identified as riots: Rochester, New York, Chicago, and so forth. And in each one of them police brutality was the cry. I will repeat that: and in each one of them police brutality was the cry.

"As the Director of Central Intelligence, I was familiar with many insurrections and disturbances in many parts of the world: Panama, Dominican Republic, Saigon, and elsewhere. And in every one of these police brutality was the cry. This raises a question in my mind: if this isn't a device, and if you are not supporting a device that is designed to destroy the law; and after all, law is just the thin thread that holds our society together, and nothing would be more beneficial to our adversaries, those who would like to destroy the freedom that this country stands for, than to destroy the enforcement of the law and bust this thin cord which holds us together."

McCone's attitude toward civilian review boards was as fixed as his belief that the charge of police brutality is a "device designed to destroy the law." At the same hearing he attacked the ACLU recommendation for a civilian review board by observing that "when the chiefs of police of this nation met to consider this recommendation, they concluded, with little if any opposition, that the implementation of this plan would destroy the effectiveness of the police department."

Christopher says he "thought the basic underlying problem was the weakness of the Board of Police Commissioners, its failure to assert jurisdiction over the police department. The mechanism was there, but they had this commission meeting one afternoon a week, giving them ten dollars a week, and I think looking toward the chief for leadership rather than providing some leadership."

Of Chief Parker the report states: "Chief of Police Parker appears to be the focal point of the criticisms within the Negro community. He is a man distrusted by most Negroes and they carefully analyze for possible anti-Negro meaning almost every action he takes and every statement he makes. Many Negroes feel that he carries a deep hatred of the Negro community. However,

Chief Parker's statements to us and collateral evidence such as his record of fairness to Negro officers are inconsistent with his having such an attitude . . ."

Yet witness after witness had testified to quite the opposite about Chief Parker's "record of fairness to Negro officers." City Councilman Thomas Bradley, who was a lieutenant in the LAPD before retiring after many years of service, presented detailed evidence to the commission of the department's internal discriminatory practices under Parker. He pointed out that the department had never had a Negro captain, although he was "satisfied that there have been men there with the talent, intelligence, and capability to rise to this level, all other things being equal." He discussed the fact that until four years ago, "No Negro and white officer could work together in a radio car," and pointed out that as a consequence "a white officer is going to regard his Negro officer as less than a first-class man."

And if the commission had been doubtful about the authenticity of Councilman Bradley's testimony and that of the other witnesses, it had only to listen to Deputy Chief Roger Murdock, himself the object of bitter attack from Negroes. Murdock admitted that the department had been prejudiced, even though he defended it on an overall basis.

Not a sign of such testimony can be found in the report's defense of Chief Parker. Instead, the report calls "for a better understanding by the law enforcement agencies of Negro community attitudes, and on the other hand a more widespread understanding within the Negro community of the value of the police and the extent to which the law enforcement agencies provide it with security." And for specific measures, the report urges that the police commission be strengthened; that an "inspector general" post be set up to process complaints in place of a civilian review board, which would be "likely" to have "deleterious effects upon law enforcement"; that the police department should "institute expanded community relations programs," and that the county sheriff's department "should effectuate these recommendations to the extent that they are applicable to it."

McCone's and Sheridan's desire to defend the police department spilled over even into the area of "hard facts" on which they had placed so much stress. In "144 Hours in August 1965," the chronology of events which appears as one of the first sections of the final report, the description of a key circumstance—one which might well have changed the entire direction of the events—is distorted so badly that in effect the commission report lies about what happened. The specific event was a meeting held Thursday afternoon, at the very height of the rioting, in an auditorium in a public park in the Watts area. The Athens Park meeting had been arranged by staff officials of the Los Angeles County Commission on Human Relations who were working desperately to quiet the situation. According to John Buggs, executive director of the agency, the purpose of the meeting was to bring together, "clergymen, community leaders, persons who worked for social agencies in the area, political leaders, law enforcement officers, probation officers, and our staff to discuss a plan of employing these groups in a door-to-door individual contact with residents in the affected area, in an attempt to keep people off the streets and at home . . ."

The commission's "hard fact" chronology of events states flatly: "The meeting called by the Los Angeles County Human Relations Commission, at the request of county officials, for the purpose of lowering the temperature misfired." It then goes on to describe in some detail but inaccurately what happened at the meeting, without pointing out that the fundamental cause of the "misfiring" was the refusal of the police to consider seriously a suggestion which the agency staff had made earlier that day to a police official for withdrawing white officers from the area and replacing them with Negroes in plain clothes and unmarked cars. At the meeting, attended by a county supervisor, a city councilman, and the congressman from the area, there were also about 100 to 150 adults representing the groups which had been contacted. In addition, about 100 youths who had not been expected showed up, because some of the adult leaders in the community had urged them to attend, says Buggs, in the belief that the young men "would be helpful in (1) relaying to the group the feeling of those who were engaged in the rioting, and (2) because they had indicated a desire to use their influence in getting their friends and acquaintances to stop the riot."

At the meeting the proposal to ask for the removal of the uniformed white police was again discussed, this time at some length, making it the second time the police knew of it, for there were a few police officials present. After the main meeting had adjourned a smaller one was held between some of the adult leaders and the young men representing the youth gangs in the area. The gang leaders agreed to use their considerable influence to stop the riot if they could have an opportunity to present to the mass media their view of what had sparked the riot and if the suggestion made earlier of replacing the uniformed white police with plainclothes Negroes was carried out. They indicated, too, that if this course of action did not end the rioting, they would have no objection to having the white officers return to the area.

After the second meeting was over, Buggs and his staff contacted the police and were told that the proposal to withdraw the white officers had been rejected. Disappointed by the police reaction and convinced that the rioting would get worse, Buggs and two members of his staff met again with the gang leaders. In the meantime, as they suspected, the rioting showed every sign of reaching a fever pitch. At this meeting with the gang leaders it was decided that the only way "of preventing further rioting and probably bloodshed was to immediately get the police removed . . ." Buggs and two members of his staff went to the 77th Street Police Station to see Deputy Chief Roger Murdock who was in charge of the police operations in the area. At the station they were joined by a Negro minister who was present during the discussion with Murdock.

Murdock rejected the proposal, saying, according to Buggs, that he had made the decision earlier in the day with the concurrence of Chief Parker and Mayor Yorty. Further, says Buggs, Murdock told the Negroes that "We are not going to have hoodlums telling us how to run the police department, and you had no right to tell them we would send in Negro officers." The session grew angrier and angrier until the Negro leaders left the hostile police official and returned to the area, where the rioting was getting completely out of control.

But the McCone Commission's report on the two meetings in the Athens Park Auditorium omits any mention of the discussion at the first general meeting of the proposal to replace the white officers with Negroes, nor does it include the fact that the proposal had originally been made to the police earlier that morning.

In addition to omitting these extremely important "hard facts," the chronology further distorts what actually happened by giving the impression that the proposal to withdraw the white officers was made initially at the *second,* smaller meeting between the smaller group of community leaders and the representatives of the youth gangs.

In the commission's version the small group "went to see Deputy Chief of Police Murdock at the 77th Street Station where the proposals were rejected by him at about 7 P.M." There is not a single word in the commission report to indicate that the proposals had been made by the adult leaders and rejected by the police earlier in the day. And the commission's description of the meeting at the 77th Street Station fails to mention any of the hostile statements attributed to Murdock by Buggs and the others present at the meeting with him.

This is not just a slight error on the part of the commission or its staff about an unimportant incident. If the police had been willing to replace the uniformed white officers, who were visible objects of hate to the Negroes, and if they had been willing to work with the youth leaders, the rioting might have ended that night and the worst of the bloodshed and property destruction might have been avoided. At least, the police might have tried out the proposal instead of rejecting it as contemptuously as they did. And certainly, in its chronological report, the commission had the responsibility of making public the actual sequence of events, which could not be disputed. After all, the "hard facts" about what was said at the Athens Park meeting were known, just as were the "hard facts" that earlier that day Buggs had made the proposal to withdraw the white officers.

It is also not as if the commission did not have access to the facts. Buggs testified at great length to the commission, as did Murdock. And where the two men differed in their versions, it was the responsibility of the commission to acknowledge that the differences existed, for by anyone's standards Buggs must be characterized as a responsible community leader. In addition, Buggs provided the commission with a detailed "chronological report" he had prepared for the County Board of Supervisors, which gives every detail of the events as he saw them occur. Interestingly enough, that chronological report was not included in the copies of the commission's documents deposited in nine libraries in the state, although Buggs's testimony is there.

The commission's one-sided presentation of the events at and following the Athens Park meeting is the norm for its entire chronology of the riots. Wherever distinctly separate versions were presented to the commission in testimony at hearings, its report gave as the truth that version which defended the actions of the police or those other government agencies acting in the name of law and order. And when one of its own consultants prepared a report analyzing the procedures followed by one such agency, the coroner's office, the chronology merely acknowledges in a footnote the existence of the memorandum, stating "it has been forwarded to the appropriate public officials for their consideration." But there is not a single word referring to the contents of the report, which in fact attacked the procedure used in conducting coroner's inquests.

Perhaps, too, to men like John McCone, John Buggs is not as responsible a community leader as is Roger Murdock: months later, at a meeting attended by both men after another outbreak of violence in the Watts area, McCone stated flatly that he did not believe a statement which Buggs had made to the meeting about a staff member of the County Commission who had been kicked by a police officer while trying to quiet the outbreak. To McCone it is probably inconceivable that the police would do such a thing, and so he finds it easy always to accept the police version of an event as true, for they are the "thin cord which holds us together."

Another characteristic example of how the commission refused to "probe deeply" into the "immediate and underlying causes of the riots" was its report on housing. The commission lists as its consultant on housing Professor Fred Case of UCLA who has been studying housing and real estate in Los Angeles for many years, and who has also served on commissions and boards involved with land use and building operations. But Professor Case was not even approached by the commission until three weeks before the report was written, and he never met with the commission. He was given $300 for expenses to hire some graduate students to help him prepare his report. Since Case, like Bullock, was working on the material for a report anyway, he had available data, which he submitted together with his conclusions to the commission.

But Case's view of the housing problems faced by minority groups in Los Angeles is a far more dismal one than McCone and Christopher were willing to admit existed. And as had been true in so many of the other areas, the witnesses called to testify before the commission almost always tried to defend the status quo in housing and the specific role played by their own agencies.

The result shows in the commission's report: not only were the memoranda of its own staff ignored, but hardly a trace of what Professor Case reported to it can be found in the pages of what McCone has called "the little book." Instead, the report mirrors McCone's personal attitudes. For despite all the data and evidence about ghettoization, McCone still insists that "the evidence that the Negro is confined in an area of Los Angeles is more imaginary than real. If you examine the maps—and we have them for each five-year period from 1946 on—to show the expansion of the Negro-dominated area, it evidences the fact that they moved to the west and to the south and also in areas of Pasadena, Pacoima, and elsewhere and have continually spread. So there was no real confinement."

McCone's misunderstanding of the ghettoization process that has been going on in Los Angeles is matched by his ignorance of reality, for he says, "Now, to be sure, there were laws in the thirties and in the early fifties that were restrictive, but those were all extinguished. So the only obstacle that stood in the way of Negro occupancy was the owners' choice. There was no legal restriction. It was a man's option to do what he wished with his property. But to me it's just amazing to go into areas where—not as a child, but as a young man and middle-aged man—where the homes of my close friends were, that you find today is 100 per cent Negro."

The commission report on housing may also reflect Christopher's concern about a serious political problem for the Democrats. The issue of segregated housing was an extremely controversial one in the state as a result of a court case seeking to declare unconstitutional a referendum proposition which had been passed in 1964, repealing a state law against housing segregation.

"Proposition 14 was pending before the courts at the time," says Christopher. "It had been argued but not decided, and we felt a great deal of reluctance to wade into that problem because the matter was pending before the California Supreme Court at the very time there was a Superior Court judge and at least two other lawyers on our commission. And that was coupled, somewhat, with the fact that this could be one of those problems to which the solution lay so deep that it didn't seem hardly within our reach, whereas one of the useful things we felt might be done about segregation was to improve the level of achievement in the schools so that you didn't have the white people fleeing as soon as the Negro people moved into an area."

What is true of welfare, police, and housing is equally true for most of the other areas discussed in the commission's report. Health problems are disposed of in five brief paragraphs, which indicate in a few phrases that the report prepared for the commission by its consultant, Dr. Milton Roemer of UCLA, had at least been read. But a key point made by Dr. Roemer—that private medicine had failed to meet its obligations in Los Angeles—is not mentioned.

On only one question, education, did the commission report use in a substantive way the material submitted to it by a consultant. This, the lengthiest section, was written almost entirely by the staff, although it mirrors the commission's view of education as "holding the greatest promise for breaking the cycle of failure." Yet even after reviewing in detail what it believes to be the disparities between the schools in the Negro areas and those outside, the report refuses to deal with the basic problem of Negro education— school segregation. Instead, it accepts as apparently inevitable the existence of de facto segregated schools, but says, "We reason, therefore, that raising the scholastic achievement might reverse the entire trend of de facto segregation." To achieve the possibility of this objective, the commission made its two specific proposals about education: cut class size in what it would designate as "emergency schools," providing them also with "additional supportive personnel to provide special services; and establish a permanent pre-school program throughout the school year."

In another area, too, the commission was very forthright: it attacked the absence of an adequate transportation system in the city. Here again it demonstrated its willingness to take a position on any question that was non-controversial and about which no body of stereotypes existed. After all, who can be opposed to bettering ghetto schools and who can oppose a decent transportation system? As one disgusted staff member put it after hearing a lengthy discussion in the commission offices, "God damn it, you'd think that all Los Angeles needs to solve its problems is better transportation. These people seem to believe that if we just had better bus service, we'd have a bunch of happy niggers laughing in the streets and there'd never be another riot. What a mess this commission turned out to be!"

Reverend Jones, who had dissented from the other commission members about the contents of the welfare section, also disagreed with what the report said about the role of the Negro leaders in the civil rights movement. The report states: ". . . the accusations of the leaders of the national movement have been picked up by many local voices and have been echoed throughout the Negro community here . . . the angry exhortations and the resulting disobedience to law in many parts of our country appear to have contributed importantly to be feeling of rage which made the Los Angeles riots possible . . ."

This section of the report then concludes with, "No amount of money, no amount of effort, no amount of training will raise the disadvantaged Negro to the position he seeks and should have within this community—a position of equality—unless he himself shoulders a full share of the responsibility for his own well being. The efforts of the Negro leaders, and there are many able and dedicated ones among us, should be directed toward urging and exhorting their followers to this end."

To these statements Reverend Jones responded: "I do not believe it is the function of this commission to put a lid on protest registered in ghettos of the urban areas of our country . . . Protest against forces which reduce individuals to second class citizens, political, cultural and psychological nonentities, are part of the celebrated American tradition. As long as an individual 'stands outside looking in' he is not part of that society; that society cannot say that he does not have the right to protest nor can it say that he must shoulder a responsibility which he has never been given an opportunity to assume."

According to Jones, who was in San Francisco attending a meeting while the final report was being written, great pressure was exerted upon him to withdraw his two objections so that the report might appear as a unanimous one. This is denied by other commission members, who maintained no such pressure was applied.

Yet it cannot be said that everything in the commission's report is bad. Just as Bullock pointed out that the employment section had some good statements in it mixed along with very bad ones, the report as a whole is a mélange of some correct analyses and recommendations along with much more that at the least is merely superficial and at the most perpetuates stereotypes.

The story of the McCone Commission does not end with the publication of its report. After the report was issued the staff was dissolved; only Sheridan and a few of the investigators remained on the payroll, answering correspondence and handling accounting problems. Sheridan is also acting as the commission's attorney in a lawsuit in which it has become involved: a number of insurance companies are suing the City of Los Angeles and have demanded the right to see the documents accumulated by the commission during the investigation but not made public afterwards. The commission has refused to allow access to these documents.

That refusal is not limited to the insurance companies but extends to everyone else. After the commission report was issued Sheridan was given the blanket authority to decide what other documents the commission would make public, what documents should be saved, and what should be destroyed. Acting on this authority, he went through the materials, chose those he felt should be copied, and deposited the copies in nine libraries throughout the state. Thus, it is possible to read the consultants' reports, for example, or study the transcripts of testimony either at one of the libraries or by getting a microfilm copy.

But, and a big but it is, future scholars would have no way of knowing, from looking at the eleven volumes of materials available in the libraries, that Sheridan had taken out such key exhibits as John Buggs's chronology of events. Sheridan states that he destroyed only "drafts" of reports and memoranda, but that edited versions of interviews and other materials were saved. Unfortunately, until access to the materials is given, no one will know what was destroyed and what was kept but for a variety of reasons not included in the documents the commission did deposit in the libraries.

The commission is still operating at the public relations level, too, defending itself against some of the attacks which have been made upon it. That defense has devolved upon McCone, the conservative Republican, and Christopher, the liberal Democrat, who have acted in the name of the commission, even though they do not consult with the other commission members. Thus, for example, in August 1966 a "Staff Report of Actions Taken to Implement the Recommendations in the Commission's Report" was issued in the name of the commission. It was signed by McCone and Christopher but seen for the first time by the other commissioners on the day it was released to the press.

Considering that the commission never functioned like a British Royal Commission, perhaps nothing more could be expected from it than what was produced. From its start, as an idea of the governor's staff, the commission was given a limited responsibility to perform, and it was hampered even in that by the needs of short-term political expediency and anticipated acceptance; it was assumed that the whole truth should not be told to the community, lest it be rejected. And so instead of acting like a responsible public body, the *Governor's* Commission became John A. Mc-Cone's Commission. As a reflection of McCone's views the commission report is accurate; as a reflection of truth and reality it is unreliable. And its recommendations are useful only in that the commission acknowledges the need to spend money on strengthening such institutions as schools or on building a hospital. But in every case where fundamental change, not just more money, is required, the commission was silent.

But the greatest tragedy of the commission is that it may become the model for all the other commissions that have been set up by governors and the President. Indeed, Warren Christopher went to Detroit along with Cyrus Vance; shortly afterwards the President announced the formation of his Commission. It's not hard to predict what its report will be.

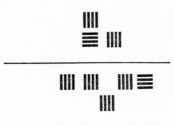

Conclusion

Enough. The failure of the McCone Commission is as good a place as any to stop. There is no real end to the story, anyway. I might have gone on to examine the parole and probation system, for these, too, are an important part of the daily lives of those inside the barrios and ghettos. I could have probed into the operations of the Los Angeles County Commission on Human Relations and shown how until the events of August 1965 it was viewed by the Board of Supervisors as little more than a public relations gimmick, poorly financed and little heeded in its advice, despite all the efforts of its staff.

But I would come out at the same place with the same agonizing conclusions. So enough.

In America, the poor and especially the minority poor live inside a pen without an exit gate. And government, rather than helping weaken or break it down, has reinforced the fence that keeps them inside it. It is true that more of those caught inside escape now than before, but the undiminished masses within are all the angrier at not getting their chance to get out too. As the pressure from within increases, the frustrations and resentments build up to an exploding point, the people cooped up inside lash out and revolt.

Since the August 1965 revolt in Los Angeles, a few meaningful improvements have taken place. A few hundred residents of the barrios and the ghettos have had an opportunity to learn some things about organization and political action through the use of anti-poverty funds; a few dozen new organizations of the poor and the minority groups are beginning to make some demands upon the society.

Yet there has been no important fundamental change in Los Angeles or any other American city.

Mayor Yorty, who like so many other mayors is more interested in furthering his political career than in solving the city's real problems, spends weeks at a time in Asia and Europe as part of his campaign for higher office. And in the last gubernatorial elections, California's white voters accurately reflected the views of white America when it elected, by an overwhelming vote, a governor who had pledged himself to cut down on welfare payments, educational expenditures, and the social services.

He has carried out his pledges, too, for he takes himself seriously. His appointments are popular ones; characteristically, the real estate broker who led the fight against fair housing was made real estate commissioner, and a county supervisor who opposed welfare expenditures is now state welfare director. The Governor authorized an investigation of "welfare frauds" and denounced rioters as "mad dogs." His actions meet with such wide public approval that he has become a serious Presidential possibility.

Still, it's not only Republicans who give a low priority to the crisis of the cities; many Democrats also oppose any large-scale expenditure on behalf of the urban poor. The War on Poverty has been more rhetoric than combat—the amount of money spent thus far has been less than $100 per poor person in the country and a sizable percentage of that has gone to administrators. And even that niggardly sum has been slashed by Congress. The War on Poverty has not had Presidential leadership either, for his priorities and those of the Congress are twisted, too.

These twisted priorities, which prevent America from curing her cities' cancers, have their roots in old but ignoble traditions in American life, traditions which have developed alongside those of a higher order. And now, confronted as we are with wars in the cities, we must honestly recognize the existence of the traditions before we can deal honestly with them.

First, we must admit that we *are* a racist country. Deep down in their visceral being, millions of white Americans believe that race *does* matter. They believe that they have a higher status and are more intelligent than non-whites.

Without extraordinary effort no one can escape the pervasive sense of white superiority that dominates American life. Thus, although Lyndon Johnson makes a speech at Howard University, carefully shaping in his mind and mouth the word "Negro" in order not to offend his audience, he *thinks* about Negroes or Mexican-Americans or Puerto Ricans as a white man who grew up in a racist country.

Along with its tradition of racism, America has always had a tradition of contempt and dislike for the poor. That tradition is a strong strain in our Puritan heritage, brought here by the first settlers and reinforced over the years by the success the country achieved through work and efficiency. Americans as a people, are convinced that only those who don't want to work are poor, since otherwise they would not be in that condition. After all, everyone can get an education in America; there are plenty of jobs for skilled workers; and finally, they think, other poor people have made it.

Indeed, those who have made it, who have come out of poverty, out of ghettos, are often the worst offenders against the people who remain.

And because so many Americans combine racism with a sense of moral superiority toward the poor, they behave as masters, either ordering how the poor shall live or suggesting, firmly, what they must do. Southern conservative racists say they "take care of their niggers"; Northern liberals say they know what's best for their "clients," the welfare recipients. Both groups share a belief that the poor and especially the non-white poor are incapable of making their own decisions, whether these decisions involve how to look for a job or how long a hambone can be kept in the refrigerator of a public housing project apartment.

We are trapped, too, by the great size and regional diversity of the country. Ignorant of each other's ways, separated from each other by sectionalism and local prejudices, we are especially ignorant about the texture of life for those who are poor or of a different color.

Discovering that ignorance was a frightening lesson for me, for I found out quickly, when I began this book, how little I knew. And while my ignorance came as a great personal shock, since I had always believed I was fairly knowledgeable about American society, such ignorance is nearly catastrophic in a more general sense: the fact is that before I began this book, I *was* fairly knowledgeable. I *was* better informed than the great majority of Americans, I did have many more Negro, Spanish-speaking Mexican-American, Oriental, and Indian friends than most Americans, and I was certainly far more aware of the existence of their problems than are most Americans. Yet I really knew very little.

Only a few months ago I was discussing this book at a meeting of liberals in New York City. One of them, a decent man who tries to behave decently, argued with me about my pessimism: "Look," he said, "it's not as bad as you say. Why, right now some of us have made it possible for eleven or twelve Negro families to live on Park Avenue."

I looked at him in shocked silence for a moment or two and then said, "Thousands of Negroes live on Park Avenue. But they're all above 96th Street. That's Park Avenue, too, you know."

But it isn't to him or to most other white New Yorkers: *their* Park Avenue ends at 96th Street.

I don't want to single out that decent man, though, for I too have had and still have my own foreshortened Park Avenues. For example, I was arrested twice during the year I was writing this book. Both times I went to jail, and it was not until then that I understood what life is like for those to whom an arrest is a more common experience, those who are not writers with bail funds and attorneys readily available.

Outside of jail I had to learn how to make my eyes and ears work better for me, too. For a whole year I looked at the walls of the housing projects in Boyle Heights on which the "chicano" gangs had spray-painted their names in huge letters and all I saw was vandalism. It was not until the year was nearly over that I saw something besides vandalism in the unique lettering style of the gangs' names. I finally learned to see that these teen-agers in Los Angeles are seeking an identity of their own, linked to their direct connection with Mexico and the Southwest. Anyone who wants to observe how an art form can develop inside a gang culture has only to go over to Boyle Heights and East Los Angeles and look at the gang graffiti.

But very few people will go. And of those who do, very few will stay to talk and listen.

Too few of the Negroes who have made it out go back, either. Middle- and upper-class Negroes are just as frightened of and alienated from the Negro poor as are the whites, just as ignorant of the lives of the Negro poor as are the whites. So, too, the new middle class of Spanish descent, whose Spanish is minimal, have very little in common with those poor Mexican farmworkers living on the eastern edge of the serape belt in Los Angeles or the Puerto Ricans in Chicago and New York. The middle- and upper-class members of minority groups may be joined by color or ethnic background to the poor minority people, but they are much more widely separated from them by class.

And my own ignorance still appalls me even though I have managed to learn a few things. Never again will I read, without suspicion, what some social scientist writes about disorganization in *"The* Negro Family" for I have seen no such unit as *"the"* Negro family. This is not to suggest that life in fatherless Negro families doesn't have enormous difficulties; obviously, the absence of a male parent in the house is going to have consequences for the family unit. But very often I have seen that absence compensated for in other ways.

And in Mexican-American family life, where more often the father *is* present, I have seen a grievous distortion of the male role, a glorification of the male, of the quality called "machismo," which stunts and thwarts the women's lives. Yet I have also been in poor Mexican-American family homes where the parents are devoted to each other, where each child is treated like a tiny saint, where love makes poverty almost bearable. Almost.

One important characteristic of ghetto life is the transiency: you can have very close friends, but in a few months they're always gone, and a year later you can't even remember their names. Because rapid turnover and mobility are a matter of course in the ghetto, neither the school nor the neighborhood nor the church exists long enough in any person's life to provide the set of values those institutions intend. That is one reason why looting and stealing and vandalism are perceived differently inside the ghetto than outside.

Of course, I have seen disgusting things, too, inside the barrios and ghettos—hate and violence, bitter, uncontrolled anger, unbridled viciousness. I have seen little children out in the street all day, without any parental control, learning the worst habits of the slums. I have observed absolute indifference to the needs of others and have watched vandalism become a way of life. One afternoon, waiting for a traffic light to change in Watts, I saw a Negro teenage boy knock an elderly Negro woman to the ground, grab her purse, and run frantically toward a car which screamed off down the street as soon as he got into it. The old woman stood there, sobbing as if her heart was going to break. Later that afternoon, as I was describing the incident to one of my Negro friends in Watts and explaining my own feeling of helplessness because I had been going in the opposite direction from the way in which the thieves had driven and couldn't turn my car around in time, he asked me if I would have chased the purse-snatchers if my car had been going the other way.

"Yes," I said, "wouldn't you have?"

"No, not in a million years. First of all, if you caught up with them, they probably would have killed you. And secondly, I wouldn't turn in anybody to the goddamn cops. That shit's okay for you white guys, but not for me any more. Maybe five years ago I might have chased after that guy and given the license plate to the cops, but not any more, not any more."

My friend is wrong, but after research for this book showed me what the police's relations are with the ghetto, and the ghetto's relations with the whole community, I see his point. I understand, too, why so many middle-class Negroes and Puerto Ricans are sympathetic to the rioters, even while they disapprove of their specific acts.

One night at the other side of the continent I saw a group of Puerto Rican kids go into a phone booth on 34th Street, in New York, rip off the dialing apparatus, and run down the street, laughing. As I continued to walk on 34th Street, I reached Seventh Avenue and saw a well-dressed middle-aged Negro couple emerge from Macy's, loaded down with parcels. The woman stood on the sidewalk, the man stepped out into the street, trying vainly to stop the taxicabs which passed him by, empty. A minute or two later he and the woman wordlessly exchanged roles and she went out into the street while he remained on the sidewalk, holding the packages. Finally, a cab stopped and he rushed into it after her.

Now, that family has a man in it and one who obviously works, for they were clearly not welfare recipients. If they have children, there is a male model in the house, a working father. Does it matter very much? Does the fact that he is working help his image or his self-image if he cannot get a cab to stop for him?

Yet that experience is perfectly ordinary and routine for almost all Negroes and Puerto Ricans in New York. Most white cab drivers and some minority ones, too, are afraid to pick up Negroes and Puerto Ricans. Their fear is understandable, for cab drivers do get knifed and shot. And so the endless circling around continues and grows worse, the fires of bitterness and hate are stoked higher for all of us caught in this trap. That is why putting larger amounts of money into the cities, although absolutely essential, will do very little good unless the expenditures are accompanied by radically new approaches to the problems.

These new approaches must be interconnected, too, for the problems are interdependent. We cannot work for a solution of the nation's educational crisis without simultaneously working for a solution of the welfare crisis; the medical needs of the people who live in Boyle Heights cannot be met without providing some form of adequate income for the residents of Watts. A global approach is required instead of the present fragmented one. But what is demanded most of all is a willingness to scrap traditional ways, to run risks, to innovate.

For example the entire welfare system, as it is now, must be abolished and a whole new view substituted, based on the principle that human beings have a basic *right* to a reasonable income even if they cannot work. To make such a change requires more than just changing the name of the welfare institution, as has just happened in Los Angeles and New York; it means changing its entire orientation. For too many years now social work and social welfare have focused on adjusting people to live within their environment instead of helping them in their own efforts to change that environment. And for too many years social workers, like teachers and those in other service occupations, have been obsessed with a phony "professionalism" based on the possession of a graduate degree as the sole important criterion of ability.

The educational system is in the same rotten condition. No amount of tinkering with it will repair its fundamental faults, although a few more children might be helped than are presently being helped. The character of the school curriculum must change radically, and the character of the teaching process along with it: no change will be of any consequence without a new breed of educators, willing to experiment, to junk what has been drilled into them by *their* teachers as the proper way to teach. Principals must be imbued with a willingness to resist administrators, teachers to resist principals, and administrators taxpayers. Above all, the priorities of the system must change, technology put into its proper place, and the citizen's education given more emphasis than the astronaut's.

The same broad general principles can be stated for *every* institution of the society with which the poor have contact. New hospitals will help, but unless the doctors stop being the kind of doctors American medicine produces today, the hospitals will be of only limited assistance.

The police system must change, too, and that means the police will need to do more than learn Spanish or send a police car to the elementary schools so that the little kids can ride around the schoolyard with the siren blowing. City government and state government and federal government all would need new perspectives, too, before any fundamental changes can take place in the lives of those caught in the double trap of racism and poverty. New tax structures are needed along with new forms of government that meet the needs of regions and cities.

These new forms might even require junking the private enterprise system in many key areas of American life. Technology is forcing us into new kinds of government, but we are not yet engaged in consciously creating these forms; instead, they come into existence in hasty and ill-conceived response to immediate pressures. Yet although I believe private enterprise may be replaced by some form of public enterprise society, I do not believe such a society would *necessarily* be free of racism. It is possible to have a racist socialist society, just as it is possible to have a poverty-free socialist society that is still destructive of human dignity.

I am not attempting here to provide an exact blueprint of what should be done in Los Angeles and America: none are available although hundreds of good ideas, some certainly worth trying, have been suggested as possible partial solutions to the problems. But these ideas will not be effective unless the country as a whole develops the will to change. It is that *will* which is missing now, and yet without it change will not take place and the country will continue toward complete disaster.

And it is horrifying to see the complete absence of leadership, at all levels of government, from the President down to the mayors. Nearly every official in government is convinced that the urban crisis is beyond any solution within the accepted capabilities of American society, as it is today. Yet instead of facing the crisis honestly, too many political leaders of both parties have shown a shameless lust to attach themselves to the inevitable counterreaction to Negro and Puerto Rican wars on the whites. Thus, they have reinforced America's sickness, its disease of racial superiority, instead of attempting to understand government's responsibility in creating the bitterness and hatred that burst out, finally, in looting, burning and killing.

Tanks and armored cars, shotguns and rifles, billy clubs and riot helmets are the only answers that the leaders of America give to the oppressed. The President proclaims a day of prayer at the same time as he announces the beefing up of the National Guard. Cynical political expediency makes the short-term programs useless except for the professional anti-poverty bureaucrats; no long-term proposals going to the heart of the problems have been proposed. And in the midst of all the turmoil in the society are the frightened policemen, lashing out indiscriminately at hippies, peace marchers and the minorities. Chief Parker is dead but his spirit is still very much alive all through the land.

The police have reason to be frightened, too. In Plainfield, New Jersey, a white police officer was all but dismembered by an angry mob after he had killed a Negro child; in Los Angeles I heard a story of how two white officers were set upon by another mob in a housing project after the policemen had shot a kid who they said stole a car. And perhaps they were right, but it had made no difference to the Negroes who surrounded them, ripped out their car radio and threatened to stomp them to death. Fortunately for the officers, according to the story, they were saved from certain death by the arrival of two Negro project policemen who, armed only with moral authority, broke up the scene.

I do not know if this story is true or not, but it doesn't matter— if it hasn't happened yet, it might still happen. And then what will be the reaction of the LAPD to the killing of their officers? It will be much like that of the police and National Guardsmen who poured bullets into any house in Detroit or Newark where they even suspected snipers of hiding. Unless a radical change takes place, America *will* have its own Sharpeville.

Which city will be next? Which city will break the record for deaths and destruction just as Los Angeles did for the past and Detroit did for Los Angeles? Will it be your city? Yes, it will be unless the country, as a whole, comes to understand that government, as it is today in America, is still a government of, by and for the white. A Negro may be in the Cabinet and another on the Supreme Court, but the government is still white. The police departments may recruit Negroes, Mexicans and Puerto Ricans, but they will be defending a white society. And so inevitably, the non-whites in the country have started trying to build their own societies. America is polarizing at a fantastic rate of speed. And the next riot may be started by whites, burning down the Negro sections of the cities.

Only a few months ago, I sat talking with a Negro friend, who seemed very depressed.

"What's bugging you?" I asked.

"I had a nightmare last night," he said. "You know, the last time in Watts, I was out on the streets trying to cool it. Well, in my nightmare it happened again, but this time I wasn't cooling it, this time I was up on a roof with a rifle, sniping. And down below on the street, there was a white guy and I shot him, I killed him. And you know who he was? He was you. I killed you."

His nightmare is becoming our reality.

Sources

The data in this book are drawn from a great number of varied sources, including official documents of all the government agencies plus reports, analyses, and documents compiled by private groups and universities. The single most important source of general data on population, employment, and housing in Los Angeles is "Hard-Core Unemployment and Poverty in Los Angeles," a report prepared by the Institute of Industrial Relations of the University of California, Los Angeles, for the Area Redevelopment Administration of the U.S. Department of Commerce. Supervised by Paul Bullock of the Institute staff, the report was completed in December 1964, and no study of Los Angeles is possible without continual references to it. The Census Bureau's special 1965 study of the Negro and Mexican areas of Los Angeles contains much valuable data, as does the "Racial and Ethnic Survey" prepared in 1966 by the Los Angeles City Schools.

The reports made by the consultants to the McCone Commission, which the commission unfortunately did not publish, are another valuable source of data, especially Bullock's report on employment, Dr. Milton Roemer's on health, Dr. Fred Case's on housing, Dr. Kenneth Martyn's on education, and Dr. Frances Feldman's on welfare. These are available for examination at a number of libraries in California, but they cannot be circulated. The 1965 report of the California State Social Welfare Board was extremely useful in gaining an understanding of the welfare problem, as was "Welfare in Review," published by the U.S. Department of Health, Education and Welfare. The Los Angeles County Commission on Human Relations has prepared a great deal of valuable material about the tension-creating problems of Los Angeles; all of it is worthy of study.

Jerome Skolnick's book *Justice Without Trial* is the best work I have found on the police. Although it does not deal specifically with the Los Angeles Police Department, its general themes are applicable there.

Charles Abrams' book *The Future of Housing* provides essential background to that problem in America; the Urban League's survey of Los Angeles housing provides the necessary local background. In the vast field of writings on education I found the works of Edgar Z. Friedenberg and Christopher Jencks especially helpful. Much of the data for this book was drawn from interviews with officials of all the agencies, city, county, and state, I have analyzed. As always, in such cases, the interpretations of the data are my own, not necessarily shared by any of those who supplied the materials to me.

About the Author

PAUL JACOBS was born in New York City in 1918. He served a brief apprenticeship in the diamond business, leaving that to become, first, a full-time radical and then a union organizer. Since the mid-1950's he has devoted his time to writing. A frequent contributor to many magazines, Mr. Jacobs is the author of *Is Curly Jewish?* and *The State of the Unions,* and with Saul Landau, *The New Radicals.* Mr. Jacobs is on the staff of the Center for the Study of Democratic Institutions and is also associated with the Center for the Study of Law and Society at the University of California. He and his wife, Ruth, an attorney, make their home in San Francisco.